[HARDCOVER]

KOREAN CULTURE DICTIONARY

From Kimchi To K-Pop And K-Drama Clichés.
Everything About Korea Explained!

ISBN 979-11-88195-62-6

Written and Compiled by WOOSUNG KANG
Edited by EDWARD LEARY

Printed in the United States of America

www.newampersand.com
14 13 12 11 10 / 10 9 8 7 6 5 4 3 2 1

HOW TO USE THIS BOOK

We've written this book with people like you in mind, so having zero knowledge about Korea is absolutely fine! You can simply follow the sections in pre-set order and get done with the course. However, if you are the proud K-Culture know-it-all of your friend group you can put your knowledge to the test and even learn some new interesting facts to surprise your friends with by jumping between sections of your choice.We've cross linked important information so you are always guided in the right direction and will not get lost in the middle of the road. But, that's not all, folks! To maximize your learning, we've included the following in every section!

BOLD & *Italicized* — Important Names & Korean Terms You Should Know!

Taejo / Yi Seong-gye 태조 / 이성계

Taejo 태조, birth name **Yi Seong-gye 이성계** (1335 - 1408), was the founder and the first king of the Joseon Dynasty, reigning from 1392 to 1398, and was the main figure in overthrowing the Goryeo Dynasty. By the late 14th century, the Goryeo Dynasty was beginning to fall apart, with its foundations collapsing from years of war against the Mongol Empire. During the time, General Yi Seong-gye gained power and was respected for pushing the Mongol remnants off the kingdom and repelling Japanese pirates. When the newly rising Ming Dynasty demanded the return of a significant portion of Goryeo's northern territory, Goryeo was split into two factions – anti-Ming who argued to fight back and those who sought peace. Yi, the latter, however, was chosen to lead the invasion. At **Wihwado Island 위화도** on the **Amnok River 압록강**, he decided to revolt and withdrew the troops, and headed back to the capital. The military coup succeeded, and he dethroned the King. He first put a puppet king, but later exiled him, and ascended the throne, and began the Joseon Dynasty.

Epic Battle Scenes!

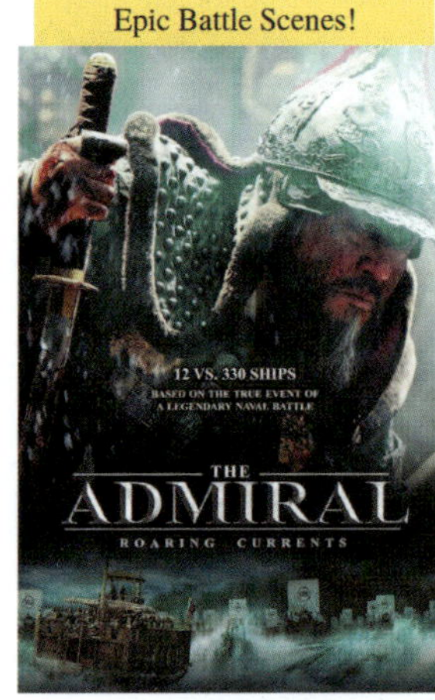

Myeongryang 명량
(*The Admiral : Roaring Currents*, 2014)

Yukryongi nareusha 육룡이 나르샤
(*Six Flying Dragons*, 2015, SBS)

K-Drama series about Yi Seong-gye's Military Coup & The Beginning of the Joseon Dynasty

Must-See Films, TV Shows & Documentaries!

Download a Free QR Code Reader on App Store / Google Play

WATCH! What Korean *Hoesik* Is Like

Scan The QR Code To See This Clip!

A *hoesik* scene from *Once Upon A Time in Saengchori* 원스어폰어타임인 생초리 (2010, tvN)

HOESIK 회식 – THE DREADED COMPANY EVENT EVERYONE WANTS TO AVOID

PREFACE

Before reading this book, you probably had some moments of curiosity in your life where you questioned certain things about Korean culture. Why is there a Pepsi logo on the Korean flag? Why do Korean kids in my class only have like… three last names (Kim, Lee, Park)?

If you are a K-Drama addict, and even took the time to watch variety shows with your favorite idols, your thoughts and interest towards Korea may have grown even deeper! What does 'Korea' mean, and who are the people on the Korean currency notes? Why do Koreans love kimchi so much?

Maybe, if you're a Koreaboo (no shame in the game) you may wonder how and why you become a year (or two years) older as soon as arriving in Korea? Why so much drama in those street tent bars (*pojangmacha*)? How do Koreans drink so much *soju* from those infamous green bottles? And, probably the question on everyone's mind in 2020, why is BTS so gosh dang popular (honorable mention: What the heck does "Gangnam Style" mean)?

Well, if you get lost in translation, you can simply look up the word in the dictionary or on the latest phone app. But what if you get lost between cultures and there's no one to kindly fill you in on what's going on? You can get by with a lucky guess, but not only is there no guarantee that you will get lucky next time, but you are also missing a valuable opportunity to learn about Korean culture indepthly!

Regardless of who you are and where you come from – a K-Pop/K-Drama fanatic, an expat living in Korea, a student who just got accepted to study abroad in Korea (congrats!), or even a second-generation *Gyopo* from the Korean diaspora, you no longer have to stay puzzled and irritated by not being able to understand the peculiarities you find in Korea overall! This book is jam-packed with over 350 essential topics and most frequently asked questions that are hand-picked from 27 categories, covering virtually every aspect of Korean culture by laying out all the details on the "Five Ws (Who, What, When, Where, Why) and How." After reading, you can fully understand Korea and appreciate its culture inside and out

By the time you've finished the last chapter, you will have learned so much about Korea, including all the minute details! (E.g., Why do Koreans love sitting on the floor? Why is it rude to pour drinks with one hand?)

An added bonus (perhaps the most important one) is that Korean dramas, movies, and K-Pop music videos and lyrics will mean so much more the next time you see them (Hey, you will have the ability to accurately identify all the Korean drama clichés)! So next time you hang out with a Korean friend, you can flaunt your knowledge by telling them why you hit the neck of the bottle with a Taekwondo chop when opening it (don't forget to turn your body away when drinking with an older person). Oh, and if someone compliments you for having a "Small face," you will correctly respond by saying "Thank you." Now let's start this book with an example of "*Bbali Bbali*" culture - hurry up and start reading!!

ABOUT THE AUTHOR

Woosung Kang is an author based in Colorado and Seoul who spent an equal amount of his life in the U.S. and South Korea. He studied Business Management at Denver University and Consumer Psychology at New York University. Woosung plans to continue his journey around the world because he believes that the best way to share Korean culture is by learning, appreciating, and respecting other cultures first. While in New York, he led a series of successful marketing campaigns promoting the beauty of Korean culture, and made TV/Radio appearances to share his story. Woosung is also the author of the best selling series 'The K-Pop Dictionary.'

E-mail: storyteller1634@gmail.com
Instagram: vivaretro0810

ABOUT THE EDITOR

Edward Leary is a K-Pop fan first and everything else second! Reporting K-Pop news for 7 years, Edward has shared his opinions and content through allkpop, kpopstarz, print magazines, and more. Residing in Korea, Edward is pursuing Korean Broadcasting as a TV personality to showcase his love of Korea through Hallyu. Using the name Hello Eddi, he has appeared in two K-Pop MVs, alongside MC-ing events, voice acting, and modeling in Korea.

E-mail: kpop.eddi@gmail.com
Instagram: Hello_Eddi

TABLE OF CONTENTS

GET TO KNOW THE FLAG

UNDERSTANDING KOREAN NAMES

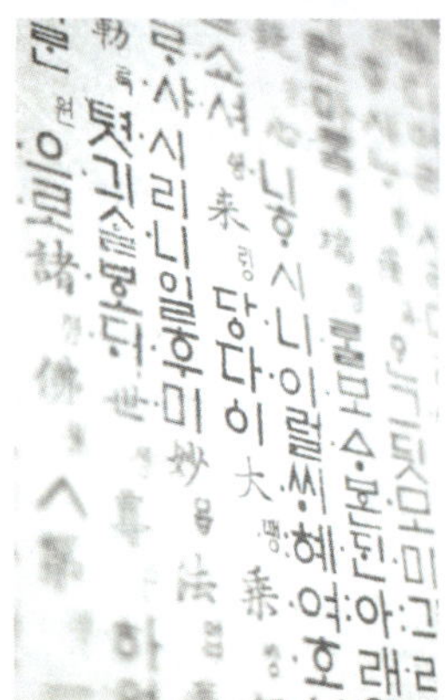

THE LANGUAGE

KIMCHI - THE KOREAN SOUL FOOD

YUGYO - THE IDEOLOGY OF THE KOREAN PEOPLE

WHAT DO KOREANS EAT?

DINING IN KOREA

DRINKING IN KOREA

WORKING IN KOREA

EDUCATION IN KOREA

FUN AND QUIRKY KOREAN SUPERSTITIONS AND BELIEFS

SPOOKY KOREAN SUPERSTITIONS AND BELIEFS

ODD QUESTIONS AND COMPLIMENTS

DEATH AND AFTERLIFE

KOREAN FUNERAL - HOW KOREANS SAY GOODBYE

JESA - REMEMBERING AND HONORING THE ANCESTORS

TYING THE KNOT - WEDDINGS IN KOREA

SPECIAL DAYS AND OFFICIAL HOLIDAYS IN KOREA

NEW YEAR'S DAY AND CHUSEOK

HANBOK – THE TRADITIONAL KOREAN CLOTHES

THE KOREAN LIFESTYLE

KOREAN HISTORY - HIGHLIGHTS AND TIMELINE

KOREAN WAR

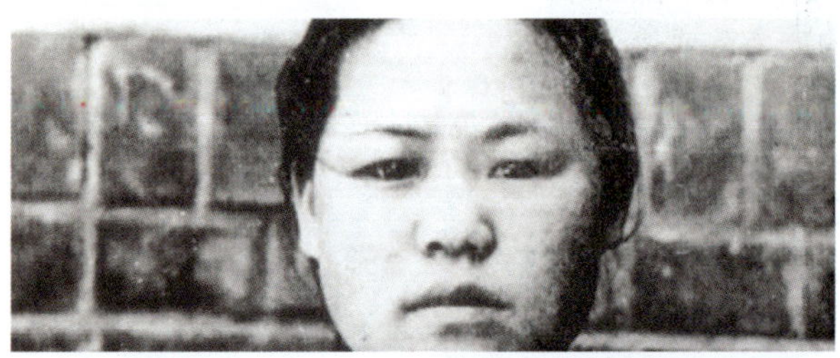

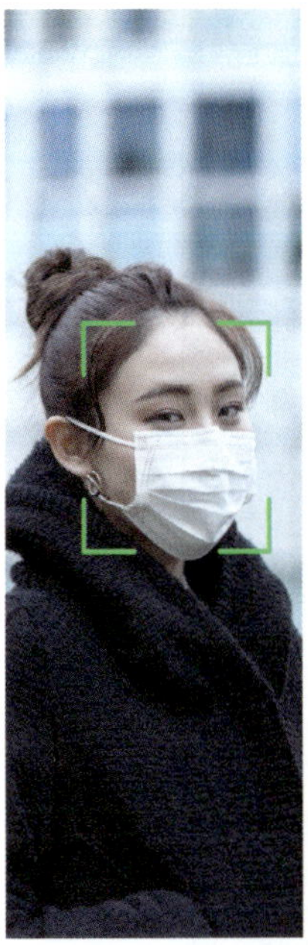

LOST IN TRANSLATION

KOREA IN THE DIGITAL ERA

SPORTS

PLACES AND THINGS

HALLYU THE KOREAN WAVE

THE RESEMBLANCE IS UNCANNY!

WHY

IS THERE A PEPSI LOGO ON THE KOREAN FLAG?

2018 Pyeongchang WInter Olympic Games Opening Event (SBS TV Screenshot)

"Hey, nice work on the ambush marketing, Pepsi!"

When two groups of performers slowly merged to form a giant circle of perfectly interlocked red and blue symbols, similar to what you would find on a Pepsi can, during the opening ceremony of the **2018 Pyeongchang Winter Olympic Games** social media exploded with a rush of tweets and posts from TV viewers around the globe. How was Pepsi, whose name was not even on the sponsor list, able to just come out of left field and make the most brazen appearance, so much so that the world-(in)famous streaker Mark Roberts, who crashed multiple Olympic events wearing a pink tutu and monkey penis, would have been dwarfed when it came to exposure? Was the International Olympic Committee (IOC) caught off guard by Pepsi's well-orchestrated ambush marketing tactics? Well, the answer is a flat no because Pepsi was in no way involved in this scene, it's safe to assume that 99.9% of those tweets were meant to be a joke (most of them made it clear by adding a footnote saying they know it's the Korean flag). But this short-lived social media fad is actually an accurate illustration of how people have this common misperception towards the uncanny similarity between the Pepsi logo and the Korean flag. So the big question is – How did Pepsi get to bear the Korean symbol on their products? Or, how did the Koreans get the right to use the Pepsi logo on the flag? I've heard many different versions, but the one I liked the most was how a Korean billionaire saved Pepsi from going bankrupt with a wad of money and demanded to put the Korean symbol in return.

It first appeared in the 1940s, during World War II, and was meant as a show of U.S. patriotism and support for the troops fighting abroad. The motif still lives on, with minor tweaks like updated type font and slight size adjustments every now and then. While it's fun to speculate, the Pepsi logo and the Korean flag have nothing to do with each other. The Pepsi logo, which is one of the most recognizable corporate trademarks in the world, features three colors - red, white, and blue (hint, hint!), forming a sphere-like shape.

HISTORY OF THE KOREAN FLAG

Meanwhile, the prototype of the modern-day Korean flag (oh, I'd like to kindly remind you that there are STILL two Koreas at the time of writing and throughout this book, by default, the word Korea refers to South Korea, but I will expressly indicate whenever I mean to talk about the scary neighbor upstairs) was first devised when Korea was still the **Joseon 조선 Dynasty** (1392-1897) whose existence was being seriously challenged by Imperial Japan's active ambition to conquer the Asian region.

In 1882, during the Joseon-U.S. Treaty, the need for a national flag to represent the Dynasty arose, as there wasn't one to serve the purpose. To rectify the situation, delegate Lee Eung-jun 이응준 took the King's order to create a national flag, and he did so by modifying the Dynasty's royal standard, *eogi* 어기, and it stood side-to-side with the U.S. Flag.

On August 22, 1882, Emissary Park Yeong-hyo rearranged the trigrams and created a scale model of the *taegeukgi* 태극기 (*taegeuk*, the red and blue circle found in the center of the flag, meaning "supreme ultimate", and *gi*, 기, meaning "flag", hence "supreme ultimate flag"), and on January 27th, 1883, the Joseon government officially promulgated *taegeukgi* to be used as the official national flag.

Then the Great Korean Empire Daehanjeguk 대한제국 (1897-1910) was proclaimed in October, 1897 by Emperor Gojong 고종 of the Joseon Dynasty, and the flag continued its service.

During the Japanese occupation (1919-1948), a flag similar to the current South Korean flag was used by the provisional Korean government based in China. Following the establishment of the South Korean state in 1948, the current flag was declared official on October 15, 1949.

The flag, just like the Pepsi logo, has been modified and adjusted throughout history but always maintained its status as a national symbol of Korea, which is why many Korean companies bear the *taegeuk* symbol as part of their brand identity.

KOREAN AIR

대한민국정부

Government Emblem of South Korea

With the brief history session, I hope all the Pepsi-Korea mysteries and conspiracies have been properly debunked and demystified, and we can take a closer look at the Korean flags and learn about what all the symbols represent!

WHAT DO THE SYMBOLS MEAN?

It's more than a sample of Korean art. It's a graphical representation of the Korean ideology and core values.

Let's start off with the South Korean flag! As we have previously covered, the local nomenclature is ***Taegeukgi* 태극기** ("supreme ultimate flag"), and the dominant color found in the background is white, which represents **brightness**, **purity**, and **peace**, which Korean people fully embraced as values into their lives, to the point where they earned the nickname "**white-clad people**" by foreigners, as the color was ubiquitously present in the daily attire ***hanbok* 한복** of the 19th century.

The circle in the center is derived from the traditional philosophy of yin and yang – the red portion represents the positive cosmic forces, and the blue counterpart represents the negative cosmic forces, thereby creating a perfect balance.

In sum, it represents the rules of Mother Nature where the whole creation revolves around the interaction between yin and yang. Lastly, a group of stripes called the trigrams represent the harmony of unity, placed around the yin and yang symbols. Each block of symbols, ***geon* 건**, ***gon* 곤**, ***gam* 감**, and ***ri* 리** (they might not look like they are in the correct order but this is the traditional way), represents the sky, sun, moon, and land, the directions, and the seasons.

Why Were Koreans Called "White-Clothes People"? P. 200

BALANCE IN THE UNIVERSE

The rules of Mother Nature where the whole creation revolves around the interaction between yin and yang.

HARMONY OF UNITY

The 4 symbols form harmony of unity, centered around the yin and yang symbol.

KOREAN MINDS

The bright white color represents the national characteristic of loving brightness, purity, and peace.

When WW2 ended with the Allied victory in 1945, Japan relinquished its 35-year-long control over the Korean peninsula leading the Soviet Union to occupy the northern half of Korea while the U.S. took control of the southern half, per Allied terms. Trying to instill their socialist ideology, the Soviet Union leaders deemed inheriting the traditional ***taegukgi*** inappropriate and decided to design a new flag. **Kim Il-Sung 김일성**, the then leader of North Korea agreed, and in 1947, a new flag was dictated from Moscow, and the North Koreans named it ***Ingonggi* 인공기**, meaning "the flag of the people's republic".

The red star is a symbol of Communism (found on the flags of many other Communist countries such as the Soviet Union, Vietnam, and China), and people's happy prospects. The white circle in the background represents the universe. The dominant red color represents the revolutionary spirit and path to Communism while blue represents the nation's commitment to peace and friendship (hm… really?). Finally, the white stripes represent the purity of the North Korean ideology, as well as strength and dignity.

All right! So that pretty much covers the ideas and meanings behind the symbols of the flags of both Koreas, and I hope it was a nice introductory session to get a glimpse of the Korean ideology!

**Who Are The "Kim Dynasty"?
P. 222**

SYMBOL OF COMMUNISM

The red star is a symbol of Communism and the white circle represents the universe.

SPIRIT OF NORTH KOREA

The red color represents the revolutionary spirit and path to communism and blue represents the nation's commitment to peace and friendship. The white stripe represents the purity of the North Korean ideology, as well as strength and dignity.

FLAG OF THE SOVIET UNION

In 1947, a new flag was dictated from Moscow, and the North Koreans named it *ingonggi* 인공기, meaning "The Flag of The People's Republic."

KOREAN NAMES

WHY DO KOREAN PEOPLE ONLY HAVE LIKE... THREE LAST NAMES?

For this topic, let's start with a little trivia - what could the Korean proverb "looking for a Mr. Kim in Seoul", possibly mean? Well, look for the clues throughout the following story and you should be able to answer it on your own.First off, if you went to school that had a lot of Korean students, grab your yearbook, dust it off, and find the index page and locate the "K" section. Lo and behold, you would immediately realize that the descendants of the **Kim** family are claiming the lion's share of the real estate.

The same can be said for last names **Lee**, and **Park**, and if you recall the names of your Korean friends (or if you don't have one, think of your favorite K-Pop star), the chances are pretty good they are one of the three. What's more, the first Korean player to make it to the Major League Baseball was **Park Chan Ho**, the first swimmer to win a gold medal at the Olympics was **Park Tae Hwan**, the first soccer (okay, football) player to play for Manchester United was **Park Ji Sung**. Notice that the Romanization of a Korean name places the last name (family name) before the given name, so for the sake of clarity, I will use the term "family name" from this point on. Of the past 12 presidents of Korea, 2 were Parks, 2 were Kims, and 2 were Lees. Guess the name of the current president of the World Bank? **Jim Yong Kim** (Kim is the family name here). Also on the list is the Olympic figure skating champion **Kim (Queen) Yuna**. All right, **Kim Jong Un**, the "supreme leader" of North Korea, is a member of the Kim club as well. And did you know that Hollywood actor **Lee Byung Hun** (*Terminator Genisys, The Magnificent Seven, G.I. Joe: Retaliation*) and **Lee Ki Hong** (*Maze Runner*) are also of Korean ancestry? Even that funny comedian **Bobby Lee** from *MAD TV* is also a Korean-American.

Based on the data I presented, you might have concluded that the Parks are great athletes, the Kims are great leaders, and the Lees are great entertainers, but that's not the point I'm trying to make here. The gist of the story is that there are only 286 family names in Korea (as of 2003, not counting those from naturalized Koreans), and the Kim, Lee, Park people make up more than 45% of the entire Korean population (**Kim at 21.8%, Lee at 14.8%, and Park at 8.5%**)! For a quick comparison, there are over 1,800 family names in Russia with the most common family name **Smirnov** making up only a meager 1.8% of the Russian population. Over 100,000 in Japan share the name **Sato** as it is known for being the most common, and all top 10 combined make up just 10% of the entire population! In the U.S., **Smith** is the most common with just 151,671 sharing this last name, close to 1% of the entire population.

If you are an avid investor, this is certainly not a well-diversified portfolio. So what's with the disproportionate population? Are Korean families inbred? Is it a case of endogamy? On the surface, such speculations don't look completely groundless, especially after knowing that there are only 286 family names available (by the way, the Korean naming conventions are patronymic, which inherits the family name of one's father, grandfather, but it's possible to adopt a mother's family name is allowed, although some tedious jumping through administrative hoops are required). With that, you have every right to wonder if all Koreans are somehow related to each other, but that's when this thing called ***bongwan* 본관** comes in to get things in order. It's a concept used to distinguish clans with the same family name, as it tells the birthplace of the first ancestor or founder of the family name (according to a survey done in 2015, there are 36,744 of them).

So members of a certain family name who also happen to share the same paternal ancestor or progenitor are said to be of the same clan. Utilizing this grouping system, one clan can be distinguished from one another, and within each clan, it gets further divided into various factions.

Also, many Korean families, or their "lineage society," keep a detailed record of family lineage in a genealogy book called ***jokbo* 족보**. By comparing your faction you can see what your familial status is and your "generation level" (more on this later). Some onomasts (people who study proper names, especially the names of people and places) often liken *bongwan* to the European naming convention that incorporates the place of origin within a name (e.g., Olivia von Westenholz = "Olivia from Westenholz"). The difference is that the Korean system doesn't display the label upfront, so it requires a little more digging into one's family history. Oh, and an interesting fact – up until 2005, a couple of the same last name and *bongwan* were not allowed to be married by law!

To put it in perspective, let's look at a real-life example.

Kim Min-ho
Hi, nice to meet you!
I noticed that you have the same last name as mine.
What's your bongwan?

Kim Gyu Ri
Nice to meet you too!
Mine is Gimhae.
What is yours?

Kim Min Ho
Oh no... Mine is Gimhae as well... I guess you and I are not meant to be...
We can never get married...

Kim Gyu Ri
Oh my! Snap out of it already! It's 2019 and, yes, we can get married if we wanted! The prohibition ended in 2005. Wait a minute... What did you just make me say?

All right, I'm sure you found the answer to the Korean proverb quiz at the beginning. If you haven't, the English equivalent of the proverb is "finding a needle in a haystack".

WHY ARE THE KOREAN LAST NAMES 이 (YI) AND 노 (NOH) ROMANIZED AS "LEE" AND "ROH"?

***Dueum beopchik* 두음법칙** ("initial sound rule") is a grammar rule to facilitate easier pronunciation for certain Sino-Korean words, including last names based on Chinese characters, that begin with ㄹ (l/r) and ㄴ (n).

1) When ㄹ (l/r) is placed in the onset position of the first syllable in a word, followed by the vowels ㅏ/ㅐ/ㅗ/ㅚ/ㅜ/ㅡ (a/ae/o/oe/u/eu), they are replaced with ㄴ (n).

Example) Mr. 로철수 Roh Cheol-su -> Mr. 노철수 Noh Cheol-su (when written in English, it takes the original sound, Roh).

2) When ㄹ (l/r) is placed in the onset position of the first syllable in a word, followed by the vowels ㅑ/ㅕ/ㅖ/ㅛ/ㅠ/ㅣ (ya/yeo/ye/yo/yu/i), they are replaced with ㅇ (no onset sound).

Example) 리철수 Lee Cheol-su -> 이철수 Yi Cheol-su (when written in English, it takes the original sound, Lee/Ri/Rhee, but some choose to use Yi, to keep the revised pronunciation.)

WHY DO ALL KOREAN NAMES HAVE THREE SYLLABLES?

Now that we've covered the family name portion of a Korean name, let's turn to how a Korean first name is composed. If you've been following Korean celebrities for quite some time, you should have noticed a pattern that almost all of their names have three syllables (family name (1 syllable) + first name (2 syllables, for example, the Korean name of a famous K-Pop star G-Dragon is Kwon (family name) + Ji Yong (first name), and might have wondered if it's something required by law or people are simply following the social norm, keeping in mind the Korean proverb "a cornered stone meets the mason's chisel."

To understand the science behind it, we need to refer back to the Korean genealogy system we've just learned - a Korean last name is indicative of one's ancestral history and *bongwan* tells which clan they belong to. So what's the role of a Korean first name? While a Korean family name provides information regarding its origin and its following lineage in a vertical direction, a Korean first name works in a horizontal direction, providing information related to a given generation.

Traditionally for each generation, the belonging members of the same sex share one syllable of a first name. This "generational name," or ***hangryeol* 항렬**, is unique by the clan and the placement location, which can be the first syllable or second syllable of a first name, is also decided and approved by the clan society (which is often not observed nowadays). Similar to a serial number of a manufactured product which tells us when and where it's made, the shared syllable serves to indicate what "generational level" one comes from. Thanks to such detailed record-keeping effort, members (not just one's siblings but everyone along the line of one's generation) of the same clan can pinpoint how far, in terms of the number of generation, one's stretched down from the first ancestor, thereby making it possible to determine one's "generational level," and the relative "rank."For that reason, even when one happens to be a lot younger but comes from an older generation (higher rank), the much older one (lower rank) has to use honorifics, and it's quite a comical and confusing situation even for average Koreans. And as for the remaining slot, it's left for the parents to freely decide.

Here's another real-life example:

With the nation's relentless endeavor for modernization and the Korean lifestyle rapidly shifting away from collectivism to individualism, however, large portions of traditional values and cultural practices are weakening, and this syllable-sharing tradition is getting less and less observed (but if you come from an extremely orthodox clan, they might throw the book at you).

Also at this point, I should make clear that the three-syllable system is not a legal requirement, and different combinations are perfectly fine. For instance, two-syllable versions of a Korean name is very common (1 syllable family name + 1 syllable first name, e.g., Kim Hwan), or two-syllable family names like Sunwoo and Namkung, four-syllable combinations (2 syllable family name + 2 syllable first name, e.g., Sunwoo Hyun Soo) are also a dime a dozen.

DO KOREAN PEOPLE HAVE A MIDDLE NAME?

More often than not, Korean people who apply for an English-based document such as an international driver's license will find a syllable missing in their name upon picking it up. The reason for this mysterious disappearance is largely attributable to a common mistake where they think of their "middle syllable" of their name as the "middle name" in English, and putting it in the "middle name" section. If your name is Yong Jin (first name) Kim (last name), the end result will be Yong Kim or Yong J. Kim, or Yong Kim, as the middle name is often initialized or omitted in the American English system.What could be the cause?

As an educated reader, you must have figured out that it's the spacing between the two syllables of a first name that creates the confusion. A popular solution is inserting a hyphen between the two syllables (i.e., Yong-jin Kim), or eliminating the space between the two (i.e., Yongjin Kim). Both are pretty solid solutions, but the hyphen method does a better job at separating pronunciations, thereby providing readers guidance (i.e., without spacing, Yongil could be read as Yon Gil or Yong Il, but hyphen eliminates that issue). And for those of you who ever wondered if there is any difference between a hyphenated and the no-space version first name, they are exactly the same.

Hong Gil-Dong - The John Doe Of Korea
P. 239

WHAT DOES A KOREAN NAME STAND FOR? HOW CAN I DECODE IT?

Now that we've successfully learned the structure of a Korean name, let's continue the winning streak and jump to another popular topic – what does a Korean name stand for and how can I decode it? To understand this concept, you need to know that more than 70% of the Korean vocabulary is based on ***hanja*** **漢字 한자** (the Korean term for Chinese characters borrowed from the Traditional Chinese that are incorporated into the Korean language with Korean pronunciation), and Korean names are not an exception – a typical Korean name has an underlying *hanja* character which represents a meaning (ideogram), while ***hangul*** **한글**, the Korean alphabet, represents the speech sound (phonogram).

For someone named Lee Mi Hwa, it looks like this:

이 Lee 李 ("Jeonju" (place)) + 미 Mi 美 ("beautiful") + 화 Hwa 花 ("flower")

So knowing just the *hangul* sound of a name is looking only at half of the picture because there are a myriad of *hanja* characters with the same pronunciation that have various meanings.

A: Hi! My name is Lee Mi Hwa. Nice to meet you.
B: Are you serious? So is mine! What *hanja* characters do you use for your name?
A: Mi, meaning "enchanting" and Hwa, meaning "harmony." And yours is?
B: Wow, that's a really beautiful name! Mine is Mi, meaning "beautiful" and Hwa, meaning "a painting." You might have guessed from my name, my Dad was an artist, but not a good one!

The example above isn't to show that you're expected to share with someone you met for the first time what *hanja* characters your name is based on (rather, just exchanging the *hangul* sound name is sufficient), but to illustrate the importance of knowing precisely what the underlying *hanja* character is and its meaning is necessary to fully understand one's name. Case in point – on some Korean business cards, especially those from an older generation, you can find a name written both in *hangul* and *hanja*. This bilingual name writing practice is also found on official documents such as the identification card.

AND THE LONGEST KOREAN NAME AWARD GOES TO...

The longest Korean name is also made purely with a combination of Korean words - Park Ha Neul Byeol Nim Gu Reum Haet Nim Bo Da Sa Rang Seu Reo U Ri 박하늘별님구름햇님보다사랑스러우리, a tongue-twisting 17-syllable long name meaning "more beautiful than the star, the sun, the moon, and the cloud in the sky."And you think your baby has a shot at setting a new record too? Sorry to burst your bubble but it's not going to be possible because the current law limits the number of syllables of a first name to five max. Lastly, we have to talk about the power of habit – in real-life conversations, Korean people will still fit a lengthy name into the more familiar three-syllable format (for the sake of convenience, but after only getting well acquainted and becoming close) – so the above mentioned Park Ha Neul Byeol Nim Gu Reum Haet Nim Bo Da Sa Rang Seu Reo U Ri will be shortened to Park Ha Neul.

All right! I hope I've covered and answered all the questions you had about a Korean name, and explained that a Korean name can be as simple as a pair of syllables, but it contains a huge amount of family history and tradition. Now that you know how to unlock and decode a Korean name, try to find out what your favorite Korean stars' names stand for!

DO KOREANS SPEAK CHINESE OR JAPANESE?

Gwanghwamun Gate

All right folks, it's time to be honest. Have you ever wondered, before you started paying serious attention to Korea, what language Korean people speak (Chinese? Japanese? Or something else, even?). Truth to be told, it's one of the most frequently asked questions I received from foreign friends (other runner-ups are "Are you from North or South Korea?" and "Do you know Karate?"), and I'm sure many other fellow Koreans had a similar experience at least once in their lifetime. Well, even if your answer to the question above is a solid yes, you shouldn't feel embarrassed because it's a very common question foreigners have about Korea and it just reflects how undiscovered Korea is to the rest of the world, compared to its neighboring countries (up your marketing/PR game, Korea!). Hoping that things will get better for Korea in the very near future (which is the main purpose of this book, fingers crossed!), now let's find out why the question keeps popping up!

WHY CHINESE CHARACTERS ARE SEEN EVERYWHERE IN KOREA?

Among all, the biggest cause of the confusion must be the ubiquitous presence of the Chinese characters found in Korea, especially so if you've been to the historical sites such as **Gwanghwamun Gate 광화문**, or **Gyeongbokgung Palace 경복궁**, and gazed up at the signboards displaying majestic calligraphy written in Chinese characters. Even in the streets of modern-day Seoul today can you find the signboards bearing Chinese characters, abundant enough to make you puzzled.

As always, knowing history helps us understand the present. While keeping their native spoken languages, many Asian countries (Korea, Japan, Vietnam, Mongolia, and etc.) adopted the Traditional Chinese characters (vs. the "Simplified Chinese" which has been in use in mainland China and some other countries since the 1950s to encourage literacy) as the written lingua franca (for both domestic and diplomatic use) similar to Latin in European history, or the role of English as the global standard today.

In Korea, *hanja* (the Korean term for Chinese characters borrowed from Chinese and incorporated into the Korean language with Korean pronunciation) was the only available means of written communication until their own *hangul*, the Korean alphabet, was invented in 1443 and promulgated in 1446.

Gyeongbokgung Palace

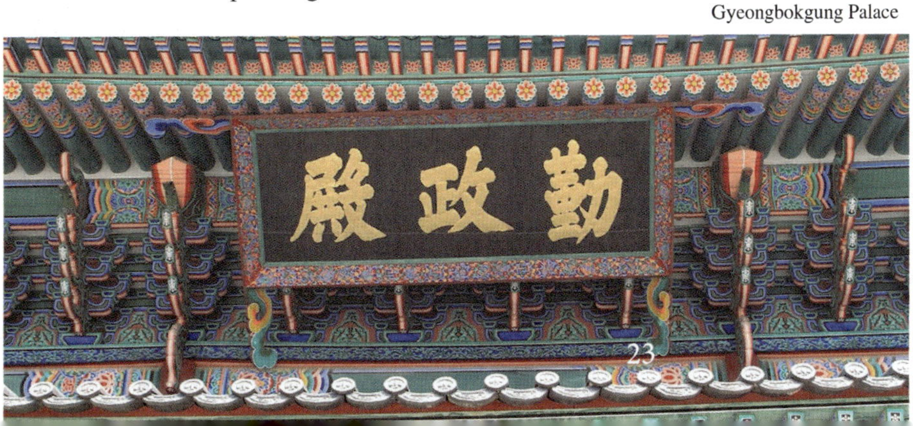

WHO INVENTED HANGUL THE KOREAN ALPHABET?

Besides the tall list of his splendid achievements, the main reason **King Sejong the Great 세종대왕** (1397-1450) is revered as one of the (if not THE) greatest rulers in Korean history is his benevolence and compassion for his people (proof can be found at the heart of Gwanghwamun Square, where his bronze statue is situated with great dignity, along with that of the biggest war hero in Korean history, **Admiral Yi Sun-shin 이순신**). Reflecting his down-to-earth character, King Sejong always deplored the fact that his people had to rely on the extremely complicated *hanja* for written communication, and how the opportunities for learning it were almost exclusively available only to the haves (noble people, or ***yangban* 양반**, scholars, and the government officials and the like) only, while the have-nots were just too busy working their socks off to eke out a living, being the illiterate portion of the society. But even with knowledge of *hanja*, for it being of foreign origin, people had trouble expressing fully and freely their thoughts and meaning which they could have done effortlessly through their native spoken Korean language.

More importantly, those at the bottom of the totem pole had no way of having their stories heard, be they legitimate complaints (e.g., I'm paying too much taxes!) or brilliant ideas (e.g., I know how to annihilate the enemies camping outside the fortress!) because the only way to get it done was through oral communication (but you would be stopped by the gatekeepers). And because recording them with ***hanja*** for posterity wasn't a viable option, much of the hard-gained know-hows of the common people (e.g., farming techniques, folk remedies, etc.) couldn't be properly passed on to the next generation, which was a huge loss to the society as a whole. Luckily for Koreans, though, there was King Sejong the Great - an earnest scholar whose vast knowledge and natural talent in a wide spectrum of subjects constantly amazed even the most brilliant experts, also happened to be a problem solver and a go-getter determined to "walk the walk." Fired up by the love and sympathy for his people, King Sejong rolled up his sleeves to rectify the problem himself. To accomplish the mission, he envisioned a set of letters that was uniquely Korean and easy enough so that people with little or no education could learn to read and write.

After countless days, he personally created a new set of alphabet consisting of 28 letters (17 consonants and 11 vowels, of which 3 consonants and 1 vowel became obsolete and fell out of use later, thus modern Hangul consists of a total of 24 letters with 14 consonants and 10 vowels), named it ***Hunminjeongeum* 훈민정음** ("The Proper Sounds for the Instruction of the People"), and promulgated it on October 9th, 1446. The preface of the proclamation well reflects the essence of King Sejong's benevolence.

That was one moving intro, isn't it? His sincerity still resonates with us today. Now, let's see how critics rated the new invention.

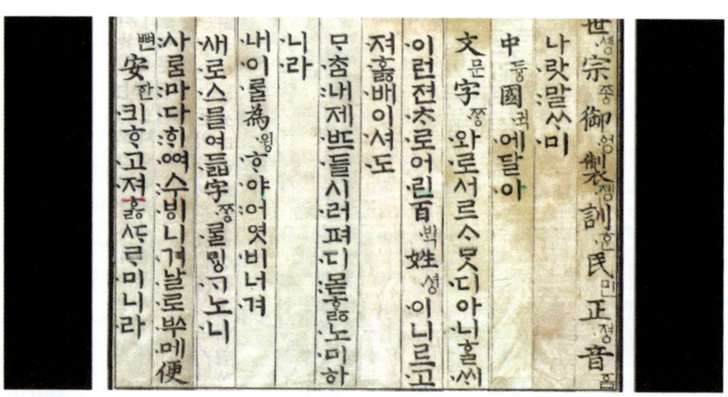

Hunminjeongeum Haerye

"A wise man can acquaint himself with them before the morning is over; even a stupid man can learn them in the space of ten days."

A commentary (well, that's what I'd call a five-star review) written by scholars from the ***Jiphyeonjeon* 집현전** (Hall of Worthies) in the ***Hunminjeongeum Haerye* 훈민정음 해례** ("Explanations and Examples of the Correct/Proper Sounds for the Instruction of the People"), hints us that King Sejong's plan to promote literacy among the commoners through an easy writing system got off to a great start (heck, you got the country's top scholars vouching for it)!

Korean Scholars Viewed *hangul* as a threat to their status

After the promulgation, however, the Korean alphabet faced fierce opposition by the literary elite and Korean Confucian (the main ideology of the Joseon Dynasty) scholars, who cherished the Traditional Chinese characters, *hanja*, as the only legitimate writing system and as the "language of scholars." More importantly, they saw *hangul* as a threat to their status – out of fear that the enlightened commoners might start a revolution.

독닙신문

But *hangul* gained popularity in the late 16th century as traditional poetry and *hangul*-novels flourished. Centuries later in 1894, fueled by the **Gabo 갑오 Reformists**' push for modernization coupled with strong support from the Western missionaries, ***hangul*** was finally adopted in official documents for the first time, and a year later in 1895, elementary schools began to teach texts written in ***hangul***. In 1896, **Dongnipsinmun 독립신문** ("The Independence (Newspaper))", became the first newspaper ever to be published in hangul.

"The language of [our] people is different from that of the nation of China and thus cannot be expressed by the written language of Chinese people.

Because of this reason, the cries of illiterate peasants are not properly understood by the many [in the position of privilege].

I [feel the plight of the peasants and the difficulties faced by the public servants and] am saddened by the situation. Therefore, twenty eight [written] characters have been newly created.

[My desire is] such that, each [Korean] person may become familiar [with the newly created written language of Korean] and use them daily in an intuitive way."

- King Sejong the Great -

東亞日報

日外務·文部省대립 표면화

국제批判시인 是正요청

再修正절대不可를 결의

日해명資料8項 마련

實業系高校 추천入學制

工農業校 정원30% 科學校는 全員

南北韓 교차承認

한반도統一촉진

Newspaper from 1982 showing ***gukhanmunhonyong***

Since this period, *hangul* and *hanja* coexisted and maintained a symbiotic relationship in the form of ***gukhanmunhonyong* 국한문혼용** (a writing style that uses a mixture of *hangul* and *hanja*), supplementing and complementing each other.

During the Japanese Occupation (1910-1945), Japanese was made the official language of Korea and the Korean language was completely persecuted – earlier Korean literature was banned from the public school curriculum, and the publication in the Korean language was also outlawed on the pretext of "cultural assimilation policy." Despite the Japanese Imperialists' effort to obliterate the Korean spirit, *hangul* was still secretly taught in schools established by Koreans, and it was one thing that held Koreans together during the difficult times. After Korea was liberated in 1945, *hangul* once again became an indispensable part of Korean culture.

Propelled by the government-wide 5-year project known as the Exclusive Usage of Hangul Act in 1968 which abolished *hanja* education while promoting *hangul*, the use of the mixed writing style has been rapidly decreasing and *hangul* took over the place where hanja used to be.

매일경제

mk.co.kr

2018년 11월 16일 금요일

토종 지배구조펀드 한진 경영권 공격

30대 기업 인건비, 1년새 8.5% 급증

Newspaper from 2018 published mostly in ***hangul***

The project was rolled out for realistic reasons - reading and writing documents full of *hanja*-based jargon took too much time and effort, and the widespread computer usage favored the simple Korean layout with just 14 consonants and 10 vowels over the complicated Chinese system.Despite the effort, however, the use of *hanja* couldn't be completely eliminated, largely due to practical reasons - Chinese characters are an ideogram (represent a meaning) Korean characters are a phonogram (represent a speech sound), and if presented only in *hangul*, it can get confusing when dealing with homonyms.

For example, the Chinese word 最高 and 最古 are both written and pronounced "*choego*" 최고 in Korean, but have different meanings - "best" and "oldest". So when presented solely in *hangul*, it's difficult to distinguish the difference without knowing the context in which it's placed. For that reason, there is a school of thought who stresses the importance of *hanja* education and demands it be included back in the public school curriculum. While it's left for the policymakers to decide, it's undeniable that *hanja* has been an indispensable part of Korean culture, and is projected to remain so in the future.

Looking back, *hangul* had one heck of a rocky ride, but it was definitely worth it – according to the CIA's report released in 2002, the total Korean population of age 15 and over can read and write, setting the literacy rate for the male at 99.2% and 96.6% for the female. This incredibly high literacy rate accurately reflects the easiness in learning the Korean alphabet and this is also great news to foreigners contemplating if learning the Korean alphabet is something achievable – most people can learn to read and write *hangul*, within just a day or two, or even in a few hours (but learning the spoken language might be more challenging). What makes it all possible? *Hangul*'s scientific design and efficiency as a writing system, which has been praised by linguists around the world, such as the **UNESCO King Sejong Literacy Prize**, an annual prize awarded to two institutions, organizations or individuals "for their contribution to the fight against illiteracy," which was founded in honor of the King. If King Sejong were still alive today, he would be smiling from ear to ear, looking at his people being able to communicate freely and fully with the Korean alphabet he invented - someone would have to explain to him what a smartphone is, though.

UNESCO

UNESCO KING SEJONG LITERACY PRIZE

an annual prize awarded to two institutions, organizations or individuals "for their contribution to the fight against illiteracy."

Story of King Sejong The Great and Hangul Creastion

Bburigipeun Namu 뿌리깊은 나무
(*Deep Rooted Tree*, 2011, SBS)

Who Are The People On The Korean Currency Notes? P. 199

Any ***Civilization*** fans?

King Sejong the Great, sitting on the Phoenix Throne at Gyeongbokgung Palace is the leader of the Koreans in ***Sid Meier's Civilization V***!

THEN CAN KOREANS UNDERSTAND CHINESE, JAPANESE AND VICE VERSA?

Having learned the role of Chinese characters as the written lingua franca in Asia, you might feel inclined to assume that the people in Korea, China, and Japan must be able to communicate freely since they have adopted and use the same Chinese characters and have a large set of vocabulary based on them. So if you managed to order dimsum at a Chinese restaurant located in Seoul, you should be able to replicate your success in Tokyo, and also in Beijing, right?

To answer, it's partially correct and partially incorrect. First off, it's highly probable that they would understand each other to a certain degree should they try to communicate through written Chinese characters, because Chinese characters, an ideogram, hold a meaning, and it has the same effect as showing a picture to someone. For example, a Korean person traveling to China and Japan could write a Chinese character 水 ("water") and show it to a server at a restaurant and get a glass of water without a problem. But here's the reason why I said "partially correct" – with grammatical differences being the biggest factor (although Korean and Japanese have the same grammatical structure), the way they are spoken is a point of divergence. For every Chinese word, there are two ways to read it – one is ***hundok* 훈독**, which represents the meaning in native Korean terms, and ***umdok* 음독** which represents the sound that resembles the Chinese pronunciation. For example, the same Chinese character 水 ("water"), is pronounced *su* 수 in Korean *umdok* and *mul* 물 in *hundok*, while it's *shuǐ* in Mandarin Chinese, and *sui* すい in Japanese *umdok* and *mizu* みず in *hundok*, adding more complexity and setting them further apart from each other.

Knowing how even this one Chinese character is spoken differently depending on where you come from, with the grammatical differences, it should appear obvious by now that communicating through just pronouncing the Chinese characters is nearly impossible, although you can get lucky sometimes as they have similar sounds across all three different languages. So back to ordering dimsum – if you want to find out how your favorite dimsum tastes in three different cities, I suggest that you either 1) have it written in Chinese characters on a flashcard and carry it with you (might not work well in Korea and leave the server "lost in translation" because *hanja* is not widely used nowadays), or 2) be adventurous and learn to say it in their local language - don't be surprised if you get something completely different from what you thought you ordered, though (um... wait... I ordered... chicken feet?).

BUT I SEE KOREANS SPEAKING FLUENT JAPANESE IN MOVIES. HOW IS THIS POSSIBLE?

If you are a fan of historical Korean movies and dramas that feature the tumultuous times of **the Late Period of Joseon** and **the Japanese Occupation Era (1897-1945)** as the backdrop ***Mr. Sunshine* (tvN, 2018), *Miljeong* 밀정 (*The Age of Shadows,* 2016), and *Amsal* 암살 (*Assassination,* 2015)** are some of the greatest titles I personally recommend), you must have noticed that Korean characters seem perfectly capable of communicating with Japanese characters in fluent Japanese, which might have led you to wonder if Koreans are somehow naturally bilingual or whether the two languages are compatible with each other, possible to switch back and forth on a whim like a reversible jacket, requiring no extra effort in translating – both are very reasonable speculations. The reason for the bilingual fluency of the Korean characters in the movies is due to the historical fact where the Japanese Imperialists obligated the Koreans to learn their language in school and even have their native Korean names converted to Japanese style during the **Japanese Occupation (1910-1945)**. Even today, there is a significant portion in the Korean population, especially those born during the time of Occupation, who are still able to carry out a conversation in Japanese – something that's been deeply ingrained in them. But fast forward to present day Korea - only those who choose to learn it know how to speak Japanese, and Koreans are much more likely to know English than Japanese, as it is part of the school curriculum. Korean and Japanese are two distinctive languages, both spoken and written, and it's not possible to communicate directly without the help of a dictionary or a translator. For an average Korean, however, the Japanese language is probably the easiest foreign language to learn, thanks to the similarities found in their grammatical structure (syntax and morphology) and pronunciation. However, the sad history made an impact on the Korean language which still lingers on – a considerable amount of Japanese

Japanese Occupation - Sad History P. 212

Miljeong 밀정
(*The Age of Shadows*, 2016)

Amsal 암살
(*Assassination*, 2015)

Mr. Sunshine (tvN, 2018)

vocabulary and expressions (labeled "the vestiges of Japanese Imperialism" by Korean people) have become part of the Korean language, and they are still being used today unbeknownst to the Korean people's knowledge. But ironically, they help Koreans learn Japanese with relative ease (no need to memorize a new word!).

WHY DO K-POP GROUPS ALSO RELEASE ALBUMS IN JAPANESE?

One thing that makes going to an ice cream parlor particularly exciting is variety – you can choose from a wide spectrum of flavors and you enjoy multiple flavors at the same time should you choose to do so! Well, that's what many K-Pop groups do, too – more often than not, they come in two flavors - Korean and Japanese! And it raises a question that is very frequently brought up by K-Pop fans around the globe: Why do K-Pop groups also release albums in Japanese? Having covered the historical aspect of the relationship between Korean and Japanese languages, we know that Koreans don't actually have a switch which they can conveniently flip on and off between the two languages. If we look at the matter from a business perspective, however, the answer seems obvious - at just over 51 million in population, South Korea is not a big market, compared to China (1.4 billion) and Japan (126.5 million) – the very reason why many K-Pop groups constantly look for an opportunity to expand their popularity outside their domestic market. Given the numbers, it might look like going to China is the way to go (imagine how much money you could make if everyone in China bought something as trivial as a toothpick!), but again, (Mandarin) Chinese is not something Koreans can learn in a short period of time. On the other hand, Japan (although politically they are like cats and dogs, they manage to maintain an amicable relationship through civil cultural exchange), is conveniently located just a few hours flight from Korea, and combined with the relative easiness ("relative" because it is so compared to other languages, and it's still not something that can be achieved overnight and would still take weeks and weeks of hard studying and dedication) of learning Japanese language, makes Japan an extremely attractive market that's also well within reach. Simply put, for K-Pop groups seeking to expand their presence outside Korea (more revenue streams), it's realistically and financially more reasonable to try out their luck in Japan first. Seasoned K-Pop heads already tried and realized that it's better received when things (promotions, advertising, connecting with local fans, and the like) are done in their native language, including the albums. Moreover, success in the larger and more international Japanese market could help them earn even more attention around the globe. So that explains why K-Pop albums come in two flavors, and it's something a K-Pop fan would definitely enjoy (except the double-spending part!).

What Is Hallyu (Korean Wave)? P. 252

kimchi

THE KOREAN SOUL FOOD

history of kimchi

KIMCHI AND KOREANS GO WAAAAY BACK!

What comes to your mind when you think about Korean food? Among many candidates, ***kimchi*** will surely be on the list. This tangy and spicy fermented side dish has become an inseparable part of the Korean lifestyle, to the point where they view it as part of their identity (heck, it even has "Kim" in it). According to the studies tracking down the origin of *kimchi*, their camaraderie dates back as far as the Three Kingdoms period (57 BC to 668 AD), when it was in its primitive form as pickled vegetables optimized for long term storage. During the time, its name was ***ji* 지**, meaning "pickled", and during the early Joseon Dynasty (1392-1897), it was first called ***chimchae* 침채** and ***timchae* 팀채**, which literally means "submerging vegetables (under saltwater)", and later became ***dimchae* 딤채**. Finally, it's believed to have evolved into ***kimchae* 김채** through palatalization, and finally became *kimchi* (here's to you, Charles Darwin!).

kimchi fun facts

KIMCHI USED TO BE WHITE

Now, what color is *kimchi*? Well, if you said red (who wouldn't?), it must be because the type of *kimchi* we encounter most frequently is the red hot ***baechu*** **배추** (used to be called Napa cabbage, but it's more frequently referred to as *kimchi* cabbage as of late) *kimchi* and ***kkakdugi*** **깍두기** (cubed radish *kimchi*). As you might have guessed, this iconic red color comes from ***gochugaru*** **고추가루** (chili powder or red pepper powder) which is liberally used as a seasoning. Having been used to this bold red color, you might be taken aback by the fact that *kimchi* wasn't all that fiery back in the old days! It wasn't until the late 16th or the early 17th century that Korea was introduced to this now-ubiquitous ingredient. As to how chili arrived in the Korean peninsula, there are many theories with convincing explanations, but one of the most widely accepted ideas is that it was the Japanese who brought it with them during their failed invasion attempts during 1592-1598. And interestingly enough, it was considered toxic for about 200 years and couldn't earn a spot in the kitchen. Only at the beginning of the 19th century did Koreans start incorporating it as one of the main ingredients, and with the invention of ***tong baechu*** **통배추** (whole cabbage) *kimchi* in the early 1900s, it started to look like the ones we see today (until that time, ***mu*** **무** (radish) was the most popular ingredient).

THERE IS EVEN A MUSEUM FOR KIMCHI

Established in 1986 with the mission to "display diverse aspects and stories of *kimchi* and enable visitors to feel, experience, and enjoy it," the **Kimchikan 김치간** has been "enhancing its renown as a prestigious museum promoting *kimchi* among people around the world." Selected by CNN as "One of the World's 11 Best Food Museums," it consists of a media room, a souvenir shop, and special exhibition halls. Among all, their ***kimchi*** making experience program sounds fun. Imagine – wouldn't the world be a much better place if men and women of all ages and colors could come together and make ***kimchi*** while singing kumbaya? (visit www.kimchikan.com for more information)

HOW MANY KIMCHI VARIETIES ARE THERE?

According to research, *kimchi* can be divided according to the 1) main ingredients 2) form 3) other supplementary ingredients. There are over 200 different *kimchi* varieties available, and it's interesting to see that *kimchi*'s from different regions of the country reflect their regional characteristics. For example in **Jeju Island**, *kimchi* made with abalone has been enjoyed as a local specialty while the residents of **Jeollado Province** have been making *kimchi* with chili, ginger, and ***yuja*** (citron) - ingredients that are abundant in the local area). If you were ordered by the King of Korea to make *kimchi* using the ingredients unique to your region, what would it be like?

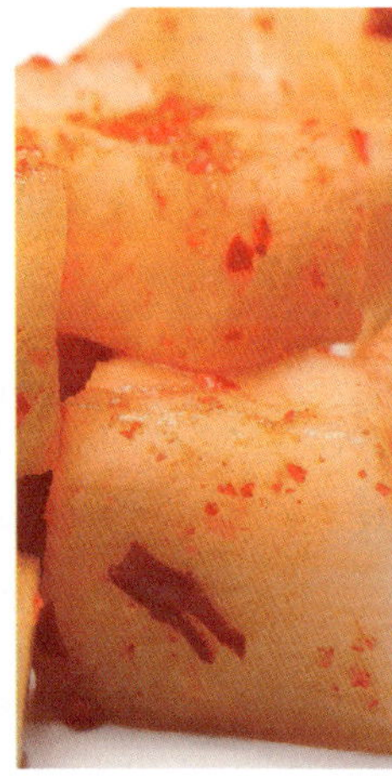

CAN KIMCHI REALLY STOP A PANDEMIC AND SAVE MANKIND?

When SARS (Severe Acute Respiratory Syndrome) and H5N1 Bird Flu swept across Asia (killing more than 700), people started wondering how South Korea was able to stay unaffected (only a few minor cases of infection reported), and people speculated that *kimchi* could be the possible answer. It became even more so after the BBC released a news report citing research conducted by Korean scientists where they fed *kimchi* extract to 13 infected chickens (Ugh… I know, but there is a Korean proverb "bitter to the mouth, better for your health") and confirmed 11 of them recovered. The researchers, however, stated that the results are not scientifically sound. While the link between *kimchi* and pandemic prevention was unclear, there were clear winners – domestic *kimchi* consumption roared and the sales of *kimchi* at Korean restaurants in China also skyrocketed. (On a side note, Japan, not a big consumer of *kimchi*, remained just as undamaged as Korea, so you be the judge).

KIMCHI – CHOSEN AS '5 HEALTHIEST FOODS' BY HEALTH MAGAZINE BUT TOO MUCH OF A GOOD THING CAN MAKE YOU SICK!

Back in March 2006, Korean people's *kimchi* pride went through the roof (again) when Health magazine included *kimchi* as one of the 5 healthiest foods in the world along with yogurt, lentils, olive oil, and soy. ***Kimchi*** was praised for being rich in dietary fiber, vitamins A, B, and C, while providing lactobacilli (a.k.a. "healthy bacteria") which is known to help with digestion. To further sweeten the deal, a recent study suggests that it may prevent the growth of cancer. But don't open your *kimchi* jar just yet - consuming too much *kimchi* can bring negative health consequences – a study suggests that *kimchi* and other spicy and fermented foods may be linked to the development of gastric cancer - most common type of cancer found among Koreans. So enjoy *kimchi* but do not overindulge in it as too much of a good thing can make anyone sick.

KIMCHI IS NOT A MEAL

But if you are the adventurous (or reckless) type and insist on overindulging in *kimchi*, here is another reason why you might want to consider not doing it - ***KIMCHI* IS NOT A MEAL.** I repeat – ***KIMCHI* IS NOT A MEAL**, and nobody in Korea eats *kimchi* alone as a meal. It would be equivalent to having dill pickles for a meal. Rather, it is one of the numerous ***banchan* 반찬** (side dishes) that are served along with rice and soup in a typical ***Hansik* 한식** (Korean cuisine). This misconception has been further reinforced by the Korean government's unrelenting effort to promote *kimchi* as a representative food of Korean cuisine (one of their favorite ways of promoting it is having an event where a group of foreigners try *kimchi* and say "delicious!" in front of a camera). The best way to appreciate *kimchi* is to enjoy it as an accompaniment to other delicious Korean dishes, like bulgogi and japchae. Mmm!

KOREANS CONSUME THIS MUCH KIMCHI ANNUALLY

So how much *kimchi* do Korean people consume? On the dining table of a typical Korean family, *kimchi* has its own reserved parking spot as most people eat it with every meal, and doubling down on the dosage is observed quite often. For example, putting *kimchi* on top of a spoonful of *kimchi* ***bokkeumbap*** **김치볶음밥** (fried rice) which already has *kimchi* as the main ingredient is a very common practice (think of dipping a chocolate ice cream bar in chocolate syrup). According to statistics released in 2013, an average South Korean consumes about 48 pounds (22 kg) of *kimchi* annually. And for comparison, the large weight plate at the gym weighs 3 pounds less at 45 pounds. The twist here is that the number actually reflects a declining trend in kimchi consumption, mainly due to a change in their eating habits. As Korean people become more and more health-conscious, the importance of adopting a low-sodium diet into their lifestyle has been a new trend, and naturally, people started to cut down on kimchi consumption, a high-sodium food. More, young people whose taste buds are well used to the Western food no longer see kimchi as their BFF (Best Friends Forever). But again, that doesn't mean *kimchi* will lose the throne – Koreans will always stay attached to *kimchi*, both physically and mentally. Case in point, many Koreans, even the younger generations who have been traveling overseas for an extended period of time without eating Korean food, will find this mysterious "***kimchi*** **craving**" forming from within them, which urges them to look for the nearest Korean restaurant. At this point, then, you must be wondering how Koreans tame their "*kimchi* craving" when they are away from home, especially in places with no Korean restaurants? Well, they pretty much take it everywhere with them.

KOREANS TAKE KIMCHI WITH THEM EVERYWHERE, EVEN TO SPACE!

When I say everywhere, I mean EVERYWHERE! At the height of the **Vietnam War** in the 1960s, South Korean troops (joined as a U.S. ally) were feeling homesick, miserable, and low in morale. **Park Chung-hee,** the then President of South Korea, realized that providing them with an uninterrupted supply of *kimchi* would mitigate the pain and restore their valor. So he personally wrote a letter to **Lyndon B. Johnson**, the then President of the U.S.A., explaining what *kimchi* means to the South Korean troops and how it is directly correlated to their fighting spirit. Johnson acquiesced and established a direct procurement of canned *kimchi* to the battleground. Five decades later, Korea sent the very first astronaut, Yi So-yeon, to space. And guess what? South Korean scientists created a special low-calorie, vitamin-rich, and bacteria-free (although on Earth they are essential for the fermentation to take place, they feared that cosmic rays might mutate them) "Space Kimchi," and she took it to space with her. Don't worry - the scientists also found a way to reduce the pungent smell of *kimchi* by one-third or half, while keeping the flavor. It was the moment kimchi went global, well, universal, rather.

"2014 Seoul Kimchi Making & Sharing Festival" by Republic of Korea

KIMJANG - A UNESCO INTANGIBLE CULTURAL HERITAGE

Among all, the biggest reason Koreans feel emotionally attached to *kimchi* must be ***kimjang* 김장**, the tradition of making and sharing large quantities of *kimchi* to ensure that every household has enough to make it through the winter because *kimchi* is an important source of nutrition during the cold days when food is scarce. It takes place between the end of November and the beginning of December when the average daily temperature stays below 4 degrees Celsius (39 degrees Fahrenheit) with the lows below 0 degrees Celsius (30 degrees Fahrenheit) - If the temperature is too high, *kimchi* ferments too quickly, and if too low, it will freeze and may turn sour. This labor-intensive task really brings the Koreans together because it involves families, relatives, and even communities, and they share activities that include washing, salting, and seasoning of the vegetables. Once finished, they are stored in earthenware jars in the ground buried just up to the neck level to prevent the contents from freezing. At the end of the day, *kimjang* is a collective practice that strengthens Korean identity while providing the opportunity to understand the importance of sharing and living in harmony with nature, the very reason UNESCO recognized it as an intangible cultural heritage in 2013.

KIMCHI IS SCIENCE
KIMCHI REFRIGERATOR

Dimchae by **Winia**

Inheriting the cherished *kimjang* culture we've just learned about, the "**Kimchi Refrigerator**" has become a staple appliance in Korean households today. That's right, there is a refrigerator made just for *kimchi*! At first, the idea of having a dedicated *kimchi* refrigerator in addition to what you already have in the kitchen might not make much sense, but when you see the science behind it, you would nod your head in agreement. First, its functions are not limited to keeping it cool to prevent spoilage. Rather, it is a sophisticated machine programmed to precisely emulate the optimal environment for storing and fermenting *kimchi*. They are designed to meet the specific storage requirements and fermentation processes unique to many different types of ***kimchi*** by providing colder and more consistent temperature as well as more humidity and less air movement than a conventional refrigerator, eliminating the need for burying them in jars in the ground. Hence, the Kimchi Refrigerator is a good example of how traditions evolve with the advancement of technology. At this point, I believe we can all agree that Koreans really got *kimchi* down to a science!

YUGYO

THE IDEOLOGY OF THE KOREAN PEOPLE

FROM BOWING TO RECEIVING STUFF WITH TWO HANDS, WHY DO KOREANS DO WHAT THEY DO?

Are you a PC user or a Mac user? On the outside, all computers look pretty much the same – they all have a motherboard, a RAM, a hard disk, a keyboard, a mouse… and many more, but what makes them different from each other is what's on the inside – the software, or the operating system that governs the overall aspect of the computer (the hardware, resources, and user experience). And when it comes to human civilization, the same can be said. While we are composed of the same parts, it's the national philosophy instilled in the people that sets one apart from one another, like the operating system of a computer. In East Asia, the countries that belong to the so-called "**Sinosphere**," or "**Chinese-character cultural sphere**", a grouping of countries influenced by the Chinese culture, **adopted Confucianism**, or ***yugyo* 유교** in Korean, as their core philosophy. Developed by the Chinese philosopher Confucius, the principles were accepted as an essential system of ethics and moral codes, and have been the backbone of the society, serving as the basis for a wide range of fields, including the national system, politics, policies, philosophy, as well as the law and order. Simply put, it's not just a philosophy but a civilization itself. And the biggest reason why it was preferred as the governing ideology is that it values hierarchy, obedience, filial piety, and loyalty – a perfect set of ingredients necessary for running a centralized government. Among such countries, Korea embraced ***yugyo*** more than any other country, adopting the fundamental concept of Confucianism as early as in the **Three Kingdoms Period (57 BC – 668 AD)**, and reaching its zenith during the Joseon Dynasty (1392-1897). They lived by the teachings and held them sacred. Now that we covered the background information, let's learn what they are because you will gain so much insight into understanding why Koreans do what they do!

What Is The Three Kingdoms Period? P. 183

SAMGANG ORYUN 삼강오륜 (THREE CARDINAL PRINCIPLES AND FIVE ETHICAL NORMS)

A *yugyo* term referring to the code of ethics and practices that must be observed between the king and subject, the parents and children, the husband and wife, the adults and children, and friends.

Three Cardinal Principles

1.*Gunwishingang* 군위신강 (君爲臣綱): Focuses on *chung* 충 (loyalty). It's fundamental for a subject to serve its king.

2.*Buwijagang* 부위자강 (父爲子綱): Focuses on *hyo* 효 (filial piety to parents). It's fundamental for a son to serve his father.

3.*Buwibugang* 부위부강 (夫爲婦綱): Focuses on *yeol* 열 (faithfulness to husband). It's fundamental for a wife to serve her husband.

Five Ethical Norms

1.*Bujayuchin* 부자유친 (父子有親): There should be intimacy between parents and son.

2.*Gunshinyueui* 군신유의 (君臣有義): There should be a sense of righteousness between the king and his subjects.

3.*Bubuyubyeol* 부부유별 (夫婦有別): There should be a distinction between husband and wife.

4.*Jangyuyuseo* 장유유서 j(長幼有序): There should be order between an adult and a child.

5.*Bunguyushin* 붕우유신(朋友有信): There should be faith between friends.

The modernization efforts in the 19th century caused the existing *yugyo* order to collapse considerably because Korean reformists blamed the misinterpreted and often abused *yugyo* customs for falling behind other advanced countries, and saw them as a major hindrance to the growth of Korean society. Some of them are:

Strict Hierarchy: Difficult to question superiors means loss of opportunities for possible innovation/improvement and slower decision-making processes.

Looking Down On Commerce and Favoring Scholars: Disrespect for manual labor, commercial and materialistic activities slowed down the progress in the field of natural sciences.

Patriarchal Society: Gender inequality leading to limited career opportunities for women and an uneven balance of domestic responsibilities.

Preferring Family/Personal Ties Over Formal Legality: Nepotism, factionalism, regionalism lead to corruption.l Collectivism: Prioritizing the interest of a group at the expense of an individual's,

For this reason, in modern-day Korea, *yugyo* also carries a negative connotation for something outdated. But like the operating systems that improve through constant updates and patches, Koreans also have been effectively maintaining a society built upon the core *yugyo* values through accepting and making necessary changes. Let's take a look at some of the examples of the unique things Koreans do that are based on yugyo customs!

남녀칠세부동석 NAMNYEOCHILSEBUDONGSEOK

"A Boy And A Girl Should Not Sit Together After They Have Reached The Age Of 7"

You're watching yet another "time-slip" Korean drama. This time, Seho, a boy from modern-day Korea, accidentally gets sucked into a time portal while looking for a place to pass water in the distant forest. Hours later, he finds himself in the Joseon Dynasty era. While struggling to go back, he finds a beautiful girl around his age and they start to develop feelings for each other. When Seho takes up the courage to hold her hand in the middle of the street market, she hurriedly shakes his hand off, saying, "I was taught that a boy and a girl should not sit together after they have reached the age of 7!" and the camera zooms in on Seho's face which has turned bright red.

This cliché is based on the ***yugyo*** notion ***namnyeoyubyeol* 남녀유별 男女有別** ("There should be a distinction between male and female") which dictates the differences in the duties, roles, and space between genders. Stemming from the idea is ***namnyeochilsebudongseok* 남녀칠세부동석 男女七歲不同席** – "A boy and a girl should not sit together after they have reached the age of 7," which some argue that the original meaning was not to have a boy and a girl over the age of 7 share the same bed, but whichever you choose to follow, their purpose was identical - solidify the gender roles, not to create gender inequality but to strengthen the social and domestic responsibilities so the society can maintain its structure. As shown in modern-day Korean dramas, the idea surely seems way outdated - young Korean couples are not afraid of PDA (Public Display of Affection), although their parent's generation would still find it uncomfortable and raise an eyebrow! If you could choose between the two versions of Korea, which one would you choose?

WHY DO KOREAN PEOPLE ASK FOR YOUR AGE AT THE FIRST ENCOUNTER?

If you are meeting someone for the first time in Korea, don't panic if you are asked for your age at the very first encounter.

While straight-up asking someone's age can be very personal and even offensive, there is a good explanation for this habit. As we previously covered, the *yugyo*-based Korean society is strictly hierarchical and puts a strong emphasis on the senior person's roles and responsibilities of taking care of the junior in the relationship, while the junior is expected to show respect and discipline towards the senior in return. Hence, the "How old are you?" question is crucial in gauging and determining how one will interact with the new person. One of the biggest perks of hanging out with older Korean friends is that they would often insist on paying for your meal. In return, you can show respect by setting the utensils and filling up the water glasses (many casual Korean restaurants have a "self-service" system where you have to do the table setting). And there are always those mean-minded people who try to abuse the system - they would go as far as lying and overstating their age in an attempt to have the upper hand in the relationship, but it often gets found out by bumping into a mutual friend who is the same age. Another K-drama cliche.

WHY DO I GET A YEAR, OR EVEN TWO YEARS OLDER WHEN I LAND ON KOREAN SOIL?

As soon as you arrive in Korea, you are immediately a year, or two years older!

And nope, the sliding door you just came out of at the Incheon International Airport was not a time-travel portal. Let's find out the reasons behind this mad science, but brace yourself because there are THREE different age-counting methods available in Korea.

First batter up! It's called ***man-nai* 만나이** (***man*** means "full" and ***nai*** means "age"). As you might have guessed, you get a year older only after a full year or 12 months, or 365 days have passed since your last birthday. This is how most countries count age, so let's call this the "International Age"

Next is ***seneun-nai* 세는 나이** (***seneun*** means "counting" and ***nai*** "means "age"), so it literally means "counting/counted age." This is how it works. First, you are 1-year-old as soon as you are born and every year you get a year older. This counting method is unique to Korea, so foreigners call this the "Korean Age." Let's put this in perspective.

Suppose you were born on **December 31st, 2019.** The very first day of your life, you are

man nai – 0-year-old
seneun nai – 1-year-old (you're 1 year old as soon as you're born)

A day later, it's a new year. **On January 1st, 2020**, you are

man nai – still 0-year-old
seneun nai – 2-years-old (you get a year older with the year change)

On your first birthday, **December 31st, 2020**, you are

man nai – finally 1-year-old
seneun nai – still 2-years-old (birthdays don't add a year)

Again, with the year change a day later, on **January 1st, 2021**, you are

man nai – still 1-year-old
seneun nai – 3-years-old (you get a year older with the year change)

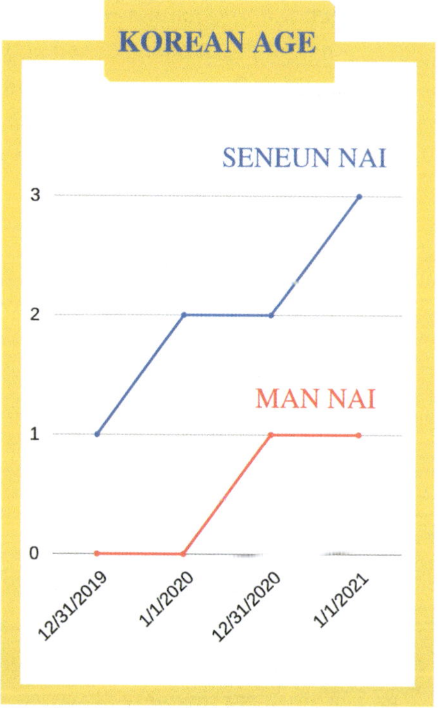

As you can see, the two babies born on the exact same date can have an age difference of up to 2 years! Not a good news to those sensitive to their age, and from a practical point of view, it's not a head start but a disadvantage because putting 1-month-old baby and 11-month old baby or 13-month-old baby and 23-month-old baby in the same bracket isn't fair considering what difference a day makes for babies.

Then where did this practice come from? There are various theories regarding the origin of the "**Korean age**". Some claim that recognizing the fetus as a human being is the reflection of the humanistic perspective of the ancestors, while some argue that it's just a system based on the lunar calendar. While there's no historical record to provide a cut-and-dry answer, one thing is for sure, this method was widely used not only in Korea but also in many other countries across Asia. China, Japan, Vietnam, and Mongolia were among them, but the system has long been abolished except for in Korea.

But here's a twist – in Korea, the ***man nai***, or the "**International Age,**" is actually the only legal age counting method, but the ***seneun nai*** is just so deeply embedded in the daily lives of the Korean people, it's extremely difficult to prohibit the use. In 1962, when Korea switched from the traditional **Dangun Year** (named after the legendary founder of **Gojoseon 고조선**, the first Korean kingdom) to the **Domical (Western) Year** system, the ***man nai***-only rule was ordered by the government, but to no avail.

Okay, so much for that. Let's talk about the third kind now. Called ***yeon nai* 연나이** (***yeon*** means "year" and ***nai*** means "age"), it refers to the counting of age by subtracting your birth year from the current year. This method is used as a standard for some laws, such as the **Juvenile Protection Act and the Military Service Act**. For example, regardless of your birth date, if you were born in 2001, you become 19 years old on January 1st, 2020. It's used for the convenience it provides. By grouping everyone by the year, it's easier to see if someone meets certain criteria. It's different from how ID-checking is done in the U.S. To be able to purchase tobacco, you would have to be 18, and the birth date matters too. But in Korea, as soon as your 18th year starts, you're automatically qualified.

Although more options are better in many situations, the co-existence of multiple age-counting systems isn't quite the case. In fact, it results in high social costs and frequent administrative errors, not to mention the nuisance of having to put extra effort to find out what age one's referring to when people meet for the first time! So ***jjajungna* 짜증나** (annoying)!

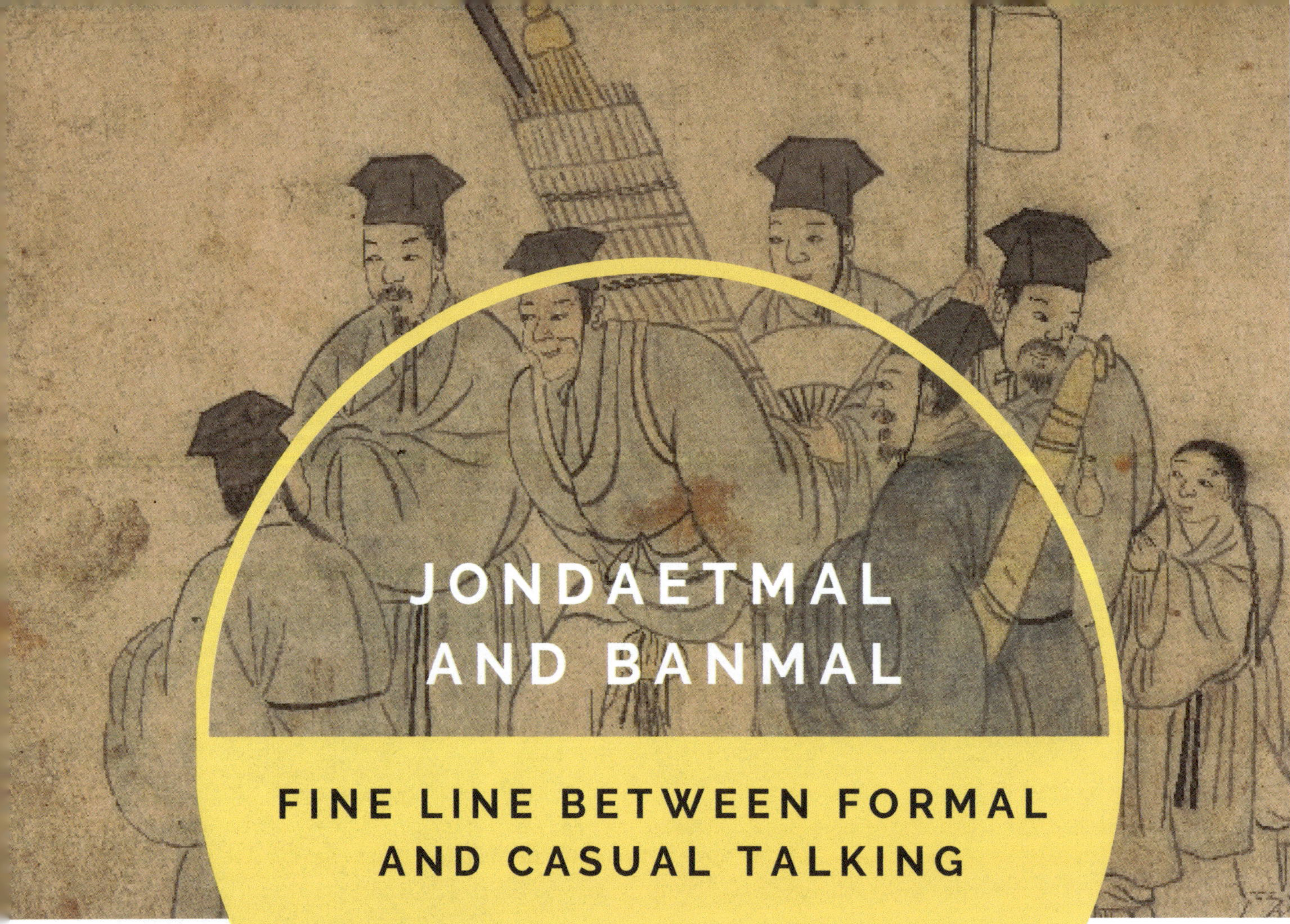

JONDAETMAL AND BANMAL

FINE LINE BETWEEN FORMAL AND CASUAL TALKING

We've just learned that age determines the relative hierarchy between people and how they interact with each other, but there's one more thing that needs to be adjusted – how they speak to each other. If you watch Korean dramas, you must have noticed that Koreans use different forms of speech in different situations, but might have found it difficult to fully understand what was going on because all the subtle nuances tend to get lost in translation, leaving you wondering: "Okay… Why does the husband speak informally to his wife while she speaks in an extremely formal way?", "They all seem to be the same age, but why do some speak formally to another while some don't?"

To begin with, there are two main types of speech. ***jondaetmal*** **존댓말** ("polite/formal speech," which typically ends in *~yo, ~nida, ~kka*?) is used when talking to someone older, higher in rank, strangers, and anyone who you aren't close to (even if you are the same age), but it can also be used to someone way younger, like an elementary school kid and someone way lower in rank, like a high school intern, should you choose to be formal and polite, and show respect. There is a similar concept in other languages, such as "tu vs. usted" in Spanish and honorifics used in Japanese, but the Korean system is far more complicated because it involves a myriad of honorifics to choose from, different personal pronouns which get "upgraded" and "downgraded," as well as the verb stems that change constantly, depending on the person you talk to, and it's a Rubik's cube even for native Korean speakers.

Conversely, ***banmal*** **반말** ("informal/casual speech,) literally means "half-speech," and it indeed requires fewer words to convey the same message (e.g., "May I please have a hot dog?" vs. "Give me a hot dog."). Hence the colloquial expression, "Your speech is getting shorter." This is an indirect way of saying, "Hey, are you dropping formalities with me?" *Banmal* can be used when talking to someone younger, the same age as you, lower in rank, or anyone who you have developed a sense of closeness and intimacy with.

Now, pay attention to how I said it can be used - just because you're older or higher in rank doesn't automatically give you the right to "drop the *jondaemal*." A man of character would first ask permission to switch to the informal *banmal* speech, not to offend the other person. Most of the time, the other person would gladly accept the request. Some think they are given the right to skip the recommended due process and jump straight to *banmal*, but this can be seen as rude and even condescending, sometimes leading to a full-blown brawl. In other cases, Korean people are straight forward with when to drop the formality – at a point when they have developed enough closeness, or for the sake of convenience when they realize that they are the same age, one could propose to "lower the speech," or "drop the *jondaetmal*."

Simply put, *jondaetmal* is used to show respect and politeness and creates a psychological barrier or social distance because it has restrictive feelings embedded in it, while *banmal* frees up the speaker so *banmal* indicates friendliness and intimacy and brings people closer. Noticing which form is used speaks volumes about a particular relationship, so pay special attention when switches are made as they indicate a change in the underlying relationship!

Let's take a look at a K-drama example. Youngho and Sumi work at the same company and they felt an instant connection and were irresistibly drawn to each other when they first met. Not wanting to risk their professional career, they choose to stay professional and keep their distance by talking to each other in ***jondaetmal***. But the harder they try, the more difficult it gets – Youngho, who can't hold his emotions anymore, gets soaked in ***soju*** and shows up at Sumi's place, and Youngho surprises her by dropping the *jondaetmal* and speaking to her in ***banmal***. Youngho, feeling liberated, wants to get everything off his chest and tells her about the feelings he has towards her and says he wants to be on the *banmal* basis with her, just like any other couple. Sumi nods in acceptance, and they are official. Of course, it can work the other way around too. It's Youngho and Sumi's 10-year anniversary. Instead of blowing candles and drinking wine, they are standing in front of the divorce court in Seoul. They must have grown apart and decided to go separate ways. Youngho says, "Sumi... Are you sure you want to do this?", and Sumi replies, "Of course, Mr. Kim, that's what we agreed on, isn't it?" We can all see how Sumi reverted to using *jondaetmal* to Youngho, and it signifies that Sumi wants to keep a distance from him.

It's also interesting to learn that social hierarchies are wholly replicated and maintained through the spoken language, but some critics say it's what creates the generation gap in Korean society. Take a case in point – Guus Hiddink, the Dutch football coach who took charge of the Korean national football team during the 2002 FIFA World Cup and brought the team to the semi-finals, pointed out that the driving force behind the unprecedented achievement was the dismantling of the strict hierarchy among the players, which he thought was hindering the younger players from making creative moves on the field. He ordered everyone to "drop the *jondaetmal*" and call each other by the first name, putting everyone on an equal footing to create an atmosphere of equality and solidarity, and it worked!

SOCIAL HIERARCHIES REPLICATED

What about family members? Many families allow children to talk in *banmal* to their parents, while many other families enforce a strict in-house rule requiring the children to talk to the parents in *jondaetmal*, but they usually switch to *jondaetmal* as they grow up. Between husband and wife, the husband usually talks to his wife in *banmal*, while the wife talks to him in *jondaetmal*, but it's mostly because the husbands are typically older than the wife. Some husbands and wives, of course, opt to talk to each other in *jontdaetmal*, regardless of the age difference. The options are there, and you are the one to choose.

Why Do Korean People Prefer Addressing Someone By Their Title And Not Their Name?

In Korean workplace dramas like ***Misaeng: Incomplete Life*** **미생 (2014, tvN)**, everybody addresses each other using their titles, like **김 과장 (kim *gwajang*) Section Manager Kim**, **최 부장 (choi *bujang*), General Manager Choi**, instead of their names. Is this a corporation's wicked plan to stifle individuality? If so, the TV series would have been a different genre, like a thriller. Along with *jondaetmal* and *banmal*, appellations were another way Koreans used to maintain social hierarchies in the spoken language. In the traditional **yugyo**-based Korean society, it was considered impolite to call each other by name, not to mention that a younger person calling an older person by name was a huge taboo. For this reason, older people also showed respect towards the younger adult males by addressing them with ***jane*** **자네** (a formal form of "you").

And many adult males, especially scholars, had a ***ho*** **호**, a pen name or alias used in place of a given name. For female adults, ***daek*** **댁**, a suffix used to indicate a married woman who comes from that region, or ***buin*** **부인**, also a suffix indicating whom (which family) she is married to, was used. You might have seen in Korean dramas that Korean people, although not related at all, call each other using familial terms like ***hyung*** **형** (older brother), ***nuna*** **누나** (older sister), ***samchon*** **삼촌** (uncle), ***imo*** **이모** (aunt), leaving many non-Korean viewers wondering if all Koreans are related to each other. It's just a way Koreans show affection and get along with each other. Now, the tradition has been handed down, and titles serve an important role for Koreans who need to quickly assess and properly situate the people they meet. In the era of globalization, some companies adopted the English-name-for-everyone policy to convert the hierarchical "vertical corporate culture" to "horizontal corporate culture." Below is a handy table of some of the most common Korean appellations you will hear in Korean dramas.

korean appellations

E. Example	*M2M = Male to Male
L. Literal Meaning	*F2M = Female to Male
C. Colloquial Meaning	*M2F = Male to Female
U. Common Usage	*F2F = Female to Female

OO 엄마 EOMMA

E. Seho eomma
L. Seho's Mom
C. Mrs.
U. Between Neighbors

OO 아빠 APPA

E. Rina appa
L. Rina's Dad
C. Mr.
U. Between Neighbors

OO 댁 DAEK

E. Busan daek
L. Married woman who comes from Busan
C. Mrs.
U. Between Neighbors

OO 부인 BUIN

E. Kim-ssi buin
L. Wife of Kim Family
C. Mrs.
U. Between Neighbors

사장님 SAJANGNIM

E. KIM sajangnim
L. President/Owner
C. Mr. / Sir
U. To customer/client

어르신 EOREUSHIN

E. eoreushin
L. Elder
C. Sir
U. To a senior citizen

이모님 IMONIM

E. imonim
L. aunt
C. Ma'am
U. To summon a waitress at a restaurant

선생님 SEONSAENGNIM

E. KIM seonsaengnim
L. Teacher
C. Mr. / Sir
U. To someone older / Client

어머님/아버님 EOMONIM/ABEONIM

E. eomonim/abeonim
L. Mother/Father
C. Ma'am/Sir
U. To woman/man around your mom/dad's age / Your friend's mom/dad

형 HYUNG

E. Seho hyung
L. Older brother (M2M)
C. Brother
U. Older male friend

누나 NUNA

E. Rina nuna
L. Older sister (M2F)
C. Sister
U. Older female friend

아저씨 AJEOSSI

E. ajeossi
L. Middle-aged man
C. Mr.
U. To a male not close

아줌마 AJUMMA

E. ajumma
L. Middle-aged woman
C. Mrs.
U. To a female not close

오빠 OPPA

E. Seho oppa
L. Older brother (F2M)
C. Brother
U. Younger female friend

언니 EONNI

E. Rina eonni
L. Older sister (F2F)
C. Sister
U. Younger female friend

WHAT DOES A KOREAN FAMILY LOOK LIKE?

No matter what part of the world you live in, home is where the drama is, and Korean homes are where the K-Dramas are! While they exist in similar forms beyond cultural borders, some things are culture-specific, so knowing what a Korean family looks like and how it functions will shed light on some of the scenes that made you scratch your head.

FAMILY STRUCTURE

Traditional (Joseon Dynasty period) Korean family has been a patrilocal stem family, a large family composed of multi-generations, typically composed of the grandparents, their eldest son and his wife, and their children living together under the same roof. Because Korea was an agricultural society that required a lot of labor force, families with multi-children were the norm.

WHO WEARS THE PANTS IN THE KOREAN FAMILY?

Who wears the pants in the Korean family? It's the males in descending order of age. The reason is largely due to the patriarchal family system built upon two major principles: male shall dominate female and elder shall dominate the younger. The importance of having male children, for only they can continue the family line led to the son preference, and sonless couples wouldn't stop until they finally have a son, reason why there used to be families of as many as six or seven female children with the youngest male child.

Among the male children, the eldest male child, ***jangnam* 장남**, was regarded as the major pillar of the family and received preferential treatment. He could inherit most of, if not all, the family estates, and had the biggest voice in decision making – a Korean drama cliché where younger male children complain to the old-fashioned dad over the unfair distribution, saying "is *jangnam* the only son you have?" But with great perks comes great responsibilities. It was *jangnam*'s duty to live with the parents after getting married, while the younger sons could separate into different residences. Moreover, *jangnam* was responsible for holding a ***jesa* 제사** ceremony after his parents passed away. Not to mention he was expected to live next to the parent's gravesite for quite some time after the funeral. In the case where there was no son, the grandson ***jangson* 장손** assumed the role of *jangnam*.

Up until the **Goryeo Dynasty**, women's status in the family was on par with that of men, but with the adoption of yugyo principles, it became significantly lower, with their roles mostly limited within the domestic sphere. This was mainly due to the idea that there should be a distinction between male and female, which led to the segregation against women. The main idea of ***samjongjido* 삼종지도**, the *yugyo* moral code that specifies the status and role of women used to play in the *yugyo* culture before modern times. "Before marriage, a woman has to obey her father; after marriage, her husband; after husband's death, the son." This clearly depicts the women's status/role during the **Joseon Dynasty**.

Another example is that it was only the husband who could legally divorce his wife, and there were "seven valid vices that serve as the ground for divorce," known as chilgeojiak 칠거지악. They are disobedient towards in-laws, inability to bear a son, adultery, jealousy, hereditary disease, talkativeness, and theft. But there were exceptions – if she has no place to return to, or if she was together during the three-year mourning period for her parents-in-law, or if she contributed to the previously impoverished family but helped amass a fortune.

Despite their lower status and limited roles, they were the object of reverence and respect. As a wife, they were in charge of the family finance and domestic matters, and as a mother, the education of their children. The female children did not receive a systematic *yugyo* education, but the content of their education focused on internalizing *yugyo* virtues granted to women. At the same time, they learned their role as a woman by learning household chores such as weaving from an early age. From childhood, boys and girls had different educational processes and roles.

Times have changed and so has Korean society. What has been long considered as the social norm is now regarded as something unfit. While there have been significant changes in many aspects such as the women's status and having to live next to the parents' gravesite, there are still traces of *yugyo* ideas in the life of modern-day Koreans, thus creating confusion to the non-Korean viewers. But this imbalance is an honest snapshot of Korean society which is going through a transformation. Who knows? Maybe you're witnessing an important turning point in Korean history!

JONGGA - THE HEAD HOUSE

***Jongga* 종가** refers to a head house of a clan that has been continued down only through the eldest sons for generations. As a head house of a clan, the responsibility to carry on the clan's strict discipline and tradition, and to take charge of important family events such as *jesa* ("ancestral rites"), is enormous, but they take great pride in doing it. On the contrary, it can exert the greatest influence. In Korean pop culture, the word refers to the originator of something. For example, many restaurants market themselves as having the "original recipe."

KOREAN ETIQUETTE BASICS

WHY DO KOREANS USE BOTH HANDS WHEN GIVING AND ACCEPTING THINGS?

Like bowing, using both hands when giving and accepting something (even if it's as light as a piece of paper) to and from an older person or someone of higher rank is a sign of respect, and is one of the first things a Korean child must learn growing up. As to how it's done, it varies depending on the situation. First, the standard practice is grabbing an item with both hands. That's the very basic form. Now, suppose if the other person is a little far away from you, and you would have to extend one of your arms, to reach the person. If this is the case, you can place your second hand either under the wrist or elbow of your extended arm, as if you're supporting it. You can also pass muster by placing your second hand just below your armpit. Now as for the origin of this bizarre but specific behavior, there is an interesting speculation. ***Hanbok* 한복**, the traditional Korean attire, has an oversized sleeve that hangs low. So when pouring alcohol for someone else, you had to pull it a little bit so it doesn't touch the food, and the habit passed down to become what it is today. But what about between people of your age? If you met them for the first time, use both hands. Once you establish closeness, then you are free to use one hand.

Hanbok - The Traditional Korean Clothes P. 154

WHY DO KOREANS USE BOTH HANDS WHEN SHAKING HANDS?

This is pretty much self-explanatory because it goes hand-in-hand (pun intended) with the topic we just covered. Use your right hand for handshake and place the left hand either under the wrist, elbow, belly, or armpit of the right arm. An interesting point is that handshaking is a Western custom and one-hand handshake is the standard practice, therefore Korean people engaging in a both-hands handshake (sometimes with a 90-degree bow) is a good example of "cultural glocalization".

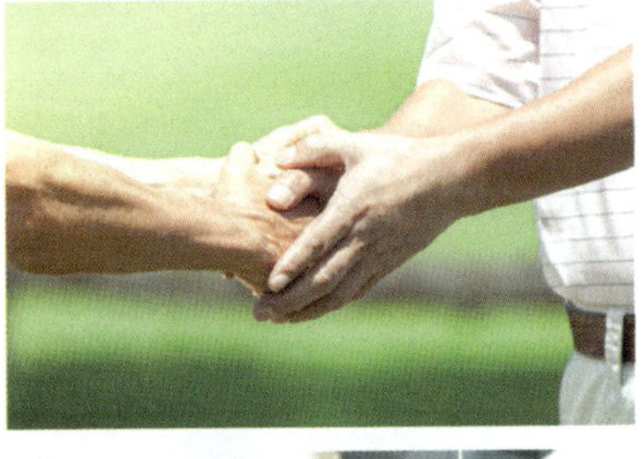

DON'T PUT THE FEET UP ON FURNITURE OR SIT CROSS-LEGGED

Korean people find it rude and insincere because it looks disrespectful to the person you are having a conversation with. It's acceptable between friends.

DON'T TOUCH AN ELDER ON THE HEAD

Touching an elder, no matter how close, on the head is considered rude and must be avoided. It's acceptable between friends.

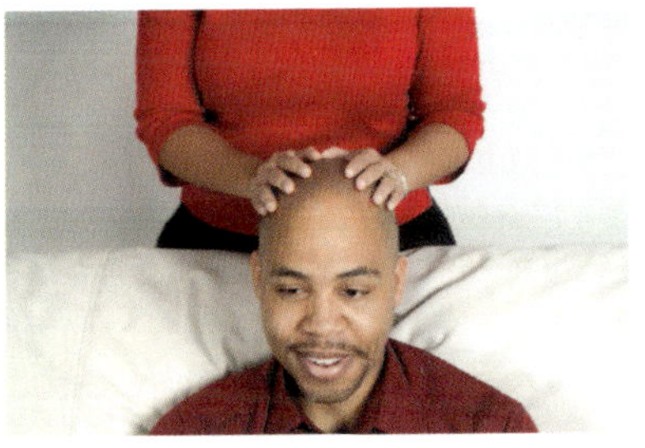

DON'T BECKON WITH YOUR PALM FACING UP OR WITH AN INDEX FINGER

The Korean way of saying "come here" is the opposite of the American style. With the palm facing down, hold your hand up about head-high and fingers stretched out and wave in and out. Never use an index finger! It's considered insulting as it's for beckoning dogs.

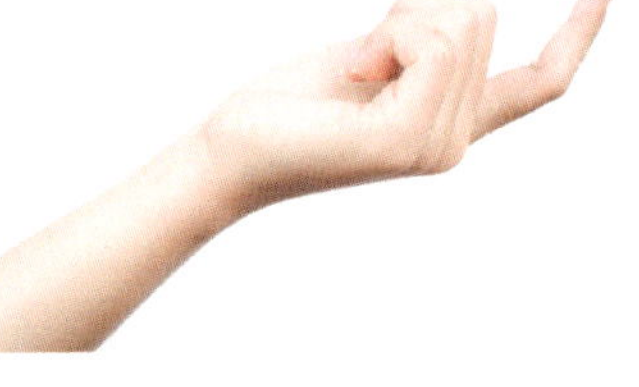

BUSINESS CARD ETIQUETTE

Business cards are handed and received with both hands to show respect. It is recommended that you rotate your business card to the other side so that the receiving person can read it right away.

Business cards should be handed from the person of lower rank to the person of higher rank. However, if you happen to be visiting, it is recommended that you, the visitor, first present the business card regardless of your status.

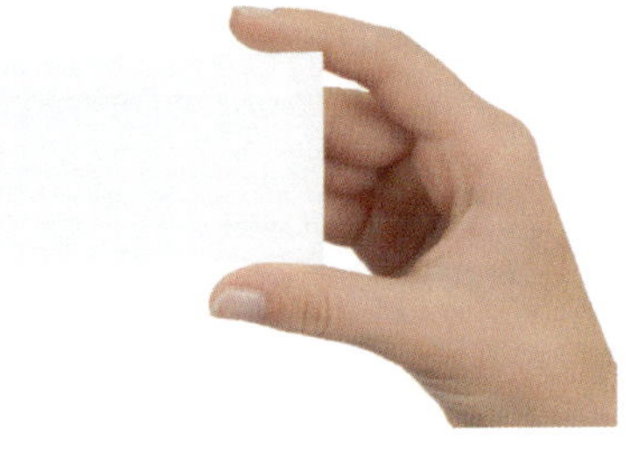

When receiving business cards, it is polite to stand up and receive even if the other person is of lower rank. When exchanging business cards simultaneously, give with your right hand, receive with your left hand, and make sure that your fingers are not blocking the other person's name on the card.

Upon receiving, quietly repeat to yourself the person's name and position printed on the card.

Finally, don't put your business card in your wallet or pocket right away, but put it in the lower right corner of your table, and pick it up upon departure.

THE ART OF BOWING

The fact that Koreans sweep all gold medals in archery at every Olympics Game proves that they surely know how to handle a bow, but it's not the only type of bow they are experts at – Koreans are masters of all kinds of bows, from casual bows to belly-button bows to half-bows to full-bows. Let's learn then all!

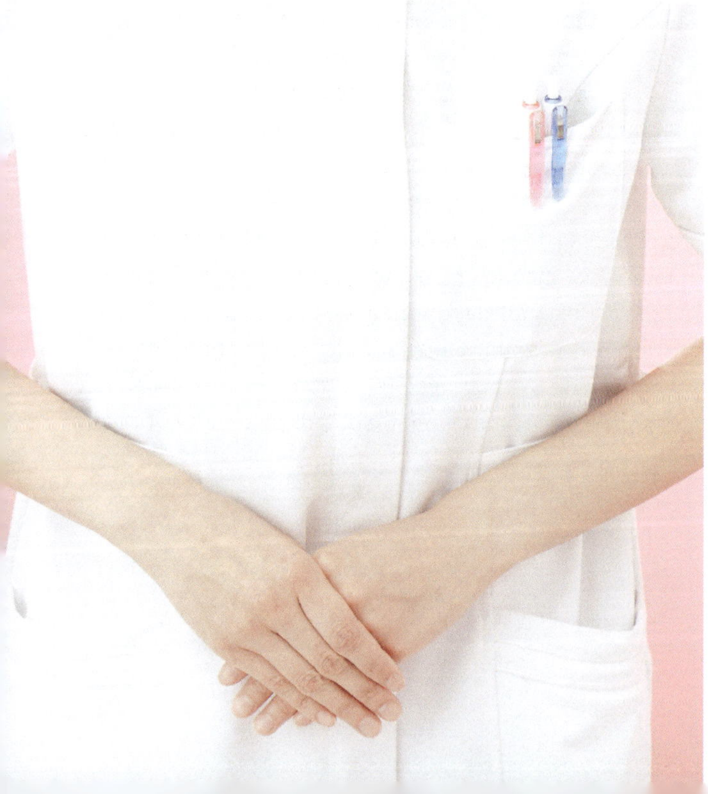

Traditionally every bow to an elder or at a ceremony begins by placing one of your hands on top of the other (left on top for male and right on top for female) and resting them below your waist. This is called ***gongsu* 공수**, and is also the default form when adopting a polite attitude. These days, however, people also place their hands straight on the side of their legs when bowing.

There are two main types of bows Koreans perform for greeting, showing respect, remorse, and gratitude, and they are standing bows and sitting bows.

The standing bows are used in everyday situations, while the knees-to-the-ground sitting bows are performed on special occasions like traditional holidays, ceremonies, and *jesa*. Due to the differences in the design of the traditional clothes, *hanbok*, they were performed differently for men and women.

경례
gyeongrye

STANDING BOW

반경례

ban gyeongrye
"Half-Bow"

Bend your waist
15 degrees

When returning a bow
Elder to a younger /
lower rank person /

평경례

pyeong gyeongrye
"Standard Bow"

Bend your waist
30 degrees

When greeting someone older
or higher in rank

큰경례

keun gyeongrye
"Big Bow"

Bend your waist 45 degrees

When you want to show
your utmost respect

의식경례

euisik gyeongrye
"90-Degree Bow"
"Folder Bow"

Bend your waist 90 degrees

Performed at ceremonies such
as a wedding and a memorial
ceremony

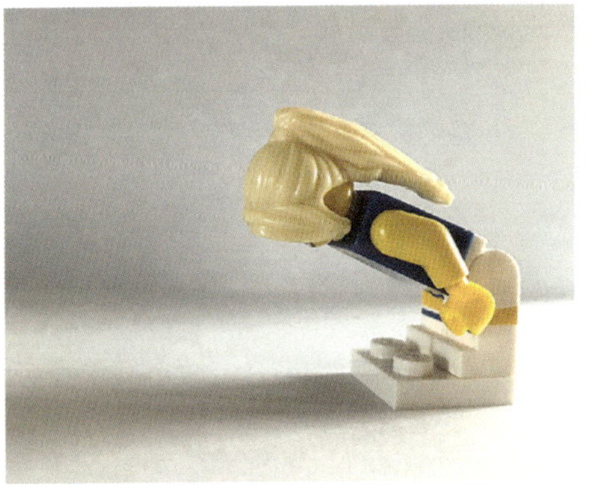

In Korean dramas, it's performed in an exaggerated manner by gangsters and junior employees who want to please their boss. Also used when asking for forgiveness.

배꼽인사

baekkop insa
"Belly Button Bow"

It's performed by service personnel such as department store employees upon greeting guests. It's termed so because you have to politely place your gongsu hands where your belly button is located.

절 jeol SITTING BOW

*For men, the left hand is placed over the right; for women, the right hand is placed over the left.

큰절 keunnjeol "Full/Big Bow"

Most formal and polite.

To whom: Elders who don't have to reciprocate when they take a bow. Husband's lineal ascendants / Spouse's lineal ascendants / Collateral ascendants within the third cousins

When: Ceremonial events / New Year's Day / Ancestral rites / Seeing each other after a long time

평절 pyeongjeol "Standard Bow"

The standard bow. When greeting someone older or higher in rank. For males, it's performed in the same way as in a big bow, but you don't stretch out your *gongsu* hand at the beginning and you get up immediately when your forehead touches the back of your hand.

To whom: Someone who must bow back with the standard bow or the half-bow. Older adults, such as teachers, elders, superiors, spouses, older siblings, sisters-in-law / People of same age / Friends / If not related, and if the age difference is less than 15 years, they will bow to each other with the standard bow.

When: Seeing each other after a long time

반절 banjeol "Half-Bow"

Performed as a Return Bow to someone younger.

To whom: One's students / Friend's children / Children's adult friends / Younger siblings / Extended family members within 10 years of age difference

When: Upon taking a bow from a younger person

*If the younger person is a minor, then the older person can give a verbal greeting instead, but it's required to return a half-bow to an adult.

SCAN THE QR CODE TO SEE HOW IT'S DONE ON YouTube

WHY

DON'T KOREANS MAKE EYE CONTACT?

Making eye contact is probably the most important interpersonal etiquette in Western culture, as it is a symbol of mutual respect and a way to build trust between each other. For that reason, deliberately looking away or avoiding eye contact is considered rude and inappropriate, and could lead the other person to thinking that you are not interested or being disingenuous.

Meanwhile in Korea, making direct eye contact can be received differently. Especially when a situation involves an older person and a younger person, the younger person tends to avoid direct eye contact as it can be interpreted as being hostile or defiant, thus lack of respect. This is especially true when an older/higher rank person (e.g., a teacher) is scolding a younger/lower rank person (e.g., a student). If you look directly in the eye while getting scolded, you can expect to hear, "How dare you look me in the eye while I'm talking to you?"- while the exact opposite is true in the West. Not surprising that it's the most discussed topic among English teachers from the West teaching in Korea (i.e., "My students keep ignoring me when I scold them!").

You can see these two cultures collide when drinking. Watch carefully – you will notice that people from the West try to make eye contact while clinking glasses (e.g., in Germany, breaking eye contact while raising your glass for a toast is believed to bring seven years of bad luck, and in Denmark maintaining eye contact is considered a courtesy to your host) while Korean people focus on the glass.

DOES A WILD ELDER ASK - "AIN'T YOU GOT NO PARENTS?"

"Ain't you got no parents?" It's a cliché expression and an indirect used by angry elders when giving a lesson to an ill-mannered youngster. As with any other idiomatic expressions, don't take it at face value – they are not interested in knowing whether you have parents or how they are doing. Rather, it's a euphemism for "You're one rude son-of-a…" because Koreans believe that proper character education starts at home under parents' supervision, so being unmannerly, especially to the elders, completely defies the Korean *yugyo* principles valuing respect for the elders. Hence the question asks whether or not one had the opportunity to learn all that through proper upbringing.

WHY

IS SMOKING IN FRONT OF AN OLDER PERSON / HIGHER RANK FROWNED UPON?

Before the late 17th century Joseon Dynasty, everyone was free to smoke without any restrictions. But as the society became more patriarchal and hierarchical, the need to discriminate the act of smoking between classes arose. The aristocrats wanted to clarify their status by using a long smoking pipe because that meant you had a servant to light it. As a result, very long smoking pipes, as long as 3 meters (10 ft), became popular. Also, they made them out of precious materials and put colorful decorations on it. But these were not enough, and it led to the imposition of strict rules and customs that defined the distinctions between classes, so they could maintain their status system and patriarchal authority. Some of them are: "You can't smoke in front of your father or older brother, not to mention the elders.""It's rude to have your tobacco pipe in front of you when you meet your elders on the street, so you must immediately hide it behind your back.""A woman shouldn't smoke in front of a man." "A commoner can't smoke in front of a nobleman." While they were not legally stipulated, they have been passed down by social conventions, and they are instilled in the minds of the Korean people.

ARE FEMALE SMOKERS FROWNED UPON?

Also, female smoking, especially in public places, has a social stigma attached to it and is often frowned upon even today. Continuing from the previous story, everyone was free to smoke regardless of status and gender at the beginning, but as society became more patriarchal and hierarchical, the noble class started viewing female smoking as something vulgar, which should be reserved only for the low-class commoners. By the time this stigma nestled down, the country was going through the modernization phase which brought the collapse of the class system. Consequently, female smoking disappeared dramatically because doing so would voluntarily signify that you come from the lower class. And this old idea is why some old Korean grandpas and grandmas go off on female smokers smoking on the street, saying, "Only the low-class commoner girls smoke!"

WHY ARE KOREANS THE SAME?

It's lunchtime at work, and the ***bujangnim* 부장님** ("team manager") calls for a team lunch at a nearby Korean restaurant. Everyone's seated and ready to order, and *bujangnim* starts off by saying "All right, I think I will go with *kimbap* today! What do you all want, guys?" As if everybody's been craving for *kimbap* the whole morning, they take turns and say, "I will go with *kimbap*, as well!" On the surface, you might think that Koreans are the people of unity and teamwork! But on the inside, it's the result of the Korean people's tendency to conform to the norm. As the proverb "an angular stone is bound to be hit by a chisel (a nail that sticks out gets pounded), is the Korean idea that values harmony and conformity which puts the group's interests before those of an individual. Good or bad? It has its pros and cons.

On the positive side, it facilitates harmony and a faster decision-making process, but the downside is that it stifles individuality and less chance of innovation because it's difficult to "think outside the box." Some of the interesting examples you can observe on the streets of Korea are the "long-padding craze" that took the Korean teenagers by storm – they all wore similar looking long padded coats as if they were a school uniform! Added to that is the same hairstyle they want to have, which changes every time a celebrity introduces a new hairstyle on a TV drama series. When the TV drama series becomes a hit, then the hairstyle gets a name after the character from the TV drama, and you can expect to see that on the streets the following week after it airs. And a few years ago, there was the "Honey Butter Chip craze," where people lined up to get their hands on a newly introduced potato chip! The demand just skyrocketed that people had to wait for days, and the resale price more than quadrupled in a secondary market. As you can see, Koreans love to be part of a group, because such "belongingness" gives them a sense of unity and security. Their dire effort to keep up with the latest trends is also related to the idea. While some find the sense of "belongingness" at the expense of one's individuality undesirable, there are companies out there that are smart enough to capitalize on the Korean characteristic.

Knowing that the Korean people are one of the trendiest early adopters on earth, many global corporations choose Korea as the testbed for their upcoming products to gauge the probability for success, thinking that if it becomes a hit in Korea, then the rest of the world must jump on the bandwagon, too!

WHAT IS
SAVING FACE?
KOREAN PSYCHOLOGY EXPLAINED

"Did you have to correct my mistake in front of my business partners? I totally lost my face today!"

"Thank you for talking me up to my girlfriend today. You really saved my face!"

"Face" used here is a conceptual representation for "social standing," "reputation," "honor," "influence," and "dignity" – known as ***chemyeon* 체면**, and is extremely important in Korean culture. As noted previously, Korean society is hierarchical which is determined by the dynamics of relationships among the members of a circle. For that, how one's perceived is very important, and maintaining and preserving one's reputation in front of others is also crucial. For this reason, not making others "lose face" is equally important as "saving your face." To avoid this, it's best to engage in indirect expressions when in front of other people. For example, when refusing or rejecting an offer from someone, do not outright say "no," but find an indirect route to express your thoughts. Also, try to avoid direct confrontation when dealing with someone older or higher in rank even if the older/higher rank person is clearly at fault. Pointing out their mistake in private will be much appreciated. It's always a good idea to allow the elders to lead the decision-making process and honor their opinion if possible, such as when they insist on picking up the tab after a meal because Korean society runs on a set of unwritten rules of hierarchy, and letting a senior do what they are expected to do would help them "save their face."

KOREAN EMOTIONS EXPLAINED

“JEONG IS PROBABLY THE MOST MYSTERIOUS WORD IN KOREAN DRAMAS”

***Jeong* 정** is probably the most mysterious word in Korean dramas because it gets translated differently (e.g., “affection,” “intimacy,” “sharing,” “generosity,” “love,” “emotional bond,”… You name it.) every time it pops up! Because it connotes such a wide spectrum of meanings, even the most advanced Korean language experts find defining it quite difficult, let alone explaining it to foreigners who don't have a deep understanding of Korean culture to fully comprehend the context in where it’s used. As a result, the concept is often chalked up to “cultural idiosyncrasy” and gets introduced to foreigners as something unique to Korean culture which can’t be understood unless you are Korean, keeping it shrouded in mystery. But is it really? Let’s look at the journey of Maria, an exchange student from Texas, who had a series of accounts of the mysterious Korean *jeong*.

Day 1 in Korea – “I arrived at the boarding house located in Seoul. The landlady ***ajumma* 아줌마** seemed like a very caring person but a little nosy at the same time. She asked a lot of personal questions like if I have a boyfriend or not, when my birthday is, what my blood type is (creepy!), how old I am, how tall I am, how much I weigh and stuff, things I would share only with my doctor, but I decided to look on the bright side and believe she was showing genuine interest in me! She even told me to call her my “Korean mom,” which I thought was a really kind gesture. I almost cried. This must be the Korean *jeong* they are talking about?”

Day 5 in Korea - “Today I got totally flabbergasted when I came back home from school! I opened the fridge to grab a bottled water and what the heck? There were a bunch of Tupperware containers sitting in the fridge! Inside them were different types of ***kimchi*** and all sorts of Korean foods which definitely were not mine. I immediately knew that someone broke into my room so I thought about calling the police but reached out to the landlady for help. She came down to my room and to my surprise, she said, “Oh, I put them in there for you! I make extra for everyone here. They are very yummy! You should try them all!” Wait… So she just arbitrarily decided to barge into my room without my permission and put them in my fridge? I didn’t know what to say so I just said thanks but I couldn’t wrap my head around it for quite some time. I spoke to another exchange student from Brazil, and she said that’s the Korean ***jeong***! She also said she had the same experience, and got used to it and she likes it now. All right… When in Seoul I should do as the Seoulites do then!”

Day 8 in Korea - “I stopped by my favorite ***tteobokki* 떡볶이** place for a quick lunch and the owner ***ajusshi* 아저씨** greeted me with a huge smile, as always. I ordered a *tteokbokki* but he also gave me a roll of ***kimbap* 김밥**, saying that it was a “service,” which means “complimentary/on the house!” This must be the awesome Korean *jeong* again!

Day 9 in Korea - “I went to an evening class and sat next to my favorite Korean friend Min-su. During the break, I took out a bag of BBQ-flavored potato chips and an energy bar I brought for dinner. I asked Min-su if he already had dinner, but he said he wasn’t hungry. I finished my snacks just before the break ended, so I crinkled and tossed them into a trash can. When I got back, Min-su said, “Oh my god… You absolutely have no ***jeong***! You didn’t even offer me a bite…!” I was like… What? Sir, you said you weren’t hungry…? Was I supposed to insist on sharing it with him? This *jeong* thing really confuses me…! After a long day of culture shock, I finally got home to chill and watch Netflix. I tuned to this Korean family drama that’s all the rage these days. In the drama, this old couple constantly

Popular Korean Dishes You Must Try P. 59

quarrels over the most trivial things. The wife leaves the house in a huff, and her worried daughter chases her right after. On a park bench, the daughter asks her, "Mom, why don't you just divorce him then? Don't worry about me, I just want you to be happy!" Then the mom says, "It's not because of you, sweetheart! It's because of this damn *jeong*..." Okay, so there's that *jeong* again and this time it really came out of nowhere. I'm just way too tired to process all this... so I'm just going to call it a night and go to sleep!"

Day 98 in Korea – "Today's my birthday and I got the biggest birthday gift ever. I woke up to a call from the owner *ajumma* inviting me to have breakfast with other housemates. I went down to the dining room in my jammies, and was greeted with everyone in the boarding house, all shouting, "Happy birthday, Maria!" My eyes flooded with tears and I said, "How in the world did you know it was my birthday?" Natasha from Russia answered, "***Ajumma*** remembers everything about us, and for us! She's our Korean mom!" Oh my goodness... I flashed back to the first day I got here – All the questions she asked... and the birthday, she still remembers it... "Don't cry, Maria and have your birthday ***miyeokguk* 미역국**! This is what we eat on our birthday, as a means to celebrate and honor your mom." I lifted my spoon and had a sip of my first *miyeokguk* in Korea and it's something I never experienced before - This is what the Korean *jeong* must taste like!"

Eat Seaweed Soup On Birthdays P. 99

That was quite a journey Maria had, wasn't it? I believe her experiences of *jeong* could help you get the drift of the concept. In the beginning, we briefly touched that some of the popular translations for *jeong* include "affection," "emotional attachment," "bond," and "generosity," and we can see that they all point in the same direction: humanistic values. Then the real question is – are these something unique to only Korean people? Of course not. They are the basic universal emotions all humans possess regardless of race and culture, but how they were displayed is different – it was the style that's uniquely Korean, and it's called *jeong*. It's similar to how different cultures create stunningly different dishes using the same ingredients that are universally available, when mixed with their own unique cultural elements. The interpretation is a dish unique to their society! *Jeong* is no different – it's the Korean interpretation of the universal ingredients, mixed with unique Korean cultural elements like *yugyo* values, social hierarchy, collectivism, and the co-existence of traditionalism and modernism. And just with any ethnic food, first-timers might find it too foreign. *Jeong*, too, can come as a shock for many (a possible red flag for the invasion of privacy, lack of respect for personal space and life, etc.), especially those who come from an individualistic culture. But like an acquired taste, many find *jeong* to grow on them once they understand and decide to embrace the concept.

This ***jeong*** has been the glue that kept the Korean people together through history, looking after each other and helping each other, even without explicit request – ***dure* 두레**, a farmer's cooperative group during the Joseon Dynasty is a prime example. Again, this notion – acting proactively on one's own assumption to help and care and expect the same from another is the key point here. A popular catchphrase for a chocolate-pie advert, "***malhaji anado alayo* 말하지 않아도 알아요** ("You don't have to say it for me to know it")," captures the essence of the ideology. It's good to know that there's someone who's looking out and cares for you like a family, but it also has a downside – the excessive attention and concern for others can be burdensome for many, and even many Korean people find it unfit for the modern-day Korean lifestyle where individualism is of higher priority than of the agriculture-based family-oriented traditional society. Reflecting the change in sentiment, the use of the term ***ojirap* 오지랖** ("nosy", "meddlesome", "intrusive") and a newly-coined term ***kkondae* 꼰대** ("fogey" or "Boomer" as in "*OK, Boomer!*") are popularly used.

So... What do you think? It looks like showing love is important, but how you show it is even more important, and *jeong* would be something everyone would enjoy if proper balance were achieved, like using ***gochugaru* 고추가루** ("chili pepper powder") which adds a unique flavor to Korean dishes.

HAN

ANOTHER TERM THAT GETS MENTIONED OFTEN AS A UNIQUELY-KOREAN EMOTION IS 한 HAN.

Another term that gets mentioned often as a uniquely-Korean emotion is ***han* 한**. While also difficult to find the perfect word-for-word translation, it's usually described as "pent up emotions," composed of a combination of resentment, regret, grief, longing, and sorrow largely coming from being hopeless in one's struggle and suffering (some say that *saudade* in Portuguese and *тоска* in Russian are quite similar in meaning, and also note that it's different from ***wonhan* 원한** ("grudge") whose focus is revenge and retaliation). Although it's described in Korean pop culture and literature as a national trait embedded in the Korean people's DNA, some historians find its roots from modern Korean history. According to Sandra So Hee Chi Kim, "[H]an did not exist in ancient Korea but was an idea anachronistically imposed on Koreans during the Japanese colonial period." Added to that was the fratricidal tragedy of the Korean War, and the "shared suffering and struggle" of the Korean people gave birth to the notion of *han*. In Korean dramas and literature, *han* is also associated with "not being able to achieve or get something that one earnestly longed for or desired.". For example, old people who can't read or write because they had to work to support the family during difficult times say that it's been their *han* all their life that they never got the chance to go to school. And the opponents of the idea that *han* is the national trait of Koreans say that Koreans are actually the people of ***heung* 흥** ("fun/joy") because Koreans always find a way to bring joy and excitement to wherever they are needed! If you want to experience the Korean *heung*, try any sporting event and you would find yourself wondering if you are in a giant karaoke because everybody sings the cheering anthem and chants the players' names non-stop. With such overflowing energy you would surely doubt whether "resentment, regret, grief, longing, and sorrow" even exist in the Korean dictionary.

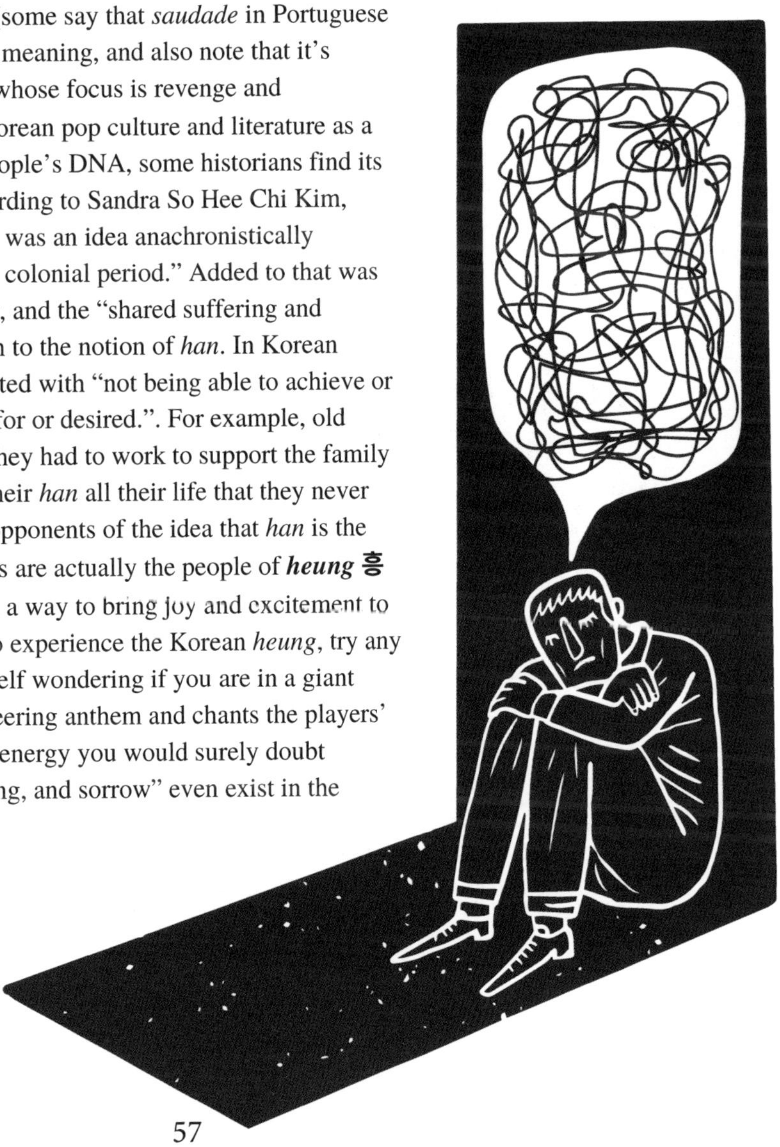

WHAT DO KOREANS EAT?

HANSIK

TRADITIONAL KOREAN CUISINE

"Namdo Hanjeongsik" by Republic of Korea

WHY DO KOREAN RESTAURANTS GIVE YOU FREE SIDE DISHES?

"Hm, I don't think I ordered these..." If you take someone to a Korean restaurant for the first time, this is the type of response you would get. The assortment of colorful small side dishes are called ***banchan* 반찬**, and they are served along with the basic Korean table set-up which includes rice, soup, ***kimchi***, and ***jang*** (sauce) to complement the main dishes like ***galbi* 갈비** and ***bulgogi* 불고기** and a stew. They are complimentary (yay!) and are presented in the middle so they can be shared. As for the origin, it's believed to have received a Buddhist influence (as far back as the Three Kingdom Era, 57 BC) which strictly encouraged vegetarianism, giving birth to the vegetable side dishes to complement rice and soup. Depending on the number of **banchan** offered, the table setting with side dishes, or ***bansang* 반상**, is called 3 (***sam***) ***cheop*** 첩, 5 (***oh***) ***cheop***, 7 (***chil***) ***cheop***, 9 (***gu***) ***cheop***, 12 (***shibi***) ***cheop bansang***. According to history, Korean kings had 5 meals a day, 2 of which were the 12 (***shibi***) ***cheop bansang***, which had a special name called ***surasang* 수라상**, meaning "royal meal". If you want to taste the essence of Korean *banchan* culture and feel like a Korean king, you should visit a ***Hanjeongsik*** 한정식 (Korean Table d'hôte) restaurant!

POPULAR KOREAN DISHES

YOU MUST TRY

Naengmyeon 냉면
Chilled Buckwheat Noodle

Yukgaejang 육개장
Spicy Beef Soup

Galbi Gui 갈비 구이
Grilled Beef Ribs

Tteokbokki 떡볶이
Stir-fried Rice Cake

Bibimbap 비빔밥
Rice Bowl With Meat & Veggies

Samgyetang 삼계탕
Ginseng Chicken Soup

Kimbap 김밥
Seaweed Rice Roll

Sundubu Jjigae 순두부찌개
Silky Tofu Stew

Samgyeopsal Gui 삼겹살 구이
Grilled Pork Belly Slices

Sundae 순대
Stir-fried Korean Sausage

Bulgogi Gui 불고기 구이
Grilled Marinated Beef With Vegetables

Pajeon 파전
Green Onion Pancake

Japchae 잡채
Stir-fried Glass Noodles & Vegetables

Bossam 보쌈
Boiled Pork Wrap

Jeyukbokkeum 제육볶음
Stir-fried Marinated Pork

WHY DO KOREANS EAT SIMMERING HOT SAMGYETANG ON THE MOST SWELTERING DAYS OF SUMMER?

How do you beat the heat of a hot summer day? A can of ice-cold beer or some ice cream (with a brain freeze!) seems like an obvious choice, but Koreans have a vastly different strategy! Instead of taking the "cool road," Koreans eat a simmering hot ***samgyetang*** **삼계탕** ("ginseng chicken soup"), a type of ***boyangsik*** **보양식** ("health food" Koreans eat to boost up the stamina and energy), on the most sweltering days of the Korean summer, known as ***boknal*** **복날** ("the dog days of summer").

WHAT IS BOKNAL?

THE "KOREAN DOG DAYS OF SUMMER"

Boknal comes in three parts, or ***sambok*** **삼복**("three *bok* days") - ***chobok*** **초복** ("first *bok* day") ***jungbok*** **중복** ("middle *bok* day") and ***malbok*** **말복** "last ***bok*** day." They fall between mid-July and mid-August with 10 days and 20 days in between the first and the middle, and the middle and the last *bok* days, respectively. Interestingly, it perfectly fits the term "dog days" because the Chinese character for *bok* **伏** is a dog lying on its stomach, maybe exhausted from the heat.

伏

Iyeol Chiyeol - "Fighting Fire with Fire"

The logic behind this counter-intuitive tactic called ***iyeolchiyeol*** **이열치열** ("control heat with heat," or "fight fire with fire"), is all about maintaining a proper balance within our body. According to traditional Korean Medicine, ***haneuihak*** **한의학**, the heat in the body during the summer is concentrated under the skin and makes our body relatively cold on the inside. Thus, eating cold food will only provide temporary relief, but worsen the situation in the long run. Instead, a hearty bowl of simmering hot *samgyetang* will help you restore the balance and replenish your body with the essential nutrients. By the time you put down the bowl, you would be all soaked in sweat, and you know you are ready to make it through the Korean summer!

보양식 BOYANGSIK "HEALTH FOOD"

Chueotang 추어탕
Loach Soup

Jeonbokjuk 전복죽
Abalone Rice Porridge

Nakji Bokkeum 낙지볶음
Stir-fried Octopus

Jangeo Gui 장어 구이
Grilled Eel

Dakjuk 닭죽
Chicken Rice Porridge

JANG - KOREAN SAUCE AND SOUP BASE

***Jang* 장**, the Korean sauce and paste (and a popular last name) is the staple of Korean cuisine. As a sauce, it nicely compliments other food such as vegetables and raw fish, and as a paste, it becomes the base of numerous Korean soups and casseroles, including ***doenjangguk* 된장국** ("bean paste soup") and ***kimchijjigae* 김치찌개** ("*kimchi* casserole"). Traditionally, this versatile ingredient comes in 4 different types.

Ganjang 간장 - soy sauce

Makganjang 막간장- Common soy sauce made by dipping ***meju* 메주**, bricks of fermented soybeans.

Gyeopjang 겹장 – Thick, aged soy sauce made by mixing soy sauce with *meju.*

Eoganjang 어간장 - Soy sauce made from fish which is fermented for more than a year with salt.

Doenjang 된장 - bean paste

***Tojang* 토장** - Made by mashing the *meju* that's not been used for making *ganjang*.

Makdoenjang 막된장 – Made by mixing *meju* after using it for making soy sauce with salt, barley rice, and chili powder.

Cheonggukjang 청국장 - fermented bean paste

***Cheonggukjang* 청국장** - Made by crushing the salted boiled beans that were fermented for 2-3 days.

Dambukjang* 담북장** – Made by adding minced radish and ginger to ***cheonggukjang.

- The fundamental difference between *cheonggukjang* and soybean paste lies in the fermentation period and the salt content.

Gochujang 고추장 - made with red pepper powder, glutinous rice, meju powder, malt, and salt

Chogochujang 초고추장 – Made by mixing *gochujang* with vinegar. Popularly used as a dressing for ***hoedeopbap* 회덮밥** ("rice bowl with raw fish") and a dipping sauce for raw fish.

Ssamjang 쌈장 – Spicy paste made by mixing *gochujang* and *doenjang*, along with sesame oil, garlic, scallions, and onion. Used when eating ***ssam* 쌈** – food wrapped in a leaf.

***Meju* 메주 -** A brick of dried fermented soybeans that serve as the basis of Korean *jang*. It's made by crushing, pounding, and kneading the cooked soybeans into a brick shape, which then goes through the fermentation process. Colloquially, maybe because of its bumpy and rough texture, meju is used as a metaphor for an ugly person.

WHY DO KOREANS EAT DOGS?

It wasn't until very recently that ***samgyetang*** became synonymous with "health food." There always had been an undisputed No. 1 king - ***boshintang* 보신탕**. The soup, which uses dog meat as its main ingredient, has been believed to provide rich nutrients to the heat-weary Koreans while promoting stamina, as the name "invigorating soup" implies (the original name is ***gaejangguk* 개장국** ("dog soup"), and *boshintang* is one of the less direct/offensive names people used). The soup is very similar to another Korean dish, ***yukgaejang* 육개장** (made with shredded beef with scallions, fernbrakes, onions, and *gochugaru* (chili powder).

However, with the hosting of international events such as the 1988 Seoul Summer Olympics, voices grew for establishing a food culture that conforms to the global standard, mostly fueled by the condemnation from the Western media. As a result, *boshintang* restaurants had to take a renaming strategy into consideration because of city-wide ban and crackdowns of such "abominable food." They chose to use different names such as ***yeongyangtang* 영양탕** ("nutrition soup") or ***sacheoltang* 사철탕** "four-season soup" to stay off the radar. And this is when ***saymgyetang*** found the opportunity to jump in and become the successor to the throne, which used to be an alternative option for those who didn't want to choose *boshintang*.

Today, *boshingtang* still maintains its existence, especially in the rural parts of Korea, but voices opposing dog meat are louder than ever. Partly due to the unsanitary environment and inhumane methods in the slaughter process, but the dramatic shift in the perception towards the domesticated animals, from livestock to family members has been the driving force. Considering that there are over 10 million pet owners in Korea, such change seems totally natural. And at this rate, many project that *boshintang* will soon disappear in Korea.

HISTORY OF DOG MEAT

While Korea has been widely perceived as the only country in the world that eats dog meat (again, up your marketing/PR game, Korea!), there were and are many countries that ate and are still eating it in other parts of the world (hats off to Korea for taking the rap for other countries?). For example, in mainland China, over 20 million dogs are slaughtered for meat every year. In Taiwan, dog meat consumption used to be allowed, but was outlawed in 2001, and a law banning all consumption was passed in 2017. In the markets in Vietnam and the Philippines, dog meat is sold as regional delicacies.

Even in Europe, which vehemently opposes eating dog meat, there is a historical record of consuming dog meat, as part of the food culture, but mostly as an emergency source of food to survive special circumstances such as famine and war. Whatever the case, the most important thing is that these countries have a long history of banning dog meat from being sold and consumed, and are also calling for other countries to join in the battle for better treatment of animals. Dog meat advocates argue that it's an imposition of Western culture on their unique food culture, but this argument is losing steam.

During the Siege of Paris (1870–1871), food shortages caused by the German blockade of the city caused the citizens of Paris to turn to alternative sources for food, including dog meat. There were lines at butchers' shops of people waiting to purchase dog meat. Dog meat was also reported as being sold by some butchers in Paris in 1910.

Dog meat has been eaten in every major German crisis since, at least, the time of Frederick the Great, and was commonly referred to as "blockade mutton". In the early 20th century, high meat prices led to widespread consumption of horse and dog meat in Germany. In the latter part of World War I, dog meat was being eaten in Saxony by the poorer classes because of famine conditions.

The consumption of dog meat continued in the 1920s. In 1937, a meat inspection law targeted against trichinella was introduced for pigs, dogs, boars, foxes, badgers, and other carnivores. Dog meat has been prohibited in Germany since 1986.

In 2012, the Swiss newspaper Tages-Anzeiger reported that dogs, as well as cats, are eaten regularly by a few farmers in rural areas. Commercial slaughter and sale of dog meat is illegal, and farmers are allowed to slaughter dogs for personal consumption. The favorite type of meat comes from a dog related to the Rottweiler and consumed as Mostbröckli, a form of marinated meat. Animals are slaughtered by butchers and either shot or bludgeoned.

In his 1979 book Unmentionable Cuisine, Calvin Schwabe described a Swiss dog meat recipe, gedörrtes Hundefleisch, served as paper-thin slices, as well as smoked dog ham, Hundeschinken, which is prepared by salting and drying raw dog meat. It is illegal in Switzerland to commercially produce food made from dog meat.

source: en.wikipedia.org/wiki/Dog_meat

SO, WHY?

To understand, it would be meaningful to explore how dog meat became a popular ingredient in the history of many countries, including Korea. First, cows were the most important farming tool and asset in agricultural countries and thus the slaughtering was regulated by law. Although beef consumption was quite substantial, it was difficult for ordinary people to enjoy unless it was a special occasion like someone's birthday or a wedding. What about pigs? Pigs were also not a common food ingredient because it was a difficult animal to raise in private homes because what they eat completely overlapped with what people eat and they eat a lot (double the food expense!). They also provided no use for an agricultural society. Naturally, the ideal candidates for meat were limited to chickens and dogs. But because chickens are small in size and lay eggs every day, it made more sense to take eggs everyday than to eat them. Considering all that, dogs were a choice left for meat. If it's any consolation, most of the dogs consumed for meat are the yellow mongrel breed named ***hwanggu* 황구** or ***nureonggi* 누렁이** "yellow one," which is raised specifically for meat. As previously mentioned, with the abundance of other meat alternatives and improvements in animal rights, dog meat consumption is rapidly decreasing.

why do Koreans drink MAGGOT JUICE?

The Internet went crazy when a foreigner couple traveling in Korea posted a picture of a milky drink on their social media, dubbed "Koreans drink maggot juice," which they later said was just a harmless prank and officially apologized (but the damage was done). The drink in question was ***shikhye* 식혜**, a traditional sweet Korean rice punch. The grains of cooked rice are part of the drink that stay afloat -and, most importantly, they are not maggots!

what are some ODD THINGS Koreans eat?

***Sannakji* 산낙지**- In Park Chan-wook's thriller flick **Old Boy (2003)** what shocked the viewers more than the wicked plot is the grotesque scene where the revengeful protagonist Oh Dae-su crams a squirming live octopus, *sannakji* into his mouth and mercilessly chews it while pulling off its tentacles desperately clinging to his face for escape. Is this how Koreans eat an octopus? Well, Koreans do enjoy eating live octopuses mostly as an ***anju* 안주** (food eaten with drinks) to accompany *soju*, but without the "eat-or-be-eaten" fight because it's chopped into small pieces and sprinkled with sesame oil. Even after that, the severed tentacles would keep on squirming, not because they try to reclaim their pieces but because of reflex actions. For this reason, eating *sannakji* poses a significant risk of choking, and reports of deaths are not uncommon. It is a delicacy that needs to be had with extreme caution!

***Beondegi* 번데기**– In the year 2310, the civilization of the earth was devastated by nuclear war, and mankind struggles to find food. What comes to the rescue is... silkworm pupa! Well, that sounds more like an opening scene from a Bear Grylls episode, doesn't it? Well, silkworm pupa, called *beondegi* in Korean, is a street food, prepared either boiled or steamed and served in a paper cup with a toothpick. It's something not everyone likes due to the repulsive, primal look (dead bugs!), but they are rich in protein, vitamins and amino acids, as extolled by the futurologists. They also come in canned forms, so you might want to consider stocking up to survive the future nuclear apocalypse...

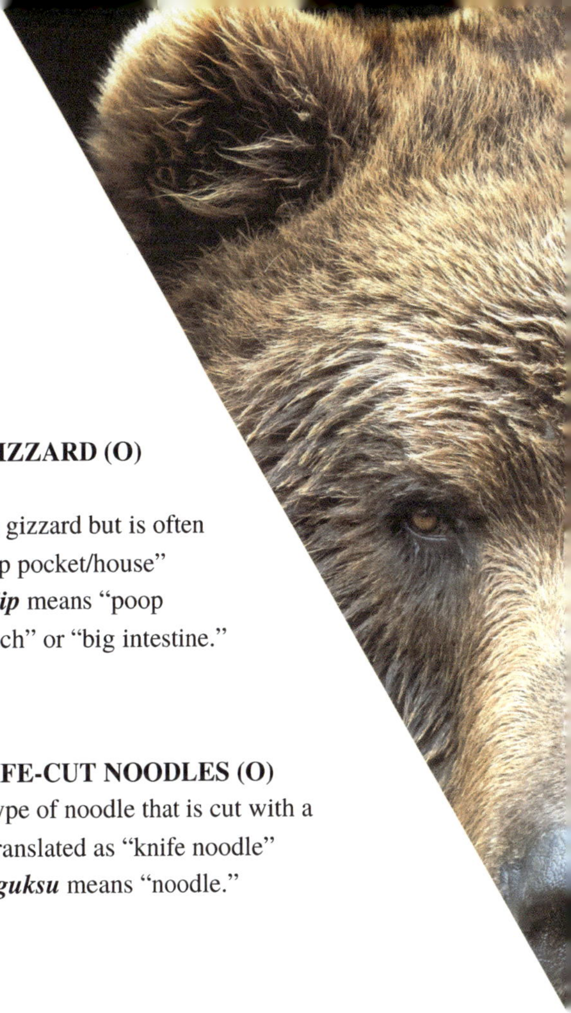

it's just a BIG
MISUNDERSTANDING!

CHICKEN ANUS (X) – CHICKEN GIZZARD (O)

Dakttongjip* 닭똥집** refers to the chicken gizzard but is often erroneously translated as "chicken's poop pocket/house" because ***dak means "chicken" and ***ttongjip*** means "poop house," which is a vernacular for "stomach" or "big intestine."

KNIFE NOODLES (X) – KNIFE-CUT NOODLES (O)
Kalguksu* 칼국수** refers to the type of noodle that is cut with a knife, but is often erroneously translated as "knife noodle" because ***kal means "knife" and ***guksu*** means "noodle."

BEAR SOUP (X) – BEEF-BONE SOUP (O)
Gomtang* 곰탕** to the type of soup that's boiled for a long time, but is often erroneously translated as "bear soup" because ***gom meaning "well-boiled" happens to be a homonym with the animal "bear."

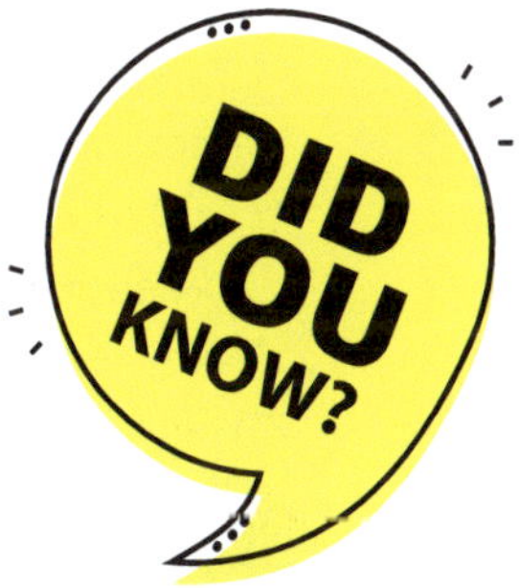

'L.A. GALBI' IS NOT FROM LOS ANGELES

L.A *galbi* (above) is a delicious **Korean BBQ** that's mistakenly thought of having originated from Los Angeles due to its name, but the abbreviation actually refers to "lateral," because that's the way the meat and bone are sliced. So it's not "Los Angeles-style *galbi*," but "laterally sliced *galbi*," compared with the regular *galbi* (below).

WHAT ARE THE TYPES OF TTEOK (RICE CAKES) AND THEIR MEANINGS?

MADE BY STEAMING IN A SHIRU 시루 – A LARGE EARTHENWARE STEAMER

***Baekseolgi* 백설기**

Meaning "white snow rice cake," made of white rice. It's considered a "sacred food" as the word ***baek* 백** means both the color white and number 100, symbolic of "purity" and "completeness," respectively. Used for children's first 100-day celebration, ***baekil* 백일**, and traditional rituals.

***Patshirutteok* 팥시루떡**

Made of rice, glutinous rice, and topped with red bean. Popularly used for business opening events, and passed around to neighbors after moving to a new place as the red color of the red beans are believed to chase away evil spirits.

Sultteok 술떡

Made with ***makgeolli* 막걸리**, unfiltered rice wine. The flavor of rice wine stays after steaming, but the alcohol content is almost non-existent.

MADE BY POUNDING RICE OR GLUTINOUS RICE IN A MORTAR OR POUNDING BOARD

***Injeolmi* 인절미**

Made with glutinous rice and coated with bean powder.

Why Do Koreans Eat Tteokguk On New Year's Day? P. 148

***Garaetteok* 가래떡**

A long white cylindrical (traditionally by hand-rolling) rice cake made with white rice, often cut into smaller portions. The long shape symbolizes "longevity" while the sliced pieces symbolize "prosperity" because of their similarity to the traditional Korean coins.

MADE BY KNEADING DOUGH INTO DIFFERENT SHAPES, AND BOILED OR STEAMED

***Songpyeon* 송편**

Half-moon shaped rice cake that contains sweet fillings such as red beans, soybeans, chestnuts, or honey. They are steamed in a steamer over a layer of pine needles. Traditionally, families would gather around to make them during **Chuseok 추석** (Fall Harvest Festival). There's a belief that if a single woman makes a pretty *songpyeon*, she will find a great husband, and if a pregnant woman makes a pretty *songpyeon*, she will have a pretty daughter.

***Gyeongdan* 경단**

Small ball-shaped rice cakes filled with red bean or sesame paste, coated with black sesame or bean powders.

MADE BY PAN-FRYING

"Hwajeon_Cooking_10" by Republic of Korea (flickr.com/photos/koreanet) licensed under CC BY 2.0 (creativecommons.org/licenses/by/2.0/)

***Hwajeon* 화전**

Thin, mini pan-cake like rice cakes made of glutinous rice, decorated with flower petals.

BONUS STORY

SHINTO BURI - PRODUCES FROM KOREAN SOIL ARE BEST FOR KOREAN BODIES?

Similar to the concept of "locavore", the practice of only consuming locally grown food, ***shintoburi* 신토불이** literally means "the body and the land (soil) can't be separated," often mistaken as a traditional ideology, it is believed to have originated as a campaign slogan during the 1980s to revive the nation's agricultural industry by promoting the consumption of local produce which was losing market share to imported agricultural products due to lowered tariffs. There is a very popular namesake song by the singer Bae Il-ho.

WATCH IT ON YouTube

eaten by presidents and beggars alike

RAMYUN

Enjoyed by presidents and beggars alike, ***ramyun* 라면** (instant noodles in Korean) is a truly versatile food that can be had as a snack or as a meal. The best thing about these curly noodles that come in a shiny polypropylene packaging is simplicity: Just bring 2 1/2 cups of water to a boil, add the soup base powder (they also have it in liquid form these days), and dried vegetable mix. Let it boil for just about a minute or two and carefully drop in the noodles (purists don't break it in halves!). Gently submerge them with a utensil, cover the lid, and let them waltz for 3 minutes tops unless you want them soggy. Oh, many people choose to add an egg for protein to what is otherwise a mostly-carbs meal. Voila! You just made yourself a bowl of perfectly cooked ***ramyun***! As for eating it, many Koreans swear by kimchi as a perfect accompaniment. And believe it or not, they also love to add an extra bowl of rice when the noodles are all gone but have lots of soup left (low-carb dieters should jump to a different topic now).

Okay, here are some fun facts about Korean instant noodles you can read while enjoying your own.. The first instant cup noodles ever made in Korea was **Samyang Cup Ramen** (the first instant cup noodles was introduced by the Japanese company **Nissin** in 1971, which also developed the world's first instant noodles in 1958). Back then, it didn't receive a warm welcome because it was fairly expensive compared to the living standards of the Koreans, and wasn't in line with traditional Korean table manners where everything has to stay on the table and not in mid-air. Despite the criticism, it steadily gained popularity as people started warming up to it, and it peaked when **Nongshim** came out with their **Yukgaejang Sabalmyeon 육개장 사발면**, which had the taste of traditional Korean hearty, spicy beef soup and a container similar to a traditional bowl.

In 1988 during the Summer Olympics in Seoul, it received worldwide fame when NBC introduced it as Korea's favorite fast food. Today, Korean instant cup noodles are available all over the globe, including the least expected places like the summit of the Jungfrau and Golf Resorts in Brazil. It was also served by international airlines such as American Airline, Air France, and British Airways. **Paldo's Dosirac 도시락** has been one of the most sold cup noodles in Russia for quite some time. So, how much *ramyun* do Korean people consume? According to a research by Instantnoodles.org, Korea consumed 74.6 servings per capita in 2018, which is the highest in the world, followed by Vietnam and Nepal with 53.9 and 53 servings.

Why So Many Retired Korean Ajusshis Run Fried Chicken Restaurants? P. 98

WHY DO KOREANS LOVE FRIED CHICKEN SO MUCH?

Fried chicken, a meal/snack which Koreans love so much, to the point of giving birth to a newly-coined word ***chineunim* 치느님** "Chicken God ("fried chicken is the real deal")." **Korean Fried Chicken** ("**KFC**") is also popular outside Korea and among those visiting Korea. When Cheon Song-yi's said, "***Chimaek* 치맥 (chicken and beer)** on snowy days..." in the mega-hit K-Drama ***Byeoleso On Geudae* 별에서 온 그대 (*My Love from the Star*, SBS, 2013)**, the reaction from the Chinese viewers was beyond incredible. People lined up in front of Korean fried chicken restaurants in Shanghai, and the *Chimaek* Festival in Ningbo, China, attracted over 460,000 visitors over 4 days. Did I mention there is a popular tourist spot called the "Chicken Camp" in Korea where you can try Korean Fried Chicken in many different ways? Korean fried chicken also has been capturing the picky taste buds of American diners, with unique flavors like soy-sauce and *gochujang*. Then why did fried chicken get so much love in Korea? People say that chicken is a "community food" that is shared with others. At the same time, it's also capturing the needs of the lone-diners who are rapidly rising in numbers, as another newly coined term "1 person 1 chicken" proves its point. To sum it all up, the popularity of Korean fried chicken is a result of both traditional and modern Korean dining culture, fueled by convenience (delivery!) and the help of beer (what doesn't taste good with a can of ice-cold beer?).

PAJEON AND MAKGEOLLI ON RAINY DAYS?

If it were a rainy day, Cheon Song-yi would have said, "***pajeon* 파전** (pancake) and ***makgeolli* 막걸리** (rice wine) on rainy days..." While the *chimaek* and snowy days are more of a marketing catch phrase to promote the fried chicken consumption, the *pajeon* and *makgeolli* combo has been a long time Korean favorite. As to the origin, there are many theories because it's not clearly recorded in the history book, but these are some of the most plausible ones. The first theory is that it's the result of the "effect of association." The sound of the rain is similar to the sizzling sound of a pancake making, so when it rains, *pajeon* automatically comes to your mind. The second theory has to do with traditional agricultural culture. When the farmers were not able to work due to the rain, especially during the rainy season of Summer, they made *pajeon* to soothe their hunger and accompanied it with *makgeolli*, a farmer's favorite drink. Naturally, it became a seasonal food, and the tradition must have been passed down to this day.

WHY DO KOREANS BELIEVE KOREAN GINSENG GIVES MYSTERIOUS POWER?

The genus name for ginseng or ***insam* 인삼** in Korean is "Panax ginseng," and the word "Panax" is derived from the Greek word meaning "panacea," As the term suggests, ginseng has long been considered to have mysterious healing properties in the West. Just like the flavor of wine differs by its "terroir," the environmental factors such as the soil, weather, and cultivation method, and the amount of nutrition in ginseng varies by where they are grown. Compared to other ginseng grown in China, Canada, and America, **Goryeo 고려** (an old kingdom of Korea, 918~1392) **ginseng** is the most famous for its superior nutritional and medicinal properties. While American ginseng contains 13 types of ginsenoside, a unique vegetable saponin which is a major antioxidant active ingredient, Goryeo ginseng contains 36 types, proving why it's considered to be of the best quality in the world. When ginseng was exported to Japan during the Joseon Dynasty, payments were made in silver. If the price of ginseng was on the high end, payments were made in gold! These accounts show how popular Goryeo ginseng was. In China and Vietnam, the emperors were said to have used it as an aphrodisiac. ***Shimmani* 심마니** ("ginseng digger") refers to a person who professionally digs ***sansam* 산삼** ("wild ginseng"), which is believed to have more powerful medicinal effects than artificially grown ginseng. Upon finding rare wild ginseng, they could sell it for a whopping amount of money (it was like winning the lottery!).

HONGSAM (RED GINSENG) THE SUPER IMMUNE BOOSTER

***Hongsam* 홍삼** ("red ginseng") is made by steaming and drying ginseng. The origin of this practice is said to be to meet the demands of the Chinese consumers in the past, to prevent it from going bad. As a result of the process, the color gradually changes to red, and the concentration level of ginseng properties go up. It's believed to boost your body's immune system, but the medicinal difference between regular ginsengs has not been clearly identified. Also, the bitter taste of ginseng goes away, making it easier to take. *Hongsam* has been made into many different varieties, including hongsam candy and gummies.

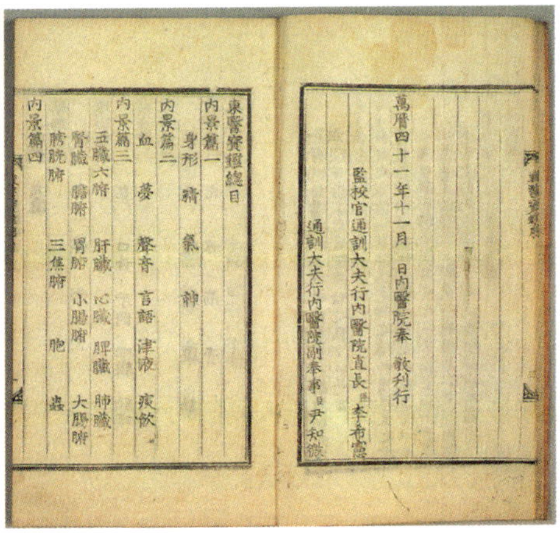

DONGUIBOGAM
THE KOREAN MEDICINAL BIBLE

Donguibogam* 동의보감*: Principles and Practice of Eastern Medicine is a Joseon-era medical book compiled by the royal physician **Heo Jun 허준**, per the royal order of **King Gwanghaegun** in 1610. It involved intensive researching and editing of Chinese and Korean medical books, and a total of 25 books were published using wood type in 1613. It's a systematic training and prescription book based on the ingredients available on the Korean Peninsula, taking into account the physical, cultural and dietary characteristics of the Korean people. It's designated as the **National Treasure No. 319** and **the UNESCO Memory of the World** and is considered one of the best medical books in the world. You can retrace Heo Jun's epic voyage by watching a hit TV drama ***Hur Jun* 허준 (*The Legendary Doctor*, 1999, MBC)**.

***Hur Jun* 허준 (*The Legendary Doctor*, 1999, MBC)**

WHAT ARE THE LITTLE GOLD BALLS KOREANS TAKE WHEN THEY FEEL LIKE FAINTING?

In Korean dramas, the main character is at an interview and is about to faint – "His palms are sweaty, knees weak, arms are heavy, there's vomit on his sweater already, mom's spaghetti, he's nervous." (Homage to the one and only Eminem!). But not to worry – he's got an ace up his sleeve. He quickly whips out a little ball wrapped in paper, unwraps it to reveal a beautiful gold ball that looks like a Ferrero Rocher, pops it into his mouth, and munches it. After a minute or so, he's calm as a cucumber, as if nothing happened, and he aces the interview. In another situation, the elderly father passes out when he hears the news that his daughter wants to marry the son of his sworn enemy. The appalled family quickly unwraps the gold ball and carefully puts it in his mouth and helps him take it with water. Moments later he magically gets back on his feet and continues to yell at her ingrate daughter. So, what's this miracle ball? Named ***woohwangcheongshimwon* 우황청심원**, meaning "a ball made with ***woohwang*** ("cow bezoar") which clears up the mind and spirit," is a traditional Korean medicine used in emergency situations involving stroke, paralysis, speech impairment, coma, high blood pressure, mental anxiety, acute/chronic palsy, and autonomic neuropathy. In other words, it's a first aid medicine and psychotropic drug.

korean folk remedies

Pricking Fingers

For severe indigestion, prick the skin just above the root of the fingernail with a sanitized needle, and squeeze out the blood. If the symptom doesn't improve, do it to all ten fingers. It's believed to force the blood circulation and the movement of digestive muscles, like jumpstarting a car.

Doenjang on Bee Stings

Surprisingly, ***doenjang* 된장** (bean paste) has been used as the first aid treatment for bee stings in Korea (not so much nowadays). The effectiveness hasn't been tested scientifically, so don't try this at home.

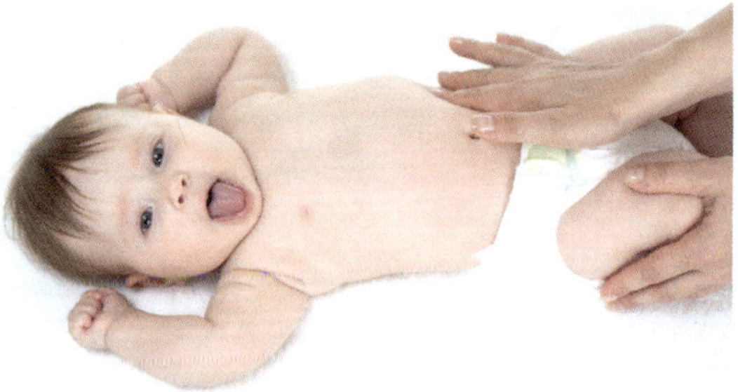

Rubbing Stomach for Stomachache

***Eomma soni yaksonida* 엄마 손이 약손이다** – "Mom's hands are the healing hands." As Korean moms/grandmas would say, the stomach rubbing is believed to relieve stomach aches. Maybe it's their love that makes the miracle?

The Content is not intended to be a substitute for professional medical advice, diagnosis, or treatment. Always seek the advice of your physician or other qualified health provider with any questions you may have regarding a medical condition.

korean
Dining etiquette

Don't lift your utensils before the eldest of the group does (during the Joseon Dynasty, ***gimisanggung* 기미상궁**, a food-tasting court lady, always tasted the royal table before serving the king to detect poison).

Don't leave the table before the eldest does.

Blowing your nose is rude, but burping is excused, but avoid loud and intentional burping in front of older people.

who picks up the tab?

- It's usually the senior of the group who'd insist on picking up the tab,. While it's a kind gesture to offer to pitch in, insisting too hard might make them "lose their face."

how young people split the bill nowadays

1. Taking turns
2. Dutch pay, or more commonly known as *en bbang* 엔빵 ("1/n" = dividing the total amount by the number of people)
3. Mobile banking - account transfer

WHY DO KOREANS EAT OUT OF THE SAME POT?

One peculiarity found on the Korean dining table is people eating out of the same pot when sharing things like ***kimchi jjigae*** (kimchi stew) or ***doenjang jjigae* 된장찌개** (bean paste stew), using their own spoon rather than a communal ladle! The proponent of this practice says that it creates an emotional bond, but the naysayers try to avoid it at all cost and demand separate bowls for each, for hygienic reasons. As a matter of fact, Koreans have an extremely high infection rate of Helicobacter pylori disease, which can cause stomach cancer, and the food-sharing culture is suspected as the main culprit. Then, where did it all begin? During the Joseon Dynasty and up until the Japanese Occupation period, Korea maintained the tradition where everybody dined on a separate mini table, known as ***doksang* 독상** ("solo table"). It was in line with the yugyo philosophy where the strict distinction between the old and the young and the men and women were defined

Doksang ("solo table")

외상을절대폐지

가족이한식탁에

영양을취하고분량은적게

同德女高普 宋今璇氏談

Newspaper published in 1936 featuring a column that promotes the *gyeomsang* ("dining together on the same table") culture

(they could, however, dine in the same place, though). But things changed during the Japanese Occupation. The Japanese Government-General of Korea encouraged the practice of eating together on the same table, known as ***gyeomsang* 겸상** because Japan needed a lot of materials including the tableware, for their military fighting in World War II. As a result, Korean families adopted the practice of putting dishes together on the same table, sharing soups, casseroles, and side dishes with each other. It's an artificial habit rather than a tradition that's been forced upon the Korean people during the difficult times. With modernization and the abundance of products everywhere, the habit has become something that many people demand unlearned.

WHY DO ONLY KOREANS USE METAL CHOPSTICKS?

"Excuse me! Do all Asian (chopsticks) look the same to you?" Well, these pairs of thin long sticks that have been picking up the 5,000 years of Asian culinary history might look similar to one another, they are very different if you look closely. The Chinese version is made of bamboo and is the longest because it's most suitable for picking up and not dropping the food from the sharing plate placed in the middle of the table. The tips are hexagonal because it is believed to attract wealth. Meanwhile, the Japanese chose wood as their main material, and the sticks are shortest in length with sharp tips, best for tearing apart and deboning fish. Korean chopsticks are surely an object of scientific study because Koreans are the only people in the world that use metal chopsticks! Specifications wise, they are shorter than the Chinese chopsticks but longer than the Japanese ones, with rectangular tips. As for the history, they are believed to

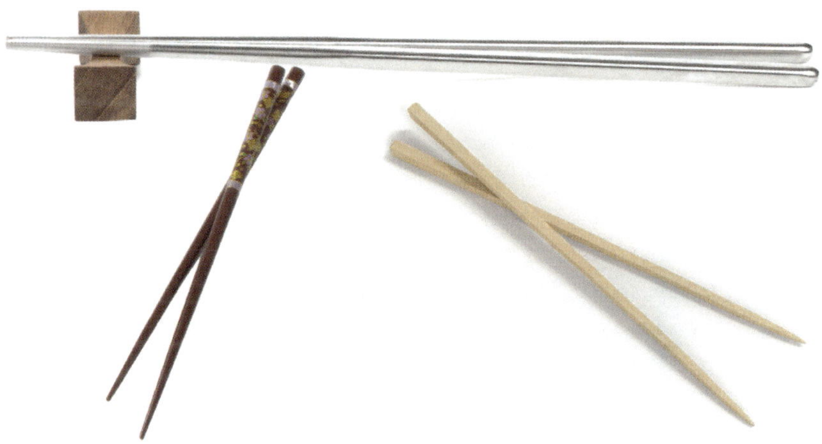

have been used as early as the Three Kingdoms Period because they were found in the remains of the royal family of the **Baekje 백제 Dynasty** (18 BC – 660 AD). During the time, the royal families and the upper class used silver spoons and chopsticks to detect poison in their food. The commoners got vicarious satisfaction by using a similar version made with a cheaper metal. Compared to wood chopsticks, metal chopsticks have more pros than cons. They are more sanitary because germs and bacteria can't live on them, and their extreme durability passes the test of time, as seen with the case of the royal remains of the ancient kingdom. The downside is that they are more difficult to use – they are a lot heavier and provide less grip compared to wood chopsticks, thus requiring more time to master. Some Koreans, when bragging about the sophisticated arts and crafts of their ancestors and the cutting-edge electric products made by their descendants, they jokingly give credit to the arduous hand-eye coordination training from using the metal chopsticks which gave them the dexterity required to perform such complex tasks.

WHY IS THERE A ROLL OF TOILET PAPER ON A RESTAURANT TABLE?

A little out of place? Don't panic when you find a roll of toilet paper on the table. Despite the psychological association with the toilet, Korean people treat it as just another type of "tissue," like Kleenex and paper napkins. Just try to contain your imagination and focus on the food.

WHAT'S THE BELL (CALL BUTTON) ON THE TABLE FOR?

Many restaurants in Korea have a pager affixed to the table commonly referred to as the "**Call Button**." Simply ring the bell and a server will be at your service! But please be respectful and don't abuse it.

THE SELF-SERVING RITUAL

Many of the no-frills Korean restaurants might not set up the utensils for you, no matter how long you wait. Don't panic, it doesn't mean they don't want to serve you -they are letting you do the honors. Most of the time, you will find a wooden case containing the utensils on the table. If you don't see one, check under/alongside the table and there should be a drawer. Just grab your favorite picks and set them up yourself. If you happen to sit next to the utensils box, flaunt your knowledge in Korean manners by setting up for your elders and others!

WHY DO KOREANS USE SCISSORS AT RESTAURANTS?

In many casual Korean restaurants that serve BBQ and ***naengmyeon*** **냉면**, it's common for the servers to use scissors to cut meat and noodles for the sake of convenience. Rest assured, though, because they are exclusively used for food only. In fact, more "kitchen shears" are finding a spot in the kitchen around the globe as a versatile cooking tool, too.

WATER IS "SELF"?

It's a funny *Konglish* expression you can find at no-frills Korean restaurants, which simply means "Water is self-service."

WHEN CALLING A SERVER

Mostly at Korean mom-and-pop restaurants, servers are ***ajumma*** ("middle aged woman"), but instead of calling them *ajumma* which doesn't sound too friendly, people use the word ***imonim*** **이모님** which means "Ms. Auntie (***imo*** = "aunt" ***nim*** = honorific suffix)," because it sounds more friendly and respectful. With some ***aegyo*** **애교**, you might score some ***service*** ("complimentary / on the house") food!

WHY DO KOREANS LOVE SOJU SO MUCH?

When a survey report conducted by Euromonitor came out in 2014 to crown the South Koreans as the biggest hard liquor drinkers in the world (13.7 shots/week of any spirit), twice as drunk as the Russians (6.3 shots/week), and four times less sober than the Americans (3.3 shots/week), everybody was taken aback, except the South Koreans themselves who didn't find the result surprising at all. (Even when considering the fact that a large portion of Korean consumption comes from ***soju* 소주**, a Korean spirit with 16-21% alcohol by volume while many other spirits usually have double that of *soju*, with 35-42% alcohol by volume, and after adjusting the data accordingly by dividing the Korean stats by half for fair comparison, Korea still comes on top at 6.85 shots/week). According to research conducted in 2017, Koreans drank 3.4 billion bottles of *soju*. When divided by the number of people of legal drinking age, that's 85 bottles per person per year, or, 1 1/2 bottles per week per person. And while heavy drinking is certainly nothing to brag about (unless you are at a frat party), it shows how much Korean people love *soju*, among all other drinks available. One of the biggest reasons is that at just 1,800 Korean Won (= 1.5 USD) a bottle at a convenience store, *soju* has always been there for the ordinary people, through thick and thin like a loyal friend overflowing with *jeong*. Hence in popular culture, the iconic green bottle has been a symbol of joys and sorrows of the ordinary people, with the magical property of helping people vent, bond, and do stupid things like falling in love. Put differently, *soju* is what causes all the drama around us. Speaking of which, here are some of the most overused Korean drama clichés featuring *soju*.

KOREAN DRAMA CLICHÉS FEAT. SOJU

DRUNK "LOVE CONFESSION" AT POJANGMACHA

A boy and a girl (let's say Junho and Youngmi, both of legal drinking age) are sitting across the table at ***pojangmacha* 포장마차** (tent/street bar) . Youngmi has a secret crush on Junho. The unsuspecting boy Junho starts talking about other girls. Youngmi, lightweight and never drank with Junho before, pours soju into her shot glass and gulps it down. Junho, dumbfounded, says, "What's wrong with you?" and grabs her wrist to stop her. Youngmi violently shakes him off and says, "Since when do you care?" An hour later, Youngmi, completely inebriated, tongue tripping, manages to blurt out that she likes him, and immediately knocks out on the table. Junho brings Youngmi to her feet but to no avail. As a last resort, Junho decides to give Youngmi a piggyback ride to his home. On the way, Youngmi continues murmuring under her breath, saying "You little b@stard, you… I like you so much… and I hate you…" The next morning, Junho is busy making breakfast for two. Youngmi finally comes to her senses and slowly opens her eyes and looks right and left. Appalled, she almost jumps out of the bed but finds herself in Junho's oversized T-shirt. Noticing she's awake, Junho says, "Good morning, my beautiful girlfriend!"

BOSS & SUBORDINATE FACE-OFF AT POJANGMACHA

"Just do as I say! I'm your superior!", says Director Kim, and Seho, his subordinate, keeps his head down to Director Kim's angry voice. Back in his cubicle, Seho is burning with a low blue flame. It's a typical scene in Korean dramas set in a Korean workplace – notoriously rigid and hierarchical, with many unspoken rules, and subordinates are expected to follow the orders from above, no matter what, because giving honest opinions and expressing candid emotions to superiors can be seen as disobedient. The scene shifts and they are at a *pojangmacha* near the workplace after work, drinking *soju*. Both quite drunk, Director Kim opens up first. "Hey, are you still upset about the order I insisted on? I'm sorry, man. I did it with our team's interest at heart.". Seho, with his eyes half-closed, manages to retort, "You know what, sir? You shouldn't have done that if you really care about the company… You know… How dare you! I thought you were a good guy but I'm disappointed… You… You…" And goes face-first onto the table. Director Kim hails a cab and puts Seho in the back seat and pays the taxi driver in advance. The scene changes again to the next morning. Seho barely makes it on time to work. Director Kim walks by and leaves a hangover-cure drink on Seho's work desk.

"MID-LIFE CRISIS" AND POJANGMACHA AJUMMA

Minsoo, 58, just got laid off from work and is alone at *pojangmacha* , drinking *soju*, with his favorite side dish ***golbaengi muchim* 골뱅이무침** (spicy sea snails salad). Fed up with life, he knocks down shots after shots, and orders another bottle, but the owner *ajumma* intervenes. “Minsoo, you already drank too much! Go home to your wife and kids!” Minsoo insists on having another bottle. “I can’t and I won’t! They don’t respect me and they won’t even care if I come home or not. I’d rather just pass out here!”Both funny and sad, these are accurate snapshots of Korean society at large, and how Korean people manage to make it through the day. For many Koreans, hierarchy, based on age and social status, makes giving honest opinions and expressing candid emotions quite difficult in many situations. But thankfully, *soju* serves as a lubricant that helps the cogs in the wheel spin smoothly - only when used in moderation. Also, Koreans are quite generous towards what’s said under the influence of alcohol. They are very forgiving and understanding, if they can remember it till the next morning. Maybe that’s why Korean people love those green bottles so much.

WHY DO KOREANS LOVE DRINKING IN TENT BARS (POJANGMACHA)?

Pojangmacha* 포장마차** (often shortened to just ***pocha), meaning “covered wagon,” is a no-frills (expect to sit on a plastic chair) mobile outdoor restaurant optimized for efficiency. It takes the form of a tented cart and is usually run by an owner-chef *ajumma* who can single-handedly make a wide variety of *anju* (food you eat when you drink), such as ***sundae* 순대**(Korean sausage), ***dakkochi* 닭꼬치** (skewered chicken), ***haemul pajeon* 해물 파전** (seafood pancake), ***kimbap* 김밥** (Korean roll), ***tteokbokki* 떡볶이** (stir-fried rice cake), ***golbaengi muchim* 골뱅이무침** (sea snail salad), and many more. The dishes are prepared fast and are relatively cheaper than dining out at a regular restaurant, making *pojangmacha* a perfect spot for Koreans who need a quick bite and a bottle of *soju* after work. This is why most of them are clustered around office buildings, but it’s also a popular dating spot because of its lively atmosphere and is quite charming especially during the sunset. These days, the number of *pojangmacha* is constantly decreasing due to sanitary concerns and taxation issues, and “indoor pojangmacha” is on the rise as a result.

YouTube

WATCH!
A Tourist Tries Out Pojangmacha!

DISTILLED DILUTED

SOJU - THE WORLD'S BEST SELLING LIQUOR 11 YEARS IN A ROW

The name *soju* means "burned liquor" because it's made through distillation. It's colorless and has just a hint of sweetness, which varies depending on the choice of sweeteners by the manufacturer, but popular choices are saccharine, aspartame, and stevia. The first version of *soju* appeared in the 13th century Goryeo Dynasty when the distilling technique was introduced during the series of Mongol invasions. Today, **Andong 안동** *soju* is considered as the direct root of the modern *soju* we drink today. Originally, *soju* was made from distilling alcohol from fermented grains such as rice, wheat, or barley. With the prohibition of the traditional distillation technique to alleviate the rice shortages back in the 1960s, diluting the highly distilled ethanol made from potatoes, sweet potatoes, and tapioca became the only method, and it subsequently gave birth to cheaper versions of *soju* that captures the majority of the market share today. The ban was eventually lifted, and many companies have been putting efforts into reviving the traditional distillation methods, and these "premium" *soju* brands are gradually gaining popularity. How fiery is *soju*? The diluted ones range between 16% to 21% alcohol by volume, while distilled ones range between 17% to 53% alcohol by volume. In 2015, fruit-flavored *soju* with a lower alcohol content (13%), held sway over the young *soju* drinkers, who didn't enjoy the strong alcohol taste of regular soju.

WHY ARE ALL SOJU BOTTLES GREEN?

Almost all (diluted) *soju* products come in a green bottle, no matter who makes them, and there are marketing and practical reasons for this. When mass-produced *soju* first appeared in the market, the bottles were colorless. They were the norm until the 1990s, but everything changed when a *soju* brand called "Green Soju" made a debut. This new contender adopted the slogan of "eco-friendliness," and provided a milder taste than regular products, and became a huge hit. Naturally, other manufacturers followed suit and started putting their liquor into a green bottle. On the practical side, when the bottles come out of the factory, they are green, and it means no further processing such as dying is necessary, and they are available for immediate use. Hence, it's the cheapest and most readily available design. In 2010, the *soju* manufacturers signed an agreement to standardize the shape and size of the bottles, so the used bottles can be shared and recycled regardless of the manufacturer.

WHY DO KOREANS SHAKE AND HIT THE SOJU BOTTLE'S NECK WHEN OPENING IT?

One of the many things that makes drinking *soju* with Korean friends more fun is that you get to watch them perform a flair bartending show! The technique goes like this:

Before opening a bottle of *soju*, shake it or swirl it fast to create a little tornado in the bottle.

Bang the bottom of the bottle with the elbow.

Twist open the screw cap and either hit the neck of the bottle with a gentle Taekwondo chop, or make a V shape with your hand and hit the neck of the bottle between them, to get the top portion of the *soju* to splash out of the bottle.

Okay, that's pretty much it for the quick Korean *soju* flair show lesson, but have you ever wondered why they do that in the first place? I mean, the bottle doesn't contain anything else inside besides *soju* itself, so shaking and swirling wouldn't mix anything to enhance the flavor like other liqueurs, right? Well, there is a very good reason why people came up with the ritual. In the past, corkscrews were used instead of screw caps, and corkscrews will get dried out and crumble if not stored properly, leaving pieces inside the bottle. As a result, *soju* bottles sometimes had little cork pieces inside the bottle. To remove them, people started to shake the bottle to get them all in one place, then bang the bottom to force them to the top, open the bottle, then let the top portion of *soju* that contains impurities splash out by either pouring it out or for more dramatic effect, hit the neck with the hand blade or the V. Having completely shifted to screw caps now, the rituals are pointless, and even many Korean people don't know why they do it, but the fact that it's still widely practiced proves that people find entertainment value in it!

WHAT ARE POKTANJU & SOMAEK AND WHY DO KOREANS LOVE THEM?

Poktanju* 폭탄주**, literally meaning "bomb shot," refers to a cocktail drink made by mixing a high-proof drink, such as whiskey, with a low-proof drink like beer. It is termed so because dropping a shot of whiskey into a glass of beer creates an effect similar to that of a bomb explosion, and also for the fact that it makes you get drunk faster. In the past, only the privileged could afford to drink whiskey, so the ordinary people looked to their friend well within reach, *soju*, as an alternative. Among many variants, ***somaek* 소맥** (soju*** + ***maekju*** 맥주 "beer") is the number one choice among Koreans who lack the time but want to reap the benefits of alcohol in the shortest amount of time possible! The 3:7 ratio (soju:beer) is the most popular formula.

WHAT KIND OF KOREAN DRINKS ARE THERE?

TYPES

***Takju* 탁주**
(unrefined rice wine)

Makgeolli
막걸리
("roughly strained drink")

***Cheongju* 청주**
(refined rice wine)

Beopju
법주
("law liquor")
= liquor made according to a certain standard

***Honseongju* 혼성주**
(compounded liquor)

Gwahaju
과하주
("summer-passing" wine)

***Gwasilju* 과실주**
(fruit wine)

Maesilju
매실주
(plum wine)

PRODUCTS

KOREAN DRINKING ETIQUETTE

For those of you over the legal drinking age, do you remember who first introduced you to alcohol? Traditionally, Korean people regarded learning "how to drink" from their elders as the proper way because it was an essential training session for the up-and-comers to master the necessary etiquettes and manners required for drinking, so they can survive in a highly hierarchical Korean society with a myriad of unspoken rules. At the same time, it was a symbol of recognition and acceptance as a mature individual and a responsible member of the society and family, making it a great pleasure for the giver and a huge honor for the receiver. Most of the customs are believed to have originated from ***Hyangeumjurye* 향음주례**, a ceremonial gathering of intellectuals during the late Joseon Dynasty which provided lessons on drinking etiquettes and manners, so learning them will not only help you avoid making social faux pas when drinking with Korean people but help you appreciate the drinking scenes in Korean dramas as well!

- When receiving and giving a drink from/to an older person, use both hands to hold the glass/bottle. Alternatively, you can use the right hand to hold the glass/bottle while the left hand gently supports the wrist of the right hand.
- If you are drinking with a younger person or someone with the same age, you can use one hand, but if it's your first time and you have not developed a close relationship yet (i.e., you're still talking in formal *jondaetmal* 존댓말 to each other), use both hands until both parties agree.
- Always fill up the other person's glass but don't pour until their glass is completely empty.
- When drinking with an older person, turn your body away and drink with two hands. If you are sitting between older people, turn your body away to the less older person.
- When drinking in shot glasses, many would say that you have to finish the first drink in one shot. It's not an obligation and you can be excused if you can't drink a lot.
- If you are the youngest in a group, be on the watch and see if other people's glasses are empty, you can grab the bottle and pour the drink, then the receiver would take the bottle from you and pour you a drink. If the bottle is too far from you, or there are multiple bottles scattered on the table, just focus on the people near you.
- Sometimes, the oldest person or the highest-ranked person in a group might drink first and then pass it around, so that everyone drinks out of the same glass! While such practice is rationalized as a way to build trust and solidarity, it's something many people, especially the younger generation, want to avoid due to sanitary reasons. It's a very difficult situation to be in, but they still choose to partake in the ceremony not to fall out of favor.

- Don't pour your own drink. If you do, people will say that the person drinking with you will have misfortunes for 3 years! Of course, it's just an urban legend of unknown origin, believed to have been made up to encourage people to actively participate in drinking by pouring each other.
- Don't drink alone and wait for the oldest person of a group to propose a toast or lift his/her glass.
- Don't drink in three separate sips as it's reminiscent of offering alcohol to dead ancestors during the jesa ceremony.
- Don't outright refuse when offered a drink from an older person because "saving face" is important for older people. Instead, say that although you can't drink it, you would gratefully accept the glass. You can then put it down on the table, and even clink together to keep pace with the other person. It's all about keeping everyone in the loop, so just play along.

WHAT DO KOREAN PEOPLE EAT TO CURE HANGOVERS?

After a night of heavy drinking comes the inevitable - Hangovers. Koreans, known for their spirit of resistance, found ways to chase away the unwelcome guest.

TRADITIONAL APPROACH

Haejang **해장** literally means "to soothe the stomach," and Koreans firmly believe in a bowl of hearty, nutrition-packed soup to rejuvenate their dehydrated, aching bodies. For this reason, any soups eaten to cure a hangover are called ***haejangguk*** **해장국** (***guk*** means "soup," so they are commonly known as "hangover cure soup"). The following are among the popular choices. Try them all and see what works best for you! (It's a good excuse to drink, right?)

Seonjiguk
선지국
(ox blood soup)

Bugeoguk
북어국
(dried pollack soup)

Kongnamulguk
콩나물국
(bean sprouts soup)

Seolleongtang
설렁탕
(ox bone soup)

MODERN APPROACH

No time to sit down for a bowl of *haejangguk*? No worries! Your hung-over Korean friends invented a variety of ready-to-drink hangover cure products you can grab at a convenience store near you. They contain ingredients such as dihydromyricetin extracted from the raisin trees in **Gangwon Province**, milk thistle, red ginseng, and medicinal herbs that are proven to help relieve, as well as prevent hangover symptoms. Try them all and see what works for you! (Hey, another good excuse to drink!)

Another product that deserves an honorable mention is the **Garamandeun Bae 갈아만든 배** ("crushed pear (juice)," more popularly known among the non-Koreans as the "ldh" drink, for that the Korean word "**배**" looks like the alphabet "**ldh**." This sweet crushed-pear juice found itself in the limelight when GQ magazine published an article introducing the Korean crushed-pear juice as a legitimate potion to prevent hangovers if taken beforehand.

WHAT ARE 1-CHA, 2-CHA, AND 3-CHA THAT KOREANS COUNT WHEN DRINKING?

When Korean people go out, they go out-out, and won't settle in just one place. Rather, they would let their party spirit guide them and visit a series of places for continued entertainment. Each changing of place/stage is called ***cha* 차** ("order, number, turn"), and the 1-*cha* (***il cha***, "first stage") typically starts at a restaurant to have dinner and drinks (***samgyeopsal* 삼겹살** (pork belly) and *soju* is a popular combo). When people start to feel the effect of alcohol, someone will shout out "let's go 2-*cha*," (***i cha***) and begin the bar-hopping sequence! Usually, they move on to a bar or pub suited for more intense drinking. By the time they are done paying respects to Dionysus, the omnipotent God of alcohol, everybody is in the right atmosphere for 3-*cha* (***sam cha***), to meet Apollo, the God of music. That's right! It's ***noraebang* (karaoke)** time! Here, the main purpose is not singing but relieving all your stress because if you've made it to this stage, you're too drunk to care what the lyrics are. Better yet, or adding fuel to the fire, most *noraebangs* serve alcohol, so you can stay tipsy throughout the session.

TYPES OF DRINKING GAMES

SAM-YUK-GU 삼육구 ("3,6,9")

Everybody goes around in order, counting out the numbers loudly. Whenever there is 3,6, or 9, you clap instead. The same applies to multiple digit numbers if you manage to advance that far. For example, you clap once for 23, twice for 33 (because there are two 3's), and three times for 639. In the same sense, for 30-39, 60-69, 90-99, you will have to clap through them!

SON BYUNG HO 손병호

Everybody holds up five fingers and goes around in order, asking if what the person says applies to you, and if it does, you fold a finger. For example, you could say, "if any of you here never had a boyfriend/girlfriend, fold your finger." The one with no fingers left has to drink.

IMAGE GAME

Everybody grabs a chopstick or use a finger instead. When a question is asked, you point the chopstick or finger at the person you think fits the image. For example, "Who here looks like the biggest flirt?"

NUNCHI GAME 눈치 게임

It's the ultimate test of quick thinking and reflexes. It starts with everyone seated, and each has to get up in order, counting out the number loudly while doing it. If two people get up to call the same number at the same time, they both take a shot. Or, if all survive, the last person to stand up takes a shot.

BASKIN ROBBINS 31

Everybody takes a turn and counts out a number loudly, in ascending order. It has to be anywhere between an increment of 1-3. As the name suggests, whoever says the number 31 loses the game.

WATCH! What Korean Hoesik Is Like

A *hoesik* scene from
Once Upon A Time in Saengchori
원스어폰어타임인 생초리
(2010, tvN)

HOESIK – THE DREADED COMPANY EVENT EVERYONE WANTS TO AVOID

1-***cha***, 2-***cha***, 3-***cha***, and even 4-***cha***? When partying with your buddies, it's all fun, but what if it becomes part of work? Would it still be fun? Well, maybe you can learn vicariously from the Koreans! In the Korean workplace, there is this culture called ***hoesik* 회식** (literally means "eating together" but can be translated as "company dinner" or "company get-together" or "company (un)happy hour"), which most people fear and try to avoid if at all possible. Wait, you get to hang out with your colleagues over dinner and it's like a little staff party? What's not to like?! Well, if used in moderation, *hoesik* can have many benefits like building a strong team-spirit and promoting a more candid exchange of opinions. But the fact that it's forced upon the subordinates at the expense of their personal lives, and how it leads to an unproductive workplace environment, makes *hoesik* feel like a boot camp for grown-ups... Here's the breakdown. First of all, mandatory attendance is expected. Of course, Korea is a free country and you can choose not to partake should you wish so, but the Korean proverb, "an angular stone is bound to be hit by a chisel," advises you not to, because doing so will mark you as someone who prioritizes themselves over the organization. Second, they will come out of left field and catch you off guard. If your superior feels like it, he/she will announce it at the last minute and consider your dinner plans canceled. "Thirsty Thursday" with your buddies? Forget it. Friday night date plans? Forget it. In Korean dramas, couples break up over this issue, but for a dishonest person, it's a perfect alibi to cover up his/her infidelity (i.e., "Honey, you should go to bed first. I'm still at *hoesik*..."). Third, the office hierarchy and workplace politics will tag along. This starts from determining where to sit - if you sit too close to your superior, you might look like an ass-kisser, and if too far from the "main" group, you risk looking like an outcast. More, you will have to laugh at every single lame joke your superior makes. Not only that, if you are the ***maknae* 막내**, or the youngest in the group, you're in charge of ordering, making ***somaek***, filling up the glasses and many more. If the gathering ends in 1-*cha*, or 2-*cha*, you are lucky! Most *hoesik* last until 3-*cha* or 4-*cha*, and thou shalt not leave before your superiors do. At *noraebang*, you are expected to sing to "liven up the mood," and it's wise to choose a song that your superiors like. But, that's not all, folks! You should also grab a taxi for your inebriated superiors who can barely walk. By the time you get home, you will only have a few hours to sleep until you have to be at your work desk in a few hours... don't be late!

Why Do Korean People Ask For Your Age At The First Encounter? P. 37

WHY DO KOREANS WORK SO DARN HARD?

For most of you who know Korea as the birthplace of the trendy K-Pop and some of the world's largest enterprises like Samsung and LG, and after seeing the city's skyscrapers soaring to the sky, it might come as a shock that the country was one of the poorest countries not so long ago. And it was not an overnight rags-to-riches, Cinderella style fairy tale. Here's the real story.

During the first half of the 20th century, Korea had nothing but a series of hardships and agony. **The Japanese Occupation** exploited the nation in every possible way, which reached the peak during the **Pacific War (1941-1945)** and **World War II (1939-1945)**. The much needed capital, the land, the natural resources, and the lives of the Korean men and women were indiscriminately procured to the Japanese military fighting in the war. The joy of liberation that came with the **Japanese surrender (1945)** was short lived. Just 5 years later, Korea experienced the fratricidal tragedy – **Korean War (1950-1953)**. This 3-year-long all-out war burned the nation to utter ashes. The **U.S. General Douglas MacArthur**, the designated commander of the United Nations during the Korean War lamented the devastation and predicted that it would take 100 years for the nation to recover. The living conditions of the Korean people were just awful. What was considered a decent meal, lucky if you could get it, was a mere hodge podge of scrounge or smuggled leftover foods from the U.S. Army base, and for starving families, dumpster diving was nothing to be ashamed of. One of those make-shift meals was ***kkulkkul-i juk* 꿀꿀이죽** ("piggy porridge'), which was a casserole made from putting together anything edible that you could find from the **U.S. Army base**. While unwelcomed elements like rubber bands, toothpicks, and shoe parts were often found, it was faithful to its duty of filling up the empty stomachs of the Korean people. While it can no longer be found on the menu of Korean restaurants, another variation called ***budaejjigae* 부대찌개** remains in existence, and in fact, is an extremely popular menu. Meaning "army base stew," *budaejjigae* is made with spam, ham, sausage, baked beans, *kimchi*, *gochujang*, and ramen noodles. As you can infer from its name and the ingredients list, the main ingredients are the surplus food supply scrounged from and smuggled through a black market around the U.S. Army base, added with local Korean ingredients to cater to the Korean taste buds (it was also called ***jonseuntang* 존슨탕** "Johnson soup" because President Lindon Johnson was said to have raved about the taste during his visit to Korea). These days, it's extremely popular as an *anju* dish (food consumed with alcohol), proof that Koreans don't associate it with the past struggle, although they are aware of it.

Another important term to know is ***boritgogae* 보릿고개** ("barley hump"), which refers to the common fear and hardship coming from the shortage of food every spring because it's the period when you run out of last fall's harvest and this year's barley (rice was scarce among ordinary people) has yet to ripen. It was termed so because the struggle was extremely difficult to overcome, which must have felt like climbing a hill.

WHAT IS THE "MIRACLE ON THE HAN RIVER"?

But Koreans are known for their indomitable "can-do" spirit. In the 1950s, the nation's feeble economy was barely sustained by U.S. aid, which started to shrink from the late 1950s. To rectify the situation, the nation began to seek ways to develop its own economy. After the collapse of the first **President Rhee Syngman's 이승만** government as a result of the **April 16th Revolution**, the Second Republic set up a five-year economic development plan, which wasn't implemented until the **Park Chung-hee 박정희** administration took over through the **May 16th military coup**. The Park administration vigorously pushed ahead with the five-year economic development plan, a growth policy that aimed to make Korea an **export-oriented country**.

At the same time, it set 'modernization' as a national policy goal and launched the Saemaul Undong 새마을운동 (New Town Movement) campaign which sought to fix, through modernization, the disparity of the standard of living between the rapidly industrializing urban areas and rural areas that were still left behind in poverty. The campaign's slogan, "Jalsarabose" 잘살아보세 (Let's try to be better-off) resonated with the Korean people and served as the driving force behind the dazzling transformation. Every day, people woke up motivated to participate in the development projects and went to bed feeling proud of the contribution they were making to the nation. As a result of the efforts of Korean workers who were able to provide quality labor at low wages, light industries developed greatly.

Outside Korea, a skilled labor force was its major export as well. In the 1960s, **miners and nurses** were sent to **Germany**, and in the 1970s **Koreans were working on the construction sites in the Middle East**. Also during this time, over 320,000 Korean soldiers fought in the **Vietnam War (1964-1973)**, and the subsidies and overseas combat allowances, along with loans received from the U.S. in return for their participants, were invested in fostering **light industries** as well as **national land development projects**. In the 1970s, **heavy and chemical industries** such as oil refining, shipbuilding, and fertilizer increased, and the automobile industry began to grow gradually. As a result of the efforts of the government and the people, the nation's economy grew at an unprecedented speed in modern world history. Korea's per capita income stood at just $67 in 1953 but surpassed $1,000 in 1977 and $10,000 in 2000. Exports topped $10 billion in 1977 and $170 billion in 2000, compared with about $22 million in 1957. It has achieved hundreds of times the growth in just over 30 years.

This period of incredibly rapid reconstruction, transformation, and economic development is known as ***hangang eui gijeok* 한강의 기적** "Miracle on the Han River," an analogy originally incorporated by the **Prime Minister Chang Myon 장면** of the Second Republic during the New Year's address of 1961 to encourage the fellow Koreans to make it through the difficult times by achieving an economic upturn similar to that of the "Miracle on the Rhine," West Germany's successful reconstruction through economic revitalization after World War II. Korea's economy kept on progressing and was called one of the "**Four Asian Tigers**," which also included **Hong Kong, Singapore,** and **Taiwan**. In 1996, Korea reached a symbolic milestone and made a statement to the world by becoming the 29th country to join the **OECD** (Organisation for Economic Co-operation and Development), which was mostly composed of advanced countries.

Korea successfully showcased its capacity by hosting a series of global events, such as the **1988 Seoul Summer Olympic Games**, **2002 FIFA World Cup Korea/Japan**, and **2018 Pyeongchang Winter Olympics**, to name a few. In 2018, South Korea was the 7th largest exporting country with the 12th largest GDP (Gross Domestic Product) and 30th largest GNI (Gross National Income).

Wonder how **North Korea**, who chose a vastly different path, is doing? Ever since 1974, which was the last time North Korea was ever ahead of South Korea in terms of GNI, the gap continued to widen and in 2018, North Koreans made a mere $1,300 USD per person while South Koreans made $29,900 USD per person. GDP wise, the North made 1/43 of what the South made. "The Miracle on the Han River" is one of the most remarkable achievements of modern Korean history, which made Korea a model example for developing countries hoping to emulate the success.

WHY DO KOREANS SAY "BECAUSE OF IMF"?

As the movie ***Gukgabudoeui Nal* 국가부도의 날 (*Default*, 2018)** accurately portrays, Korea's economic winning streak came to a screeching halt when it fell into an ambush in 1997. The Asian Financial Crisis took the region by the storm, causing a serial collapse of economic meltdown. Korea was among the countries hit hardest by the sudden blow and was on the verge of default due to the foreign exchange shortage. Countless companies filed for bankruptcy, and people were losing jobs, and families were forced out onto the streets. Korea managed to bail out through international financial supports including **IMF** (International Monetary Fund), but at a steep price. The government had to carry out extensive corporate restructuring and institutional improvements over the years, and people had to tighten their belts. This period, one of the most difficult and disgraceful times in modern Korean history, is commonly known as the "**IMF Era**," and the expression "**because of IMF**" was used by people whose life was drastically changed as a result of it.

THE GOLD-COLLECTING CAMPAIGN

Remember? Koreans are known for their indomitable "can-do" spirit! The "Gold-collecting campaign," ***Geum Moeugi Undong* 금모으기 운동**, was a national patriotic movement that took place in the wake of the 1997 financial crisis with the aim of collecting gold from the public, exporting it, and converting it into dollars to increase foreign exchange reserves to repay the foreign-exchange debt which amounted over $300 billion USD. Over 3.5 million people participated, voluntarily bringing out their cherished items like wedding rings to gold medals, and the campaign was able to collect a total of 227 tons of gold, which was double the amount of what Korea Bank had in reserve. With the unified effort of the people and the successful restructuring of the economy, Korea was able to announce on December 4th, 2000, that all the loans from the IMF were paid off and thus completely got out of the financial crisis.

Gukgabudoeui Nal 국가부도의 날 ("Default", 2018)

WHY DO KOREANS LOVE SPAM?

What would be a good holiday gift in Korea? Surprisingly, one of the most popular gifts during the holidays is SPAM. How has SPAM ham become so popular in Korea when it is treated as a "cheap pseudo-food," or "food that reminds you of war" in the U.S.? According to the NPR (National Public Radio), South Korea is the second-largest spam-eating country after the U.S.. It was during the Korean War that SPAM was introduced to Korea, when food was scarce, especially meat. At that time, SPAM was a luxury food that only the rich and those tied with the U.S. army base could afford, and for the less fortunate, ***budaejjigae***, made using leftover food from the U.S. army base, was a wonderful means as it contained SPAM, a precious source of protein. Of course, *budaejjigae* is not the only reason why SPAM is loved by Koreans. One of the reasons is that the salty taste of SPAM goes perfectly with rice and *kimchi*. The increase in the number of dual-income families and single-person households who enjoyed the convenient recipe is also a contributing factor. In addition, the series of advertisements promoting the image of 'quality processed meat' worked like a charm.

WHO ARE THE CHAEBOLS?

Chaebol* 재벌**, composed of two Chinese characters ***jae* 재 財** "wealth" and ***beol* 벌 閥** "clan/faction," refers to the **family-owned and controlled large Korean conglomerates with diversified subsidiaries**. Occupying a lion's share in various areas of the Korean economy, *chaebols* were intensively fostered by the Korean government's economic development policy in the 1960s and 1970s. During this process, *chaebols* played a crucial role as a driving force for the rapid economic growth, but because they expanded their power through strategic alliances with other political and business circles, harmful effects such as monopolization and political back-scratching have occurred. Korean *chaebol* dramas like ***Royal Family* (2011, MBC)** and ***Sangsokjadeul* 상속자들 (*The Heirs*, 2013, SBS)** portray the unique Korean management style of *chaebol*, with the most notable characteristic being the enormous amount of power and authority the owner family can exert, which often supersedes that of the management. As of 2019, the top 5 biggest ***chaebols in terms of the total assets are **Samsung**, **Hyundai Motors, SK**, **LG**, and **Lotte**, and their presence in the Korean economy is huge, with the total combined asset of the top 4 was nearly half the total GDP of Korea in 2017. The concept of *chaebol* is so unique that it's one of the Korean words listed in the **Oxford Dictionary**.

In Korean pop culture, *chaebol* is colloquially used to mean "super-rich" and it's the most popular character in a Cinderella-type story drama. A cliché scene involves a cocky, arrogant son of a *chaebol* family who believes his money can buy anything including love but changes completely after meeting an innocent humble girl, realizing that the sincere heart is the only thing that can buy love.

WATCH!
Stereotypical Chaebol
Characters in K-Dramas!

SO, WHAT'S IT LIKE TO WORK IN KOREA?

According to statistics from the OECD (Organisation for Economic Co-operation and Development), the average annual working hours per person in Korea was 2,024 hours, second only to Mexico's overwhelming 2,258 hours (hats off, I mean, sombreros to our hard-working Mexican friends!). Considering that the average annual working hours in 36 OECD countries is 1,746 hours, Koreans work 278 hours more annually than the OECD average, the report showed.

But does sitting in front of a study table longer mean you will score higher on a test? Not necessarily. Although Koreans work more hours, the productivity score of Korean workers is not high compared to other OECD countries. Korean workers' productivity score ranks 29th among 36 countries. Ireland, the top scorer, has hourly productivity of $86, more than double that of Korea. Korea's hourly productivity of its workers has been growing slightly since 2011 when it topped $30, but it is still lower than that of other advanced countries. Analysts say that longer working hours are hurting the average.

What adds to the working hours? Mostly it's ***yageun* 야근**, or working overtime at night. While Korea has a statutory working week of 40 hours and 12 hours of paid overtime on weekdays and 16 hours on weekends, many old-fashioned workplaces force their employees to work overtime because they have the wrong perception that working overtime means "working hard." In places with poor working conditions, people often work overtime and stay up all night without getting properly paid. Moreover, the fact that you shouldn't punch out before your superiors do is another contributing factor of the long working hours. But with people demanding better "work-life balance" and companies prioritizing efficiency over more working hours, the overall working conditions are constantly improving.

YOUR FIRST DAY AT WORK IN KOREA MIGHT START AT A TRAINING CAMP!

For many large Korean companies, your first day at work doesn't start in the office cubicle. Instead, as a new recruit, you will be put in a training camp and go through an intensive team-building program! More commonly known as OT (orientation) or OJT (On-the-Job-Training), new employees will stay together for a few weeks at a training facility and learn about the company – the founding ideology, history, main service & product line, values, and the company anthem! At the successful completion of the program, you will have transformed into a perfect piece for the system!

WHY SO MANY RETIRED KOREAN AJUSSHIS RUN FRIED CHICKEN RESTAURANTS?

Choegoeui Chikin 최고의 치킨
(*Best Chicken*, MBN, 2019)

In the romantic comedy Korean drama, ***Choegoeui Chikin*** **최고의 치킨 (Best Chicken, MBN, 2019)**, Park Choi-go's dream is opening his own fried chicken restaurant. He pompously quits his job working as an employee at a large corporation to pursue his dream. Although the idea of typing away at the keyboard in office cubicles to frying chickens in the kitchen may seem like an extraordinary transition, it's actually one of the most popular post-career choices Korean people seek after retirement. Why? Knowing how much Koreans love fried chicken and beer combo *chimaek*, it shouldn't come as a surprise from a pure business perspective, but there's more to it. Korean people have the tendency to identify themselves with the job they have, and the workplace is an extension of their home. For this reason, they have the notion of "**lifelong jobs**," and pursuing a continuous single career is considered a virtue. With the life expectancy going up every year and with the "60 is the new 50" idea in effect, Koreans still want to and have to remain economically active to support their post-retirement life (legal retirement age is 65 in Korea). So what do they do? Having pursued a single career, trying something new seems dangerous, so naturally, they are compelled to choose something anybody can do – a franchise fried chicken restaurant. The biggest merit is that it's supposedly a turn-key business - the franchise headquarter will set everything up for you, from selecting the location to marketing to interior design. You can just focus on frying chickens and receive a stable stream of income. What's not to love? In reality, it's not as rosy as it sounds. The competition is fierce – there are over 409 fried chicken franchise brands and over 87,000 stores, and 14,509 of their stores are in Seoul alone. For comparison, there are 1,350 Lotteria Burger stores, 436 McDonald's stores, and 442 Domino's Pizza stores in Korea. As a result, it truly became a "game of chicken," and there are more stores that close than open because if you factor in the franchise fees and royalties, it's usually the franchise that's making money. So in a sense, the abundance of fried chicken restaurants shows the reality of the limited **post-retirement options** Korean people have.

Why Do Koreans Love Fried Chicken So Much? P. 69

하이스쿨: 러브온
(*Hi! School-Love On,* KBS, 2014)

스카이캐슬
(*SKY Castle,* JTBC, 2018)

WHAT'S IT LIKE TO STUDY AS A STUDENT IN KOREA?

Your God offered you the opportunity to start your life all over again – but here's the fine print - as a student in Korea, would you take it? Well, the answer would sharply diverge depending on what type of drama you watched. If the bubbly lovey-dovey teenage romance drama like **하이스쿨: 러브온 (*Hi! School-Love On,* KBS, 2014)** was your cup of tea, you would sign the contract in a heartbeat. On the other hand, you would definitely turn down the offer and walk away from the table had you recently watched **스카이캐슬 (*SKY Castle,* JTBC, 2018)** – where the parents go as far as blackmailing, intimidating, and all sorts of hanky panky just to put their kids ahead of others to get them into prestigious colleges, and mostly to keep their egos inflated at the expense of their children's freedom. It was a shock to viewers around the world who were used to believing that everything Korean high school boys and girls did was exchanging candies and love letters. SKY Castle is not about puppy love but a reflection of the appallingly grim side of the Korean education system. While it's best to watch the whole series to understand what it's like, let me quickly walk you through an abridged version of a day in the life of a typical Korean high school student. Take a deep breath and hang tight!

The first class starts at 9 A.M., 5 days a week, but you should get there early because you have to go through a rigorous screening process which might add extra minutes. When you get to the main entrance, the teachers on duty and the members of the student council check your hair length (if it's over the certain limit, you will get a "free haircut" on the spot by the teachers), and whether it's dyed or permed (both are prohibited). Also checked is the dress code – whether you are wearing the school uniform according to the school standards. (The rules on hair has changed after ***dubaljayuhwa* 두발자유화** "Prohibition of Haircut Restrictions" went into effect in 2018).

"*Such intolerance*!" You say loudly to yourself, as you head to the classroom. Okay, you are now in the classroom, and the class promptly starts at 9 A.M. A school day consists of 7 sessions, each with 50 minutes of lessons and 10 minutes of break time in between. Lunch is from 1 P.M. to 2 P.M. and is served either in the classroom or in the student dining room. The last session ends at 4:50 PM. Yes! Free at last? Not so fast! You have to attend extracurricular activities for an hour. Then it's feeding time again! After an hour of dinner, it's already 7 P.M. It was such a long day! So... that means you can finally pack up and go home, right? Not so fast! After dinner is a 3-hour long late-night self-study session, which used to require mandatory attendance until very recently (most schools nowadays changed it into a voluntary system). Okay then, what do you do now with the precious extra 3 hours? Most students would go to ***hagwon* 학원** (after-school tutoring companies) or get private tutoring at home. If you don't want to fall behind (so much peer pressure!), you might want to consider one of the two (or both?) options, right? Oh wait... Don't forget to do your homework! Ugh!

And that's just how Korean high school students spend their day, and multiplying that by 5 is how they spend their week. The weekends aren't off days either – studying continues at *hagwons* or at home by private tutoring. But the worst comes when you reach ***gosam* 고삼** (short for "3rd year in high school," graduating class) where everything intensifies! How bad? A famous Korean saying, ***"sam dang sa rak"* 삼당사락** ("three hours (of sleep) you pass and four hours (of sleep) you fail"), will give you a pretty good idea.

So... What do you think? Does starting your life over again as a student in Korea still sound like fun? I'll leave it up to you to decide, and while you weigh up the pros and cons of each scenario, let's do some digging as to why Koreans are so obsessed with education in the first place!

WHY DO KOREANS STUDY SO DARN HARD?

Does every profession deserve equal respect? Korean people in the past certainly didn't think so. The traditional *yugyo* ideology called ***sa nong gong sang* 사농공상**, or "the four categories of occupations," (scholars, peasant farmers, artisans and craftsmen, and merchants listed in the order of their social status) dominated Korean society and led it to favor scholars, giving them more social status and prestige over those in other categories who were often looked down upon, even with contempt.

As for the noble people, the gateway to success and prestige was passing the state-wide civil service examination called ***gwageo* 과거**, to become a member of the state officials. It was of such importance that unsuccessful applicants would keep trying years after years, and many died without bearing fruit. These national traits still remain intact in the modern-day Korean society, but the fervor for education is so much greater than it was in the past. As previously learned, Koreans devote countless hours to studying so they can do well on the modern-day *gwageo* equivalent, ***suneung* 수능**, or "national college entrance exam." Like in the past, passing the exam with a competitive score will get you into a top university (the top 3 most prestigious universities are **Seoul National University, Korea University, and Yonsei University** – hence the name **SKY Castle**). Like in the drama, the parents would use every conceivable means to get their kids into one of those schools because it entails the opportunities for prestigious occupations and a connection to the successful alumni network. It was of such importance that unsuccessful applicants would keep trying years after years until they get into their dream university. For the guaranteed success and all the perks that entail, parents would invest a massive amount of money into education, hoping their investment will pay off.

SUNEUNG - THE BIG DAY FOR STUDENTS

The second or third Thursday in November every year, when the regular school curriculum is completed, is the big day every graduating *gosam* student anxiously waits for. ***suneung* 수능**, short for ***daehak suhak neungryeok shiheom* 대학수학능력시험** "College Scholastic Ability Test (CSAT)," is a national exam that tests the students' ability required for a college education. Topics include Korean Language, Korean History, English, Math, Second Foreign Language/Hanja (Chinese Characters and Classics), Social Studies, Science, and Vocational education, and the test results are an important element that affects the likelihood of getting accepted to a college. The event receives national attention (because everyone had to take the test as a student) and everybody would be walking on eggshells, which often don't make any sense to the eyes of a foreigner. For example on the test day, airplanes stay grounded or circle around the airports to avoid making noise during the listening test session. The stock markets have a delayed start time while public transportation provides an increased number of rides to prevent traffic jams so that the test-taking students can get to the testing site on time. In rare cases (but happens every year), police cars come to the rescue of a troubled student running late by providing an emergency ride. Outside the testing sites are the parents sticking ***chapssaltteok* 찹쌀떡** ("glutinous rice cake") and ***yeot* 엿** ("taffy") to the gate, both symbolic of passing the test. And while this day means a finish line for many students, those who are not happy with their scores would run the track again, in hopes of achieving the score needed to get into the college they want. Students decide to go for ***jaesu* 재수** ("second try"), ***samsu* 삼수** ("third try"), or even ***sasu* 사수** ("fourth try"). For some students, the pressure is so enormous that they would go as far as taking their own life for letting their parents down.

"FREEDOM FOR OUR HAIRSTYLES!" HAIRCUT REGULATIONS

If you are used to seeing the hot and flashy hairstyles of K-Pop idols, you might have assumed that it's what the typical Korean teenagers look like in real life! But Korean schools continued to maintain a code of strict haircut regulations until very recently. Considered as one of the last remnants of the Japanese Occupation whose education system was modeled after that of their military academy, it was criticized for depersonalizing the students, and it was finally lifted in 2018, and each school adopted more relaxed versions of regulations.

WHY DO KOREAN STUDENTS STUDY ABROAD SO MUCH?

Have you had a Korean student studying in your country? They are not a rarity because, as seen from the chart, Korean students are one of the things Korea exports a lot of! We know that studying abroad costs a fortune – the tuition,the living expenses and everything, but why do so many Korean parents still send their children to study abroad at an early age?

- To avoid the limitations of cramming education in Korea focused on college entrance and the stress from fierce competition.

- To take advantage of the advanced educational infrastructure and capitalize on the scarcity and premium of obtaining a degree from a prestigious university, which would give a competitive edge in finding a job in Korea.

On the monetary side, studying abroad was a privilege that only the wealthy could afford. For those below the middle class, it demanded an enormous sacrifice of their parents.

WHO ARE THE KOREAN "WILD-GOOSE DADDIES"?

Called ***gireogi appa*** **기러기 아빠** in Korean, the "Wild-Goose Daddies" are Korean dads who work in Korea and send money to support their underage children studying abroad and their wives who are also staying there to look after them. It's termed so because they have to take a long-haul flight to visit their family, similar to how geese migrate by traveling a great length.

WHERE KOREAN STUDENTS GO TO STUDY ABROAD

2019 – 213,000 students (Source: Veritas Alpha @ veritas-a.com)

Asia – 78,861 (37% - China 50,600 / Japan 17,012)
North America – 71,108 (33.4% - USA 54,555 / Canada 16,495)
Europe – 36,539 (17.2% - UK 11,903 / France 6,948, Germany 6,835)
Oceania - 25,431 (11.9% - Australia 18,766, New Zealand 6,645)
Africa - 604 (0.3% - South Africa 490)
Central and South America - 457 (0.2% - Mexico 229)

EATING A BLOCK OF TOFU AFTER GETTING RELEASED FROM JAIL

In ***Chinjeolhan Geumjassi* 친절한 금자씨 (*Lady Vengeance*, 2005)**, the vengeful heroine Geum-ja who had to take the rap for a crime (smothering a child) she didn't commit and serve 13 years in prison is offered a block of tofu by a pastor upon release. Eating a block of tofu after getting released from jail is one of the most frequently appearing Korean movie/drama clichés. But for every social custom, there's got to be a valid reason. On the practical side, it's believed to have started during the Japanese Occupation (1910-1945), when a huge number of Korean independence activists suffered from malnutrition caused by the hardships of prison life and persecution. Upon release, they had to find a way to replenish their body in the most efficient and economical way possible – and tofu, rich in protein, healthy fats, carbs, and essential amino acids, fit the bill. Symbolically, the white color of tofu is associated with "purity" and "peace," so eating tofu is a ceremony of wishing the ex-convict to never go back to prison again. Oh, except in the movie Lady Vengeance, Geum-ja knocks the plate of tofu straight to the ground because, well, she was on the warpath for her well-overdue revenge. Tofu and revenge are a dish best served cold.

YEOT (KOREAN TAFFY) WILL MAKE YOU PASS THE NEXT BIG EXAM

What's the hottest item among Korean students preparing for a big exam? It's the Korean taffy, or ***yeot* 엿**. Made with steamed rice, glutinous rice, glutinous sorghum, corn, sweet potatoes, or mixed grains, the belief comes from the fact that the Korean expression of "passing a test" is ***butda* 붙다**, which literally means "sticking (to the group/list of successful applicants)." By the same logic, Korean rice cake, ***tteok* 떡**, made with glutinous rice, is another popular item due to its stickiness. Nowadays, forks are a popular gift because it symbolizes "picking (the right answer)."

AVOID EATING *MIYEOKGUK* (SEA WEED SOUP) BEFORE BIG EXAMS

On the contrary, Korean test-takers will avoid eating ***miyeokguk* 미역국** (seaweed soup made with mussel, beef, or anchovy-based broth seasoned with soy sauce) on the exam day because its slippery nature symbolizes one slipping down/falling (the test rank) and failing the exam. For this reason, Koreans use an idiomatic expression "ate *miyeokguk*" when one flunks an exam.

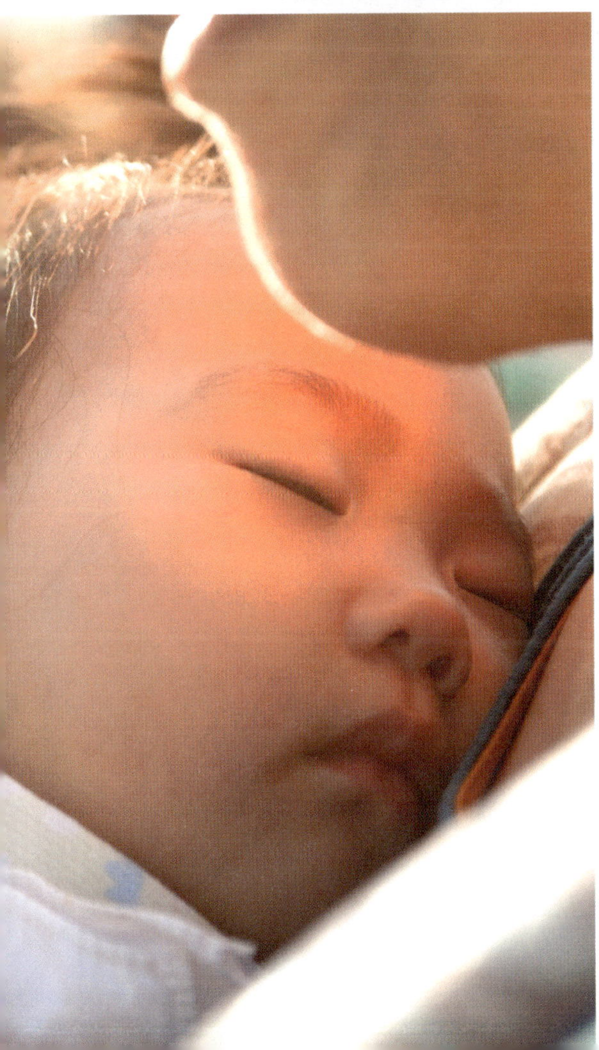

BUT DO EAT *MIYEOKGUK* (SEAWEED SOUP) ON BIRTHDAYS

Miyeok, or seaweed, is full of health benefits – it contains a substantial amount of iodine and calcium, which are the nutrients highly important for pregnant and nursing mothers in Korean culture. For this reason, *miyeokguk* has been eaten by mothers after giving birth, to rapidly restore the lost nutrition while promoting blood circulation to expedite the recovery process. Therefore, eating *miyeokguk* for breakfast on birthdays serves a dual purpose - celebrating one's birthday and honoring one's mother. That's why your friends ask whether you ate *miyeokguk* on your birthday! What should you do if your birthday falls on a big exam day? Should you eat *miyeokguk* or not...? Well, the decision is entirely yours to make, but how about eating *miyeokguk* and eat *tteok* (rice cake) or *yeot* (Korean taffy) to cancel out the bad omen!

WHO/WHAT DO KOREANS BELIEVE BRINGS BABIES?

While the storks are busy delivering babies in other parts of the world (mostly in Europe, and North America because the myth is believed to have been popularized by a piece of fairy tale written by Hans Christian Andersen of Denmark in the 19th century), there is also someone working around the clock in Korea. Known as ***Samshin Halmoni* 삼신 할머니** (grandmother goddess/spirit), where *samshin* can be interpreted as "triple god/goddess or spirits," it is known as the god who makes the blood, the god who puts the bones together, and the god who helps during labor and delivery or often depicted as just a single goddess of childbirth. Put together with *halmoni* (grandmother), she (they) represents "the goddess of conception and pregnancy who appears in the form of a loving grandmother." Compared to the storks whose duty is mostly finding babies in caves or mashes and bringing them to the mother, the Korean grandmother goddess' roles and responsibilities are quite complex. They include and are not limited to; 1) hearing out the prayers of the couples wanting a child, 2) blessing the couples with a baby, 3) looking over and protecting all babies that are still in the womb, 4) ensuring safe and smooth childbirth for both the mother and the baby, 5) protecting the baby from diseases until the age of seven (after that, they are protected by the god of Seven Stars). To pay respect and render thanks to *Samshin halmoni* for such unconditional love and care, families would offer a special table dedicated to her, presented with seaweed, rice, and freshly drawn water (and in some regions, people might also put scissors, thread, and money), from which the first meal is made for the mother immediately after giving birth.

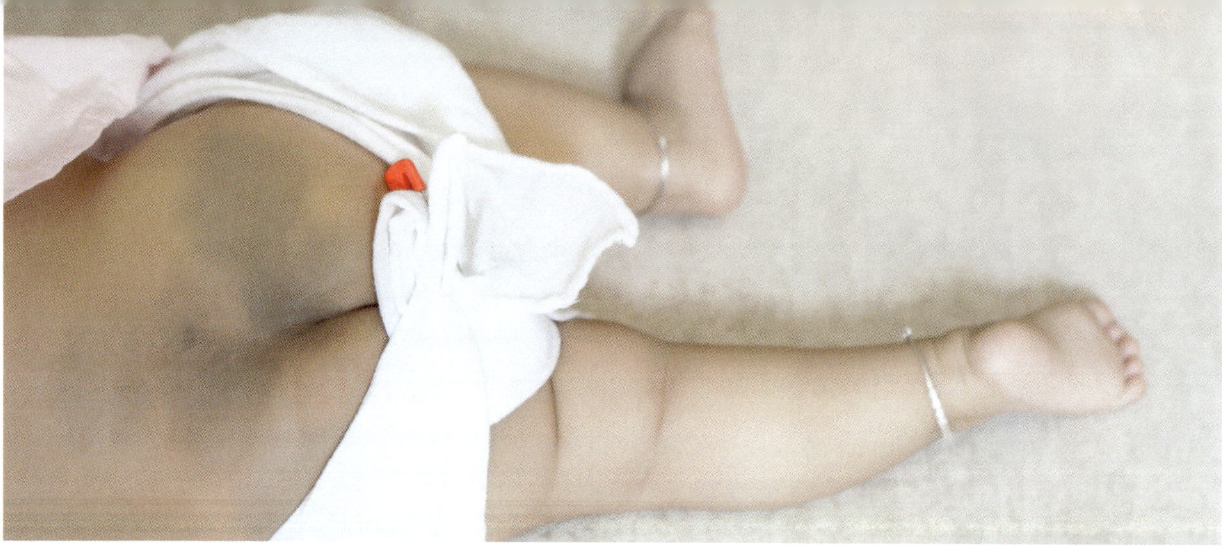

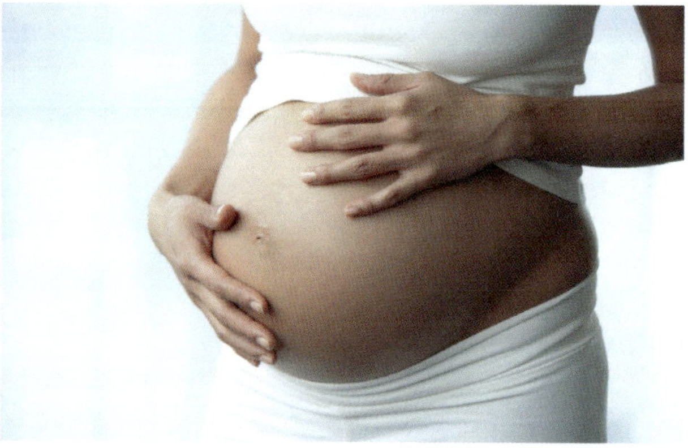

MONGOLIAN BIRTHMARKS? – THE WORKS OF *SAMSHIN HALMONI*

And our beloved *samshin halmoni* is smart enough to trademark her work through the process of branding! Almost every Korean infant (97%, according to research), regardless of gender, is born with a bluish spot or mark on various parts of the body (buttocks and torso 97.3%, arms 1%, legs 0.8%, chest and back 0.7% head and neck 0.2%), which usually fade away as they grow up. According to a Korean myth, a pregnant woman was having a difficult time giving birth, and *samshin halmoni* came to the rescue and gave her a belly rub, and voila! The baby came out like magic! But the problem didn't end there – the baby wouldn't breathe or cry! Even the seasoned veteran like *samshin halmoni* herself was taken aback because it's not something that happens a lot. As an ad hoc measure, she gave the baby a good ol' slap on the buttocks, and only then the baby started crying and breathing. And her slap was so powerful that it left a bluish spot on the baby's buttocks! For this reason, the bluish spots found on the Korean babies are believed to have come from the divine slap, and they serve as an assuring reminder that the guardian-spirit grandmother has carefully inspected the baby and put a seal of quality. In reality, the spots, known as ***mongo banjeom*** **몽고반점** or Mongolian spots, are spotted (pun intended) among the babies of other Asian countries (China 86.3%, Japan 81.5%), as well as the Native Americans (62.2%), and Latin Americans (46%) and Caucasians (5-10%). Samshin halmoni must be so busy traveling all around the world!

IPDEOT – KOREAN WAY OF SAYING "THERE'S A BUN IN THE OVEN"

At a breakfast table with all the family members present, just when the man of the house is about to lift his spoon, a young lady abruptly jumps out of her seat and sprints straight to the toilet, covering her mouth, and everyone at the dining room hears her vomiting wildly. Next, the camera zooms in on the confused faces of the family left hanging at the table, and everybody goes, "Wait a minute… Is she…?" The medical condition known as *ipdeot* 입덧, or "morning sickness" in English, is also a popularly used Korean drama cliché for saying, "Uh-oh! I think I may be pregnant!" While it's one of the many possible symptoms and hardships experienced by pregnant women during the early period, it's used most frequently due to its dramatic effect. So if you see this in a Korean drama, you know it's a telltale sign of pregnancy!

TAEMONG - THE DREAMS THAT FORETELL THE CONCEPTION OF A CHILD

From seeing a majestic dragon ascending to the sky (= making a rise in the world) to seeing a deceased ancestor with a worried face (= warning of an imminent danger/misfortune), Korean people love interpreting dreams by identifying the symbols and assigning meaning to them. And ***taemong* 태몽** (conception dream) is a special kind of dream believed to be an omen of conception, from which the baby's gender can be predicted through the interpretation of the symbols. Unlike other dreams, *taemong* can be had by other people close to the mother of the baby, such as the father, grandparents, relatives of the baby, although most of the time it's the mother of the baby who has the conception dream, and the periods when *taemong* is had can vary - before one became aware of the pregnancy or during pregnancy. Like other dreams, there are specific signs and symbols to look for but, in general, they are based on the similarities to male and female genitals (e.g., corn, eggplant, chili pepper vs. flower, chestnut burr) and their masculine and feminine characteristics (e.g., sun, tiger, dragon, carp, rooster vs. crescent, clam, bird, egg).

WHY DO KOREAN BABIES CELEBRATE THE 100TH DAY?

***Baekil janchi* 백일잔치**, literally meaning "100 days party," (*baekil* "100 days" + *janchi* "party") is a festive event involving family members and close relatives celebrating a baby's 100th-day mark since birth. Because the infant mortality rate was high in the past, making it through the first 100 days since birth was a remarkable achievement. As the number 100 symbolizes, it was an important milestone telling everyone that the baby has passed the critical mark and is expected to live a long and healthy life. Guests are offered various types of *tteok* 떡 such as ***baekseolgi* 백설기**, ***susugyeongdan* 수수경단**, and ***songpyeon* 송편** and share words of blessings for the baby. So if you are fond of *tteok*, it's an event you wouldn't want to miss.

WHY DO KOREAN COUPLES CELEBRATE THE 100TH DAY?

Given the explanation above, it must be self-explanatory why Korean couples make a huge fuss over their 100th day mark – it's a symbol of having persevered through the most critical first 100 days in a relationship. It's also a celebration and a pledge for more happy days to come. Couples usually dine out at a fancy restaurant and gift each other. For your information, these are the gifts to avoid!

WHY DO KOREANS CELEBRATE THEIR 60TH BIRTHDAY SO HUGELY?

Just like how we throw our babies a party for crawling up their way to the 100th day and the 1st year mark, our parents also deserve a celebration in their own right when they reach a milestone in their life – that is their 60th birthday ***hwangap* 환갑**. According to a research study, the average life span of the people during the Joseon Dynasty (1392-1897) was way lower than half of what we have today (78 for male / 85 for female, but keep in mind that the high infant mortality rate played a role in dragging the average down). The situation wasn't too different for the chosen ones – the average age at death of the Dynasty's 27 kings was 46.1, although there were some outliers like **King Yeongjo 영조** who lived a long 81.5 years of life. Therefore, one making it to the age of 60 was definitely something to be celebrated and congratulated on, so their children would organize lavish feasts and parties with invitations extended to family friends and village neighbors, sharing words of blessing and wisdom. With the advance in medical science and improvement of living conditions, however, the average life expectancy has dramatically increased, and the 60th birthday became less important (60 is the new 30, ya'll!). Instead of having big parties, families often opt for dining out at a fine restaurant or take a family trip. Oh, but don't you easily assume that they're done throwing parties just yet – those big parties are saved for 70th birthdays ***chilsun*** **칠순** and 80th birthdays ***palsun*** **팔순**.

*Technically, the word *hwangap* 환갑 represents the completion of a 60-year cycle of the Asian zodiac system used to calculate time in China and the East Asian cultural sphere and the beginning of another cycle.

DOLJABI - WHAT YOUR BABY GRABS DETERMINES THEIR FUTURE!

If *baekil janchi* is a small-scale private event involving just family members and relatives, ***doljanchi*** **돌잔치** "first birthday party" (*dol* "first birthday/anniversary" + *janchi* "party") is a village-wide event involving as wide a spectrum of guests as family friends and neighbors. And the highlight of the event is *doljabi* 돌잡이 = "first birthday grabbing" (*dol* means "first birthday/anniversary" + *jabi* 잡이 "to grab"). It's a traditional ceremony that takes place with a belief that the item the baby picks up from the birthday table predicts the baby's fortune/future!

THERE IS A SPECIAL PLACE WHERE KOREAN MOMS GO AFTER GIVING BIRTH

Who are the VVIPs in Korea? There might be a few you can think of, but mothers who just gave birth are definitely one of them. In Korea, the time period between childbirth and recovery is of utmost importance for the health of the new mothers, because it's difficult for the new mothers to naturally return to their pre-pregnancy health levels without proper care. For this reason, there are service facilities called ***sanhujoriwon*** **산후조리원**, which can be translated as "postpartum care centers," but provides more services than it sounds. For example, it provides services such as daily meals for mothers, babysitting, changing diapers, and bathing of the newborns. In addition, nurses are present and there are facilities to respond to emergencies. Of course, this is not a vacation hotel for the new mothers - they still have to breastfeed the baby every few hours and learn how to handle the newborn. In sum, it is an auxiliary institution that can share the burden of exhausted mothers to help facilitate their speedy and proper recovery. In Korea, where men's paternity leave is almost nonexistent, it's an essential service.

SAJU PALJA - KOREANS BELIEVE THEIR FUTURE IS PREDETERMINED!

"Should I quit my job?" "Am I going to meet someone new?" "Is this business plan going to make me rich?" Or, to be more culture-specific, "Will this double-eyelid surgery bring me good luck?" Regardless of culture, we have always been curious about what the future has in store for us, but alas, even in the age of smartphones and quantum physics, we still don't have the future-seeing crystal ball. So what do we do? We turn to the people like oracles, messiahs, and shamans who we believe possess the ability or the knowledge of predicting the future and also practice various divination methods ranging from bibliomancy (the practice of the ancient Greeks and Romans by asking a question, then opening a book at random to find the first passage you see as the answer) to oinomancy, the practice of examining the colors and patterns in wine to predict the future. Meanwhile, in Korea, people have been using a quite sophisticated method of predicting one's fate and destiny! On the New Year's Day in Korea, you can find people flock to a ***saju* 사주** shop, with a list of questions prepared beforehand. Thought to have originated from the old philosophy of China, the literal meaning of *saju* is "the four pillars of destiny" that are associated with your birth moment – year, month, day, and hour. Each "pillar" is represented by two characters - one from one of the 12 "Earthly Branches" and one from one of the 10 "Heavenly Stems," forming a combination of eight characters – the reason it's also called ***saju palja* 사주 팔자** (four pillars and eight characters). Then the "eight characters" are drawn from a pool of 60 characters, and each character has a yin or yang energy. They are further broken down into five primary elements, or ***ohaeng* 오행** – wood, earth, fire, metal, and water. Because the characteristics of each element affect the personality of the person by either weakening or reinforcing a certain disposition, it takes a skilled "*saju* reader" to accurately interpret and explain the person's fate and destiny. A *saju* reader would then lay out the interpreted meaning of your *saju* on a piece of paper, and you can ask questions about your life by category (e.g., marriage, career, health, and etc.), as well as by different time frames (e.g., 1-year prediction, 10-year prediction, after the 50's, and etc.). So next time you visit Korea, stop by a *saju* shop and have your *saju* interpreted, but don't get too excited if yours is an exact duplicate of Bill Gates', because having the same *saju* doesn't mean they will live the same life, as they are affected by many other factors such as the relationship with their parent's *saju* and other circumstantial and environmental factors (and because *saju* readers also need to have a way out, just in case). Oh, but don't get the impression that Koreans blindly trust the idea (but of course, there are people who swear by it). In general, people would take it more for entertainment purposes or to receive some helpful life advice from the wise people who came before us. Nowadays, many would rather turn to Google (or Naver, for that matter) to find an answer to their concerns about the future or how to remove Kimchi stains from their favorite shirt.

ARE WE A MATCH?
GUNGHAP - THE MARRIAGE COMPATIBILITY OF A COUPLE

***Gunghap* 궁합** "(marital compatibility)" is the analysis and the interpretation of the complex interaction between the 2 *saju*s of a couple, and an attempt to take a peek at what their future would look like. Korean couples, new and old alike, also love visiting a *saju* shop to have their *gunghap* assessed and foreshadow anything to come in the relationship - both good and bad. A *saju* reader's role is to provide an accurate measure of how well each side complements or conflicts with one another. Quite often, some traditional Korean families give it the utmost importance as a deciding factor of marriage, and it's not rare to hear breakup stories because of their incompatibility. For this reason, some would go as far as fabricating their birth certificates or even buy off a *saju* reader beforehand to have their story tailor-made to make it look like a perfect match. Such situations are frequently portrayed in Korean dramas. On the contrary, ***chaltteok gunghap* 찰떡 궁합** means "a match made in heaven" because *chaltteok* means "glutinous rice cake," and their stickiness represents perfect compatibility and harmony. Whether you believe it or not is entirely up to you, but it's a fascinating piece of Korean culture that represents the Korean people's attempt at unlocking the mysterious codes of our fate and destiny.

COUPLES BEWARE! WALKING DOWN ALONG THE DEOKSUGUNG STONE WALL PATH WILL MAKE COUPLES BREAK UP!

There's one place in Seoul which you should avoid visiting with your significant other - it's the **Deoksugung Doldamgil 덕수궁 돌담길** ("stonewall path"). On the outside, it's a lovely trail along the stone wall surrounding the Deoksugung Royal Palace, but there's an urban legend/myth that says walking down along the stone wall trail will make couples break up. Although the origin of this belief is unclear, the trail meanders to the Seoul Family Court right nearby, so a lot of couples that decide to part their ways would have to walk down the trail to get there, hence the myth.

GIFTING SHOES TO YOUR SIGNIFICANT OTHER WILL MAKE THEM RUN AWAY!

Korean couples have a strong aversion to gifting shoes to each other because they believe it will make them run away (based on the superstition that new shoes will lead them to a better place and find someone better)! Another related expression is "putting on rubber shoes the other way around," an idiomatic expression used to describe how a girl dumps her boyfriend or cheats on him while he's serving in the military. Rubber shoes were the most popular type of shoe girls used to wear back in the old days, and wearing them the other way around symbolizes the change of heart. So... if your significant other is trying to talk you into buying those fancy Gucci shoes for him/her, you can bring up this story and get out of the dangerous situation safely. You're welcome! ;)

GWANSANG - PREDICTING ONE'S FORTUNE BY "READING THE FACE"

"Freeze! You're under arrest for a crime you are predicted to commit in the next 36 hours!" Sounds like what Tom Cruise would say in the cyberpunk movie ***Minority Report* (2002)**, doesn't it? Set in the year 2054, the movie attempts to predict what our future society might look like – the Washington D.C. Police Department comes up with an amazing new technology called PreCrime, which assesses the likelihood of an individual committing a crime and apprehends them in advance. Kudos to us, we've curtailed the expected time to make sci-fi technology a reality by a whopping 30 years. In China, real-time facial-recognition technology capable of tracking down a suspect is already in use. Armed with the information obtained from "big data," stopping the bad guys beforehand is becoming a reality. Centuries before the emergence of computer technology, Korean people had their own facial-recognition system set in place. In the movie ***Gwansang* 관상 (*The Face Reader,* 2013)**, *gwansang* (physiognomy) expert Nae-gyeong is a famed face reader known for his ability to assess a person's personality, mental state, good luck, and misfortunes one's born with in order to predict their destiny. He finds himself in the middle of a Royal Court murder investigation where he's asked to use his skills to identify the murderer. After that, he assists the king (who, ironically, asked him if he had the "face of a king" before he ascended to the throne) to weed out the potential rebels and nip them in the bud. Not as high-tech as computers, *gwansang*, believed to have originated in ancient China, is the essence of East Asian philosophy. The central idea of *gwansang* is that our face is a small universe with yin and yang balance, which is divided into three parts with each part foretelling the fortune for given periods of our life – the forehead ***sangjeong* 상정** (up until the age of 30), the area between the eyebrows to cheekbones ***jungjeong* 중정** (up until the age of 40), and from the philtrum to the chin ***hajeong* 하정** (age 50 and beyond). And the characteristics of the facial features, such as the form and the shape, have different meanings and their relationships determine one's overall fortune. Some of the major reading points are:

Forehead: Reputation, Parents
Eyebrows: Interpersonal Skills, Siblings
Eyes: Love, Children Cheekbones: Ambition, Power
Nose: Wealth, Liquid Assets
Mouth: Aspiration, Talents
Chin: Realty Assets, Employees

What A Small Face / Small Head You Got! I Envy You! P. 115

Why Do Koreans Get So Much Plastic Surgery? P. 237

Like *saju*, the *gwansang* reader's role is to analyze and interpret the complexities of one's facial features to predict one's future. While it's nothing scientific, it's a common practice in Korea enjoyed by people of all ages, like tarot card reading and palm reading. But again, some swear by it, and some big companies even hire face-readers when interviewing new candidates! And according to the face-reading experts, plastic surgeries won't alter destiny, and race, culture, and ethnicity are irrelevant in the face-reading technique. So ditch your crystal ball and look yourself in the mirror, as your future is already written on your face.

HAVING A PIG DREAM = GOOD LUCK COMING YOUR WAY

Across many cultures around the world, pigs are a symbol of prosperity, abundance, and fertility, but Korean people unarguably have the strongest faith in this chubby animal; if they see a pig in their dream, 10 out of 10 will jump right out of bed and make a beeline for a lottery store. This belief is further strengthened by the countless incidents where the lottery winners claim the reason they bought a ticket was because of the pig dream! Still not buying it? Well, in Korean the Chinese character **豚 (pig)** is pronounced ***don* 돈**, which is the Korean word for "money." So **pig = money**! And for that reason, people sometimes "buy" someone else's dream in exchange for money, believing that the ownership of the auspicious dream and the associated good omen are transferred to the purchaser.

WHY DO KOREANS GIFT TOILET PAPER AND LAUNDRY DETERGENT FOR HOUSEWARMING PARTIES?

TOILET PAPER – "MAY YOUR FUTURE BE WITHOUT ANY ISSUES" because Korean word ***pulida* 풀리다** means "to unfold (a roll of toilet paper)," but also means "to resolve (an issue)."

LAUNDRY DETERGENTS – "MAY HAPPINESS BUBBLE UP"

"It was necessary to purify the house, whether it was a new house or an old house, and toilet paper or detergent took over the role."

Bae Young-dong
Professor of Folklore at Andong University

SPOOKY KOREAN SUPERSTITIONS & BELIEFS

WHERE YOUR ANCESTORS ARE BURIED CAN EITHER BRING GOOD LUCK OR MISFORTUNES TO THE DESCENDANTS!

Which direction should my couch face? Furniture arrangement is something we don't give too much thought to, but for some Koreans, it involves more precise planning because many Koreans still follow the idea of ***pungsujiri*** **풍수지리** ("wind-water-earth-principles-theory"), a Korean term for the Asian art of divinatory geomancy, more commonly known by the Chinese term *feng shui* (wind-water). In a nutshell, it's the study of topography based on the belief that one's destiny is molded by the natural surroundings. Thus, *pungsujiri* analysts are believed to be able to identify if a particular site is auspicious or not, by interpreting the relationship between life-force energy and its surroundings, and *pungsujiri* analysts claim that bad energy responsible for misfortunes can be stifled or avoided by strategic placement of various elements. According to the historical record, it was a Buddhist monk of the **Silla 신라** Dynasty (57 BC – 935 AD) who brought the philosophy of *feng shui* from China and adapted it to make it fit the Korean culture. And there is a strong Korean belief that propitious tomb spots for ancestors can bring good luck and prosperity for descendants (some even dig up an old grave and have it relocated to a more "propitious" spot when a spell of misfortune is imputed to the ancestor's jinxed old grave). This is a reflection of the Confucian culture where respecting elders, even after they are long gone, is of utmost importance. The Silla Dynasty's **General Kim Yu Sin 김유신** (595-673) who led the unification of the Three Kingdoms of Korea and **King Taejong Muyeol 태종 무열왕** (604-661) incorporated the idea of *pungsujiri* in the selection of their tombs, and the rich noble families went as far as delaying internment for months to find auspicious burial ground. A recent period film ***Myeong Dang* 명당 (*Feng Shui*, 2018")**, depicts a story where people fight over the ideal burial ground for their ancestors. Today, the tradition still lives on - high-tech Korean conglomerates hired famed *pungsujiri* analysts to consult for the layout of a new company building, and the government paid a good amount of (tax) money to hire *pungsujiri* experts before deciding where the new administrative complex should be set up. So next time you pick up your futon from IKEA, study some pungsujiri beforehand, because where you place it might affect your future…

WHAT IS THE KOREAN SHAMANISM - MUSOK & MUDANG?

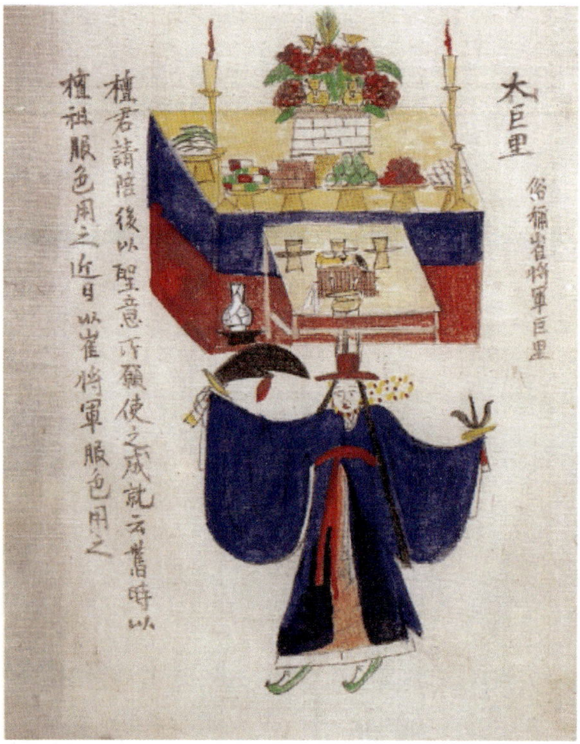

An illustration from *mudangnaeryeok* 무당내력, a compilation of the traditional Korean shaman exorcism methods in the late Joseon Dynasty (1800s). It is currently housed in Gyujanggak, Seoul National University.

"The power of Christ compels you!" In the Hollywood movie ***The Exorcist* (1973)**, fearless Fathers Lankester Merrin and Damien Karras join forces together in Georgetown, Washington D.C., USA, to desperately cast out the evil spirit from Regan, a little girl whose body is deemed to have been possessed. They fight off the evil spirit using various means such as hanging the Holy Rosary, sprinkling holy water to the body of the possessed, and reciting prayers to invoke God and angels to intervene. Now, in the Korean horror movie ***Gokseong* 곡성 (*The Wailing* , 2016)**, after a series of horrifying village-wide homicides, every suspect displays a set of abnormality, including having a weird skin rash and uttering meaningless words. A little girl named Hyojin, suffers from the same symptoms, but her conditions worsen and she starts to scream obscenities and eat excessively for no apparent reason. Convinced that she's possessed, her grandmother summons Ilgwang, to perform an exorcism. Ilgwang, wearing a ritual black garment decorated with colorful sleeves striped in red, green, blue, and yellow, is a mudang 무당, or a Korean shaman (technically, a male shaman is called Baksu Mudang 박수무당), and they are important characters of the Korean folk shamanism called musok 무속. Typically, the majority of *mudangs* are compelled to become one, rather than choosing to, and they usually go through the phase of experiencing various supernatural phenomena, (defined by scientists as "a temporary acute psychotic manic episode") called ***shinbyeong* 신병** ("god illness"), such as seeing ghosts and suffering from unknown illnesses, which completely disappeared after being voluntarily possessed by local deities or ancestor's spirits through a ***naerimgut* 내림굿**, an invocatory rite of a would-be medium from another *mudang*. A *mudang*'s job description is quite vast – they are invited to perform ceremonies called ***gut* 굿** in villages. Gut is a rite or a ritual performed by Korean shamans, which typically involves the offerings and sacrifices to various local deities and ancestor spirits, and most of the time, it's a village-wide event because it's quite a spectacle - it consists of rhythmic dances, beautiful clothes that are changed several times, mind-bending songs, mysterious oracles, and prayers. Believed to have the ability to communicate between the spiritual beings and mankind, the shamans' role isn't confined to exorcism – it's all about asking the deities and ancestors to intervene in the fortune of men, from curing illness, bringing good luck, warding off evil spirits, and a good harvest. After someone's death, a shaman also helps the soul of the departed leave the earthly life without any regrets and find the path to heaven.

By The Korea Times

MUDANG PROVIDES FORTUNE-TELLING SERVICES TOO

And a popular service provided by a *mudang* to anyone who wishes is ***jeom* 점**, or fortune-telling by communicating with the spiritual beings. It's fundamentally different from *saju* because it solely relies on the messages obtained allegedly from the otherworldly beings, as well as various divination methods such as analyzing the pattern of rice grains sprinkled on the table, and interpreting the meaning of a randomly drawn stick, whereas *saju* tries to have a systematic and deductive approach of interpreting one's fate using the objective information such as birth date, time, and year. Like *saju*, *mudang*'s fortune-telling services are very popular and some people vouch for its accuracy – but use the service at your own risk because there are many civil cases of a (fake) *mudang* talking a victim into paying a huge service fee on the pretext of tribute to appease the local deities or ancestral spirits. It's a situation often appearing in Korean dramas where a naive character gives away all his/her hard-earned money to a (fake) *mudang*. So in a nutshell, a *mudang* is a multi-purpose Korean character who serves the purposes of an oracle, counselor, medium, and shaman.

WHY DO KOREANS PUT A BOILED PIG HEAD AT A BUSINESS OPENING CEREMONY?

Tossing a few coins onto the carpet floor mat of a newly purchased car (known as "coining") and carrying around a rabbit's foot are some of the examples of various rituals and lucky charms people rely on for good luck and divine protection around the globe. Korean people also perform a blessing ritual called *gosa* 고사, which can be performed with or without the need of a mudang, and people do it for all kinds of situations – from taking your brand new car on the road for the first time, and opening a new business, to beginning a new production season for a TV show, and even when launching a cutting-edge satellite into the sky! And at the center of the table, you will find a smiling pig head because it's the symbol of fertility, prosperity (the Chinese character 豚 (pig) is pronounced *don* 돈, in Korean, which is the Korean word for "money), and good luck – nothing says "lucky" like a pig head in Korean culture. The pig head, severed and boiled, is a sacrificial offering for the local deities and ancestor spirits. It's accompanied by many other typical shamanist features such as incense, food, alcohol, visitors of the ritual stuff wads of cash into the mouth, ears, and even the nose of the pig head, as a token of offering and contribution. The money collected goes to the host of the ceremony. These days, the *gosa* tradition still lives on, but many people feel uncomfortable using a real pig head for the event due to its grotesque look and concerns about animal cruelty. Instead, people substitute it with a silicone replica or a cake made in the shape of a pig head.

WRITING SOMEONE'S NAME IN RED IS A BIG NO-NO!

Of all the colors available, there is one color that you should always avoid when writing someone's name in Korea – Red. This is especially true among the older generation and there are many theories surrounding this. First, the theory is that red is symbolic of death, as it is the same color as blood. The second theory is rooted in Korean history. When **Grand Prince Suyang 수양대군**, the second son of King Sejong the Great of the Joseon Dynasty (1392-1897) was plotting a coup, he used red ink to make a hit list of enemies on the opposing side. The third theory claims that during the Korean War, red ink was used to strike out the name of the dead civilians and soldiers killed in action. Whatever the case is, it'd be wise to choose a different color when writing someone's name!

STICKING CHOPSTICKS STRAIGHT INTO A BOWL OF RICE IS ALSO A NO-NO!

This is also a big no-no in Korean culture because it resembles a Korean funeral ceremony and ***jesa* 제사**, a memorial ceremony held on the anniversary of the ancestor's death. During the ceremony, incense burners are usually filled with rice to act as the holder, and spoons are stuck directly into the bowl of rice (some families choose to place them next to the bowl, instead). To avoid inadvertently offering the person sitting next to you a memorial service (Um… I'm not dead yet!), keep your chopsticks somewhere else, usually on top of the bowl or on the table. Often, a small ceramic rest is provided on the table.

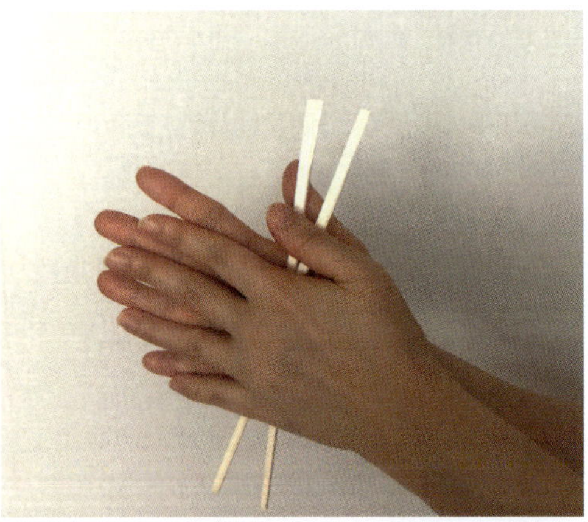

WHY DO KOREANS RUB THEIR CHOPSTICKS BEFORE EATING?

You might have wondered when you dined with your Korean friend. Why do they rub their chopsticks before eating? Is it some kind of ritual? Are they trying to start a fire? The quick answer is to get rid of the possible splinters, and for that reason, such practice only applies to wooden chopsticks, mostly the cheap break-apart type that has those itty bitty splinters sticking out. Because Koreans were the only people in the world who have been using metal chopsticks, it can be said with confidence that it's a habit acquired recently. Rubbing chopsticks isn't something that's frowned upon, but you might want to be careful when you are invited to dinner because doing so could send a wrong signal that you think the chopsticks are of subpar quality, offending the host.

DON'T WHISTLE AT NIGHT

No matter how happy you are, whistling at night is something Korean parents would stop you from doing because it's believed to attract the snakes (but if you like reptiles, try it by all means)! The logic behind the idea is that in the past snake hunters used whistling, which is similar to the hissing sound of the snakes, to lure and control them. And it's the adults who spread the rumor to elicit behavior (be quiet at night!), such as the case with Santa Claus. With most of the Korean families now living in concrete apartments and probably never getting a chance to see a snake throughout their life, the idea is pretty obsolete.

THINGS THAT MAKE GOOD FORTUNES GO AWAY - SHAKING LEGS & PLACING A SPOON BELLY UP

There are 2 surefire ways of getting a good smack from mom at the dinner table in Korea: Shaking legs and placing your spoon upside down, or belly up, because they are believed to bring bad luck. Like many other superstitions, it's difficult to track down who holds the copyright to these tales, but we can make an educated guess. In the highly Confucian society of Korea, decorum and orderliness are of high importance, and anything that falls outside the realm is frowned upon and discouraged. Shaking legs, considered rude especially in front of older people, checks every single box. Similarly, placing a spoon belly up raises the flag because Korean people have been considering eating as one of the most important elements of life, and scooping a hefty amount of rice is symbolic of health and wealth! Thus, to the Korean eyes accustomed to seeing spoons put neatly with the inside bowl facing up means "scooping up" good luck, and going the opposite direction means "scooping away" good luck.

WHY IS THERE NO 4TH FLOOR?

The Korean word for number 4 ***sa* 사**, is pronounced the same as the Chinese word "death" **死**. For this reason, number 4 is often replaced with the English alphabet "F" in elevators (and often skipped/omitted in places like hospital rooms. This superstitious practice of avoiding instances of number 4 (similar to number 13 in the Western culture) is called tetraphobia (ancient Greek word *tetrás* meaning "four," and "phobia" = "fear of number four") is commonly found in East Asian nations that use Chinese characters as part of their written language. The national railroad of Korea, Korail, left out the train number 4444 when assigning train numbers from 4401 upwards. Some Koreans would jump out of their skin if they receive a phone call from a number ending in 4444, at 4:44 AM.

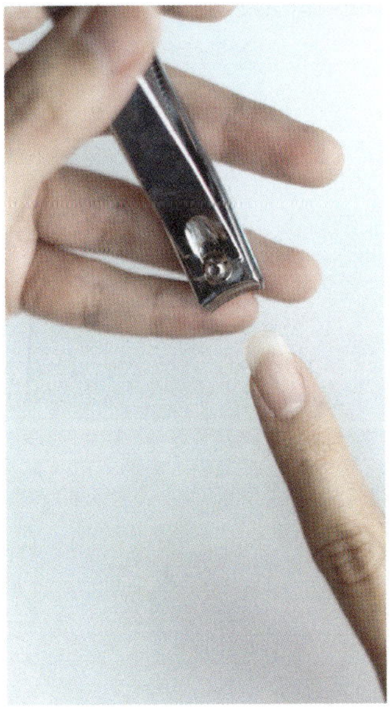

NEVER CLIP YOUR NAILS AT NIGHT

And if you thought the snakes were creepy, this is even worse. If you cut your nails at night, rats will come into your home and eat the clippings off the floor and transform into a human and take your form. Strange as it may sound, it's assumed to have originated during the time before electricity and nail cutters were invented. So naturally, cutting nails at night in the dim light was dangerous, and the cleaning up part was also difficult. Now we know that every superstition has a story behind it, and most of the time it's our parents and grandparents who come up with the ideas and share them with their children's best interest at heart, just like the story of Santa Clause! And it's just fun knowing the hidden stories because they are a snapshot of what the society looked like at the time.

FAN DEATH THE SILENT KILLER

WHY DO KOREANS BELIEVE LEAVING THE FAN ON WHILE SLEEPING WILL KILL YOU?

Can you guess the leading cause of death in the summer in Korea? Naturally, you'd think things like heat stroke, dehydration, and drowning (from drunk-swimming at pool parties) when the mercury can go above the 40 degrees Celsius mark (104 degrees in Fahrenheit) during the dog days. But Koreans would put on the top of the list something you never expected: Fan Death. First and foremost, it refers to the electric fans and not the lethal hand-held fans made of sharp sheet metal used by lady Kung Fu masters. Secondly, it's not the blades of the electric fans that cause direct physical damage to kill people. The way those evil electric fans kill people is sneakier than you think. Fan death is a belief among Korean people that sleeping with an electric fan running in a closed room with no windows open will kill the person. Proposed causes are hypothermia (body temperature is abnormally lowered by the fan), asphyxiation (suffocating due to oxygen depletion and carbon dioxide intoxication), and facial paralysis. Back in 2006, The Korea Consumer Protection Board official issued a consumer safety alert, stating that "asphyxiation from electric fans and air conditioners" was among the five leading causes of death in Korea. There have been numerous attempts by the scientific and the medical circles to debunk the urban legend, arguing that such claimed deaths were a mere coincidence, and a case of false attribution bias – they died of other natural causes but it was the running fan in the room that took the fall. But the belief is so widely held that the Korean news channels still report cases of fan death every year.

MOVING? PICK THESE DAYS TO KEEP EVIL SPIRITS AT BAY

Congratulations! You just signed the lease contract for your new apartment in Seoul and it's time to fix the best moving date! Upon calling many different moving companies for a rate quote, you quickly discover that the prices fluctuate, with some days going as high as double or triple the price of other days, but can't quite figure out what the reason is. Sometimes it's the weekend, and sometimes it just falls on the "hump day" of the week. Befuddled, you call your go-to Korean buddy and he explains what's going on. "In Korea, people have a belief that evil spirits will get in your way on the day of moving, and even follow you to your new home! According to Korean folklore, this evil spirit, called ***son* 손** (pronounced the same as "hand" in Korean), is a nasty evil spirit that roams around the four points of the compass depending on the day of the week and finds fun in bothering and harassing humans! But luckily, they're known to keep regular hours during their workdays. Every month on the lunar calendar, they are active in the East on the 1st and 2nd, in the South on the 3rd and 4th, in the West on the 5th and 6th, and in the North on the 7th and 8th. They go up into the heavens and are away from the office on the 9th, 10th, 19th, 20th, 29th, and 30th. And these are the days to shoot for. These days are called ***son eopneunnal* 손 없는날** (a day without evil spirit), and people would pay a premium to reserve these days, thereby driving the price up on those days. Well, now you know the whole story and the decision is yours to make! Would you shell out a few more bucks to make sure that no evil spirits follow you to your new place? Maybe you don't give a rat's behind and rather keep that money for a home party? Whatever the case, just don't put Mr. Son on the guest list if you're inviting me.

Odd Questions and Compliments

WHAT IS YOUR BLOOD TYPE? IT DETERMINES YOUR PERSONALITY

Many Korean people (a whopping 75%) strongly believe that blood type is closely related to personality traits and they would go as far as stereotyping people according to the blood type. If you go on a blind date, the chances are very high that you will be asked what your blood type is, so make sure to know your blood type beforehand. While many will just laugh it off and say they are just doing it for fun's sake, some are really serious about it. Okay then, let's take a close look at the story behind it. Originally, it is believed to have all started when a Japanese professor named Takeji Furukawa published his work titled, "The Study of Temperament Through Blood Type" in 1927. Although it was largely regarded as non-scientific due to the lack of credentials, the idea must have been very intriguing because it quickly gained popularity. In the 1970s, the idea was further amplified with a publication by a Japanese journalist who was an advocate of the professor's idea. Since then, it made its way over to Korea and became a popular belief. Another thing to consider is the fact that all elementary school kids have to go through a mandatory annual student health examination (which included blood type testing until 2016), and it could have contributed to the proliferation of this idea because they are more sensitive about such theory than the kids in other countries who do not know their blood type. All right, that ought to be enough for an introduction so here is the fun part. Below are the descriptions commonly used to illustrate the characteristics of each blood type. Take a good read and compare with your own self-assessment to see how (in)accurate they are.

A INTROVERTED PERFECTIONIST

- Conservative / Introverted.
- Find difficulty in expressing emotions or trusting others.
- Often called a fundamentalist and a perfectionist.
- Have a strong sense of responsibility at work, and easily gain the trust of the organization.
- Always make plans with extreme caution, but often seen as lacking flexibility.
- Look like a hard worker, but you can be a party animal in disguise.
- Can be quite adventurous when dating.

B CREATIVE AND (TOO) CURIOUS

- Inquisitive / Full of curiosity.
- Have an endless stock of topics for conversation.
- Full of original ideas.
- Exceptional ability in project planning.
- Have a strong interest in new things and often have trouble focusing.
- Sometimes called inconsistent.
- Prefer working at your own pace than in organizational settings.
- Compassionate and tender-hearted but sometimes seen as too nosy.

O COMPETITIVE LEADER

- Personality – Warm-hearted / Behavior – Goal-oriented.
- Not bothered by minor obstacles and have the ability to focus on given tasks.
- Strong sense of comradeship, often assuming the leadership role within a group.
- Often seen as a romanticist pursuing dreams, but can be surprisingly cool-headed in pressing situations.
- Hate losing and competitive- can be seen as condescending and self-complacent.

AB MYSTERIOUS AMPHIBIAN

- Unpredictable – different characteristics depending on which side of the A&B combination gets ignited.
- Superb ability to adapt to any given situation.
- Objective in making decisions, thus less prone to making mistakes.
- Often seen as someone who is easily led, but also can be wishy-washy.
- Prefer to keep personal life private and do not care much about those of others, either.

So… how accurate are they? The Korean Society of Hematology officially announced that there is absolutely no scientific basis for this belief and personality is a byproduct of environmental factors such as family and education. In fact, many experts say that it should be attributed to what's known as the Barnum effect, the tendency to embrace certain information as true and relevant to oneself. Examples include character assessment tests, horoscopes, tarot reading. The similarity between them is that the descriptions provided are so vague, they can be applied to anybody, leading people to falsely believe that they are actually tailored to their unique circumstances when in fact, they are not. Maybe it's because our desire for seeking explanations to what happens around us is deeply embedded in our human nature and these are effective tools in alleviating our uncertainties. And of course, you have to factor in the entertainment value they provide – don't we feel a little better when our horoscope (or a fortune cookie?) says something hopeful?

A bonus story – there is even a compatibility chart between blood types to show how good of a match they are (chemistry). As you might have guessed, a research survey conducted by a matchmaking company concluded it was baseless. They closely examined 3,000 couples and found that blood type had no significant impact on the possibility of a couple getting married. Well, there you have it. Do you believe the theory? Then you must be blood type B! (sarcasm)

WHY DO KOREANS ASK IF YOU ATE?

"Have you eaten? (= Did you eat yet?)". It sounds like the first thing you would hear when you visit your grandma's house. But for Koreans, it's a greeting expression used as frequently as ***annyeonghaseyo*** **안녕하세요** (literally "Are you at peace?" = "How are you?"). Why would they want to know if I ate? Many believe that it has its origin in history. In the agricultural society of Korea, meals were an important event of the day, because it did not only provide energy but served as a coagulant that brought the labor forces and community together. And through the difficult times after the Korean War which destroyed the nation to ashes, skipping meals was common, and asking if someone had the chance to have a meal naturally became a way of checking in on each other. And times have changed and so has the expression's meaning. It's the same as asking "How are you?" in English, which you would usually answer by saying "fine, thanks," even if you weren't. So when asked as a greeting, don't take it at face value and just say "I ate," or "I haven't but I will soon." And if the person asking was actually interested in knowing whether you ate, they would also say something like, "I was going to ask you to have lunch with me," so you would know the difference.

DON'T EAT ALONE

Mukbang - You Can Also Make Money Broacasting Your Eating Session! P. 241

If you decide to dine alone at a Korean restaurant, don't be surprised or offended if you find people looking at you with a strange look. In a collectivist traditional Korean society that valued the sense of unity and belongingness, meals were an important bonding ritual, so they were to be had with family, friends, or co-workers. This notion is so deeply embedded in Korean people that dining alone in a restaurant are not something they are used to seeing. So people might look at you like an oddball or the owner ***ajumma*** would even ask why you are eating alone, but it's all out of fraternal concern. But as times have changed and people are running both out of time and space, so has the meaning associated with a meal. It shifted away from a bonding ritual to a regular exercise from which you need the energy and nutrition required to make it through the day. Reflecting the social changes, many restaurants are introducing ***honbap*** **혼밥** (solo-dining) and ***honsul*** **혼술** (solo-drinking) menus and places targeting the busy modern-day Koreans.

WHAT A SMALL FACE & SMALL HEAD YOU GOT! I ENVY YOU!

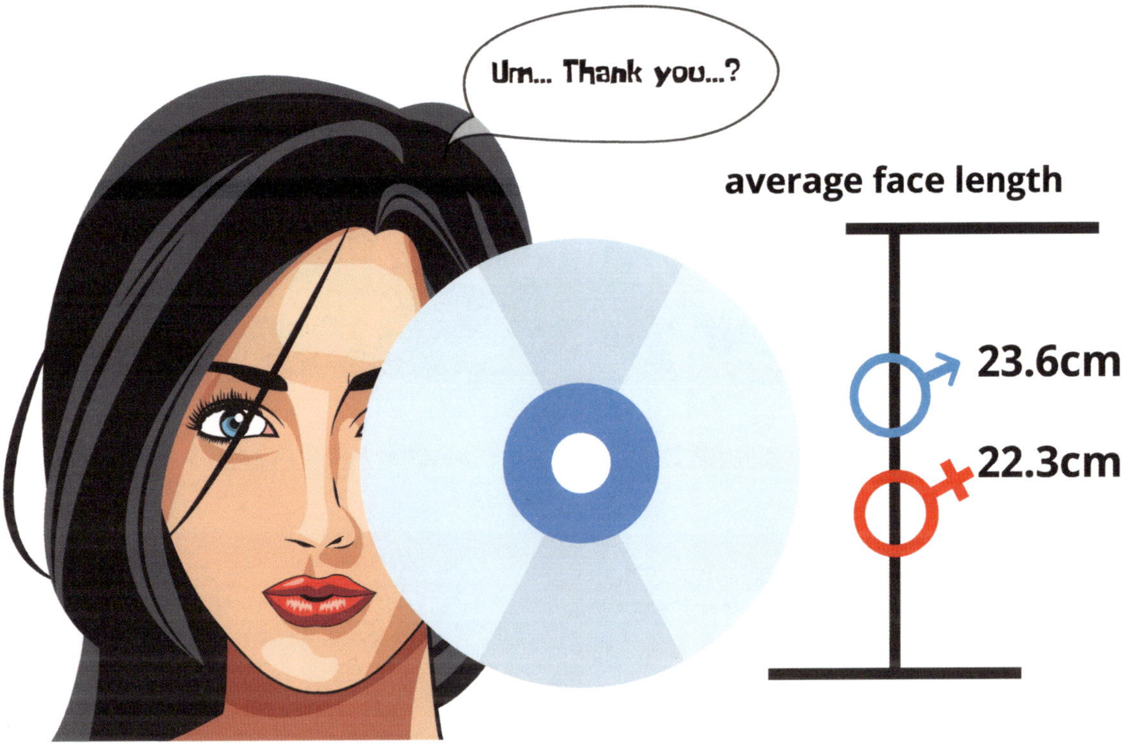

“Wow! Your face is the size of a fist!” If someone says this to your face, don’t panic because they're not trying to pick a fight with you. Rather, it is a genuine compliment coming from the heart, because one of the most important standards of Korean beauty is having a nicely proportioned body, and they consider ***pal deung shin 8등신*** ("eight-head figure")” to be ideal. Hence, having a smaller face is admired (especially among the younger generation) as it makes it easier to achieve that ideal proportion. Another belief is that having a smaller (slim and thin) face gives a more youthful look and it makes facial features look more well-defined and thus photogenic. So how conscious are the Koreans of their face sizes? Well, their fascination with small faces can be easily seen on TV, where celebrities with unusually small faces are asked to hold up an object adjacent to their faces for quick measurement, with some even whipping out measuring tools. But one of the most convenient and popular way to measure if your face is in the "small" category is to hold up a CD Rom above your face. If it totally eclipses or covers most of your face, it is super small! But this big trend over a tiny ideal doesn’t end here. There is even a study (The Standard Figure of Korean People) which measures face sizes. According to the study, the average face length of men and women was 23.6 cm and 22.3 cm, respectively. I know you already took out your ruler - how do you measure against these numbers? Do you fall within the Korean beauty standards? Uh oh… Why the long face?

Gwansang - Predicting One's Fortune By "Reading The Face" P. 105

DEATH & AFTERLIFE

WHAT DO KOREANS BELIEVE ABOUT AFTERLIFE?

Jeonseoleui Gohyang 전설의 고향
(Korean Ghost Stories / Hometown Legends, 1977~2009, KBS)

Shingwa Hamkkae 신과함께
(Along With The Gods, 2017)

One of the most popular ways for the Korean people to get through the hot summer dog days is by watching a spooky TV series like ***Jeonseoleui Gohyang* 전설의 고향 (*Korean Ghost Stories / Hometown Legends*, 1977~2009, KBS)** which is a compilation of traditional Korean folk tales, myths, and legends that are passed down from generation to generation. Aside from being super scary, they are fun learning material about the Korean people's view on the afterlife. Sampling a few episodes (but for the faint of heart, I suggest watching the movie ***Shingwa Hamkkae* 신과함께 (*Along With The Gods*, 2017)**, will layout the Korean concept regarding the afterlife.

Why Do Koreans Eat Simmering Hot *Samgyetang* On The Most Sweltering Days Of Summer? P. 60

A still from *Gimakhin Yusan* 기막힌 유산 (*Brilliant Heritage*, KBS, 2020)

JEOSEUNG SAJA - THE MESSENGER FROM THE OTHER WORLD

What happens when you die? Here's what Korean people think that happens after the last breath. First, immediately upon death, a messenger from the other world, ***Jeoseung Saja*** **저승사자** arrives to guide you to the other world (if seen while one's still alive, it foreshadows their death is imminent). Usually, they are depicted as fully dressed in black (symbolic of death, but the style of attire changes depending on the time the story takes place), with a gat **갓**, traditional Korean hat, and a face paler than a dead person. To add the numinous effects, their legs are buried in fog, masking their gait, as if they float around (in traditional paintings, however, they are painted as a prosecutor dressed in a colorful yet solemn style). Their job begins with the ID-checking to make sure that they are taking the right soul. Although they are otherworldly beings, they make mistakes like humans and often pick up the wrong person who's not supposed to leave for the other world. Knowing their "humane" side, Korean people perform a ritual called ***gobok*** **고복**, where the family of the deceased prepares 3 bowls of rice, vegetables, soups, 3 pairs of shoes, along with some money at the house entrance (an important part which illustrates that Korean people thought the messengers work in a team of 3). Through the ritual, people sought solace as they believed their offerings would soften up the messengers, ensuring that their loved one gets a hassle-free trip to the other world.

Yeomra Daewang in a Buddhist painting

YEOMRA DAEWANG - THE KING OF HELL

What makes ***Jeoseung Saja*** more relatable is that they also have a boss to report to. Once everyone is on board, they take the soul of the deceased to ***Yeomra Daewang*** **염라대왕** (King Yeomra The Great), the King of Hell, an almighty ruler (there are 10 rulers in the netherworld, known as ***Shiwang*** **시왕** "10 kings", but he's most well known) in charge of judging the sins of the deceased and deciding where they should be sent to. Because his main job is preventing the bad souls from entering the heavens, he's mostly depicted as having a wrathful look with a deafening howl of rage. While looking all cold-hearted on the outside, he has his soft side too. In some instances, he magnanimously grants another chance and revives the dead, upon hearing their pitiful stories.

MYTHICAL CREATURES & GHOSTLY BEINGS OF KOREA

HELL HATH NO FURY LIKE A WOMAN SCORNED – *CHEONYEO GWISHIN* THE "VIRGIN GHOST"

In the extremely patriarchal times in early Korea, the life of a woman was quite difficult. Taught to be subordinate to the males while receiving limited or no education, life consisted of nothing but sacrifice - serving their father, husband, and rearing children while checking off all the household chores list. As a result of their suppressed life, many Korean women in the past had lifelong resentment, grudge, or han, which further intensifies if one dies without getting married, and the pitiful soul can't leave this world and becomes a ***Cheonyeo Gwishin*** **처녀귀신**, or "**virgin ghost**." Wearing traditional white mourning clothes called *sobok* 소복, with the long pitch-black hair hanging down over their face like a curtain (only married women could pull up their hair), they wander around the people, usually the males who caused them harm, and haunt them until their resentment is satisfied. The male equivalent is called ***Chonggak Gwishin*** **총각귀신** ("the bachelor ghost").

MARRIAGE OF THE POOR SOULS

When one or both of the couple die before tying the knot, ***yeonghon gyeolhonshik*** **영혼결혼식**, or "wedding ceremony for the soul(s) (of the deceased)," a shamanistic ritual aimed to appease the soul of the deceased so that they leave this world in peace and don't become a cheonyeo or chonggak gwishin, is performed.

BE CAREFUL WHEN NEAR WATER - *MULGWISHIN* THE "WATER GHOST"

Even if you can swim better than Michael Phelps, there is a good reason to be doubly cautious when you are near water in Korea. ***Mulgwishin*** **물귀신** ("water ghosts") are the spirits of someone who drowned, and in terms of the residential environment, the cold and lonely watery depths are surely the worst. For this reason, they pull you down to their place of eternal residence, and even the most experienced swimmer can't escape from their grasp…

POOR SOUL LONGING HOME – *GAEKGWI* THE "WANDERER GHOST"

***Gaekgwi* 객귀**, or "wanderer ghost," is the haunted spirit of someone who had an untimely death while away from their hometown before reaching one's allotted span of life, or *cheonsu* 천수. Harboring a grudge, they are unable to let themselves depart the world of the living and ascend to the heavens. Caught between the two worlds, they drift amongst humans around their death site, causing harm to random passersby.

MISCHIEVOUS MONSTERS – *DOKKAEBI* THE "KOREAN GOBLIN"

***Koby-Koby* 꼬비꼬비 (KBS, 1995)**

***Dokkaebi* 도깨비**, or "Korean goblins" (who aren't anywhere near handsome as Gong Yoo, by the way) are supernatural creatures from Korean folklore that are often described as nature deities or spirits. While other ghosts or spirits are formed by the death of a human being, *Dokkaebi*s are formed as a result of the spiritual possession of non-living objects such as an old wooden poker or an old broom, from which they transform into a human shape to play pranks and tricks on humans. Despite their mischievous nature, they also have a humane side and help out the humans who are in need. The magic club they carry, known as d*okkaebi bangmangi* **도깨비 방망이**, can summon anything and transform it into any form they want. Traditionally, they are depicted as a scary creature having horns on their heads and oversized protruding fangs, but they can also appear in the form of a human being through shape-shifting. And the namesake Korean drama ***Dokkaegi* 도깨비 (*Goblin,* 2016)** does an excellent job of interpreting the traditional ideas with a modern twist, alongside romance being the main theme (it's a K-Drama, after all).

GUMIHO - THE "NINE-TAILED FOX" THAT WANTED TO BECOME A WOMAN

If a fox lives a thousand years, it becomes ***Gumiho* 구미호** (nine-tailed fox). They often appear in scary stories, but they are said to harbor a strong desire to become a human. Legend has it that it transforms into a beautiful woman and falls in love with a man and marries him because it's believed that if it can live 100 days without having its true form revealed by the husband, it will become a real woman. However, at the end of the legend, *gumiho* gets its identity exposed with I only one day left, and unable to fulfill its wishes, it ends up leaving its husband. A TV drama titled ***Nae Yeoja Chinguneun Gumiho* 내 여자친구는 구미호 (*My Girlfriend Is a Gumiho*, 2010)** is a bubbly romance story with the motif coming from the legend and is definitely worth watching. In other versions of the legend, they are depicted as evil creatures that lure men to death and eat their liver. I don't know about you, but I prefer the first version.

KOREANFUNERAL

HOW KOREANS SAY GOODBYE

TRADITIONAL VS. MODERN KOREAN FUNERALS

Time-traveling Korean dramas, like ***Daleui Yeonin - Bobo Gyeongshim Ryeo*** **달의 연인 - 보보경심 려** ***(Moon Lovers: Scarlet Heart Ryeo*** **SBS, 2016**) where the main characters go back and forth in time through a mysterious portal, actually make a great educational resource because they make a visual comparison between the traditional and modern lifestyles of Korea. But at the same time, it can create a bigger confusion if you don't understand the details. Among many, how Korean people deal with the death of a loved one has dramatically changed. With that said, a quick comparison chart should get you up to speed.

	TRADITIONAL	MODERN
DURATION	3 / 5 / 7 / 9 Days	3 Days / 2 Days
PLACE	Home	Hospital Funeral Halls
ORGANIZER	*Sangju* (Chief Mourner)	Funeral Service Provider
MOURNING CLOTHES	Hemp Dress / Hat, Straw Shoes	Black Formal Attire, Cloth Armband
WHO'S INVOLVED	Whole Village	Family / Relatives
GETTING TO THE BURIAL SITE	Village Neighbors Carry The *Sangyeo* Together On Foot	Hearse
GRIEVING	Loudly	Minimal
LEAVING OFF MOURNING PERIOD	3 Years / *Sangju* Lives Next To The Grave	49 Days / 1 Year

HOW LONG ARE KOREAN FUNERALS?

In the past, Korean funerals begin upon the departing of a loved one and can take place for 3,5,7, or 9 days (odd numbers are considered auspicious), depending on the social status and family traditions. During the time, an extremely elaborate and arduous set of rites are carried out, because they represent the essence of the Confucianist Korean philosophy that put the utmost importance on the filial piety and strict hierarchy among family members. And doing so is believed to ensure a smooth transition of a loved one into the afterlife. But due to the modernization and high-paced society where people lack both time and space, people have been leaning toward a practical approach, and traditional funerals have been simplified, with the three day-long version being the norm and occasional two day-long funerals. Despite the transformation, the essential elements remained, and they still stand as the core of the Korean funerals today. Let's take a look at the typical order of a modern Korean funeral for someone's parent:

Bugo 부고 Obituary Notice
Binso 빈소 Mortuary / Memorial Hall Set-Up
Yeomseup 염습 Clothing the Body of the Deceased
Ipgwan 입관 Placing in the Coffin
Seongbok 성복 Wearing Mourning Clothes
Munsang (*Jomun*) 문상 (조문) Receiving Guest Mourners

-- takes place on the last day of the funeral --

Balin 발인 Carrying Out of the Coffin / Procession
Anjang 안장 Burial

WHERE DO KOREAN FUNERALS TAKE PLACE?

Where they take place has changed too. In the past, funerals were held at the homes of the deceased and that's how it's still done in rural areas. In the cities, people mostly choose to spend their last days in the care of professional care centers, such as nursing homes and hospitals. Large hospitals also have funeral halls within their complex, which makes it easier for the families.

WHO ORGANIZES THE FUNERALS?

Traditionally, the ***sangju*** **상주** (chief mourner), the oldest son or the grandson of the deceased, is responsible for organizing, managing the funeral, greeting visitors, as well as looking for the best gravesite for burial. In the past, the ***sangju*** was not allowed to wash hair or shave during the funeral as an expression of grief. Today, the burden has been lifted significantly, thanks to the emergence of funeral service providers. At hospital funeral halls, they have funeral advisors who oversee every aspect of the funerals.

Bier Belonging to the Goryeongdaek House of the Jeonju Choe Clan, Sancheong, Important Folklore Cultural Heritage of Republic of Korea No. 230
국립민속박물관 (National Folk Museum of Korea) / KOGL Type 1 (kogl.or.kr/open/info/license_info/by.do)

WHO'S INVOLVED WITH KOREAN FUNERALS?

In the past, funerals involved the whole village. When the grieving family members were busy carrying out a myriad of rites, preparing food and greeting guests (and on top of that, doing it for 3,5,7, and even 9 days drains their energy to complete exhaustion), people from the village gathered together and offered help. Today, with the help of professional service providers, grieving families can focus more on the greeting of the guests. As a result of the change mentioned above, getting to the burial site has changed significantly. In the past, ***sangyeo*** **상여** or the funeral bier was carried together by the village neighbors on foot. The process has been replaced by a hearse.

WHAT DO PEOPLE WEAR AT KOREAN FUNERALS?

What to wear is different, too. In the past, ***sangbok*** **상복** (mourning barb) made of off-white ***sambe*** **삼베** (hemp cloth) was worn. It was composed of hemp dress, hemp hat, called ***gulgeon*** **굴건** and ***jipshin*** **짚신** (straw shoes). According to Professor Lee Cheol-yeong at Eulji University, hemp clothes were traditionally worn by sinners, and you are a sinner who lacks filial piety because you "let your parent die." and the hat is put on to hide the head and face from the heavens. Today, grieving families wear modern formal attire, black in color. The ***sangju*** **상주** (chief mourner) puts on a hemp armband with stripes, although it's unclear what the origin of the stripes and their meaning are, it's considered a result of a mixture of traditional and modern elements.

VISITOR'S GUIDE
RULES AND ETIQUETTE
AT A MODERN KOREAN FUNERAL

OBITUARIES are sent out via Kakaotalk, email, phone calls, and even social media channels like Instagram, detailing who passed away, where the funeral is held, and when the funeral procession and burial is.

3-DAY FUNERAL is most common, but some families do a 2-day funeral. Make sure to attend the funeral within three (two) days of the announcement.

WHAT TO BRING

JOEUIGEUM / BUEUIGEUM 조의금 / 부의금 (CONDOLENCE MONEY)

50,000 KRW-100,000 KRW ($50 - $100) is the norm.

FLOWERS

Individual guests are not required or expected to bring flowers. If you happen to represent a large company, you may send pre-arranged chrysanthemum wreaths through flower delivery shops.

DRESS CODE

STICK WITH DARK COLORS

Black is the color of mourning, if not available, wear dark (i.e., dark gray, navy, brown) clothes, and avoid colorful clothes.

BEING THERE IS MORE IMPORTANT

There are instances where you can't keep the dress code (e.g., became aware of the news last minute while you were out). In this case, it's better to pay a visit than skipping because your presence would be much appreciated, and people will understand.

BLACK TIES AND SOCKS

One thing people often overlook is wearing black ties and socks. Socks are especially important because there are more instances where your socks are exposed than you might expect. So choose the ones that are long enough to cover your ankle.

BE CONSERVATIVE

For females, if wearing a skirt, avoid those that are either too short or too tight.

1 SIGNING THE GUESTBOOK

Upon entering the funeral hall, you will be asked to sign the guestbook.

Tip: Write down your name vertically. If someone made a mistake and wrote their name horizontally, just write down your name vertically right underneath it.

2 ENTER THE MEMORIAL ROOM 빈소 BINSO

After signing the guestbook, you'll be guided to the memorial room. You must take off your shoes before entering, just as if you were entering a house. You should expect to stand in line outside the memorial room if you happen to visit at a crowded time.

3 FLOWER OFFERING AND INCENSE BURNING

Upon entrance, give a slight nod to the chief mourner. Proceed to the altar and grab (or you will be given one) a flower from the altar and place it in front of the portrait of the deceased, with the bud facing it, and offer a brief moment of silence. If visiting as a group, the oldest person can do it on behalf of the group.

Once done, kneel before the small table in front of the altar, pick an incense stick (traditionally 3, but 1 is okay these days), and light it up using a candle. DO NOT blow out the flame. Use the other hand (usually the left hand) to wave it out. Then stick it upright in the incense burner.

4 PAY RESPECT TO THE DECEASED

Step back from the altar, and:

- Do 2 full-bows ***keunjeol* 큰절** (for females, ***banjeol* 반절** is also acceptable), getting down on both knees, palms touching the floor, with right hand on top of the left for males and left hand on top of the right for females.

- Bowing is skipped if the deceased is a minor.

Turned to face the grieving family, and:

- Do 1 full-bow to the chief mourner (he will reciprocate the full-bow at the same time) and offer words of condolences.

Tip: Even if the chief mourner is your close friend, use ***jondaemal*** or honorifics.
Don't ask too many details about the deceased or the chief mourner. You can do this at a later point in time.

5 CONDOLENCE MONEY

Similar to ***chukeuigeum* 축의금** ("congratulatory money") at Korean weddings, the amount to give depends on your relationship with the grieving family, but as a rule of thumb 50,000 - 100,000 Korean Won (50 - 100 USD) is a safe range. But again, you're welcome to contribute more should you feel compelled, as the money will go to the family to cover the funeral expenses. ***In many cases, condolence money can be given immediately after signing the guestbook.**

AMOUNT: GENERAL RULE OF THUMB

DEATH OF A...

Family member of a co-worker – 50,000 KRW
Family member of a friend – 100,000 KRW
Family member of a very close friend – 100,000+ KRW

Tip: Have Cash Beforehand – Cash is the only means expected, so make sure to visit an ATM machine beforehand, or if that's not an option, borrow from someone.

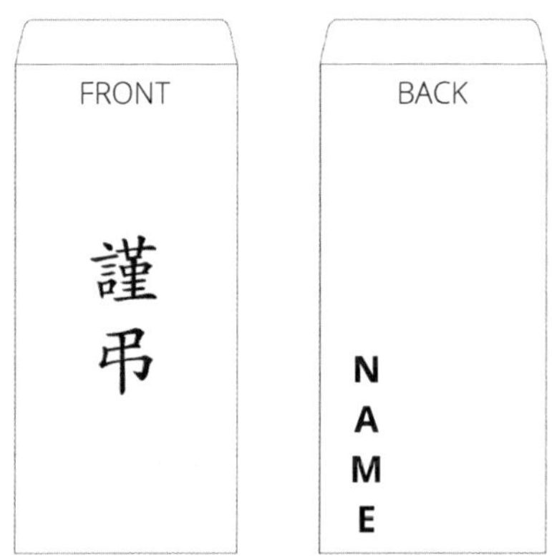

Don't give the condolence money directly to the chief mourner or grieving family.

① **Grab an Envelope for *joeuigeum / bueuigeum* 조의금 / 부의금("Condolence Money")** - If you haven't prepared an envelope, you can get it from the reception desk.

② **Write Down Your Name On The Envelope**- On the bottom left corner on the back of the envelope, write your name down.

③ **Put Money In The Envelope and Drop It In The Box** - Make sure not to fold the paper bill and drop it in a box provided. The receptionist will collect it and record your name and the amount to reciprocate at future funeral events (which certainly isn't something we look forward to).

6 DINING AND DRINKING

Now you will be guided to the dining area attached to the memorial room. Here, you will be served on disposable plates a set of dishes like rice, ***yukaegaejang* 육개장** (spicy beef soup), ***jeon* 전** (Korean pancakes), ***tteok* 떡** (rice cakes), and various ***banchan* 반찬** selections, along with ***soju*** and other soft drinks.

Don't clink glasses when you drink with other guests.

WHY DO KOREAN PEOPLE WAIL SO MUCH AT FUNERALS?

One notable difference about Korean funerals is the expression of grief. In the past, female family members of the deceased were supposed to demonstrate their grief by continuously weeping and wailing because it served as an indication of the deceased person's value and importance. On the contrary, male family members were not allowed to show their grief and were expected to suppress their emotions. The trend at modern funerals has been leaning towards the reduction in the overt display of excessive grieving.

WHY DID KOREANS LIVE NEXT TO THE PARENT'S GRAVE FOR THREE YEARS?

Lastly, the time required for ***talsang* 탈상**, or "taking off the mourning clothes" (= leaving off mourning period) is different. In the past, to pay respects for the debt of gratitude owed to one's parent and as repentance for the impiety committed as a child, the *sangju* built a mud hut next to the parent's gravesite and dwell in there, taking care of the grave for three years, while wearing the hemp mourning clothes. Upon fulfillment, the *sangju* could finally take off the mourning clothes, and it was a reverent ceremony. Today, it's usually done right after the burial, or on the 49th day or the 1-year mark of the passing, with *jesa*, a memorial service for the deceased.

WATCH TRADITIONAL KOREAN FUNERAL ON YouTube

"추억의 영상포엠 - 전통 장례 김제 성덕면 학성강당 | 투데이전북" BY KBS 전주

WATCH MODERN KOREAN FUNERAL ON YouTube

A FUNERAL SCENE FROM
YUNAEUI GEORI 유나의 거리 (STEAL HEART, JTBC, 2014)

Some say that funerals should be lively and boisterous ("the more boisterous, the better the funeral") because being so is considered a way of consolation. For this reason, you will often find people playing card games and talking loudly. But again, it depends on the situation, so use common sense (or ***nunchi* 눈치**) and gauge how others act and take that as the yardstick.

Tip: In case of the death of a family member of a co-worker, the juniors of the co-worker's team are expected to offer help at a funeral. It could be anywhere from guiding visitors, cleaning the dining tables, and neatly lining up the shoes of the guests.

WHY DO KOREANS EAT YUKGAEJANG AT FUNERALS?

***Yukgaejang* 육개장**, or spicy beef stew, is considered to be a staple food for funeral parlors, for which there are two theories regarding its origin. First, the red color of the soup is believed to expel evil spirits. Second, to serve many visitors, a food that is not easily spoiled had to be chosen, and *yukgaejang* fit the bill as it contains a lot of red pepper powder and salt which act as natural preservatives.

WHAT DO KOREANS PREFER? BURIAL OR CREMATION?

Although traditionally Koreans prefer natural burials in the countryside, the rate of cremation is rising due to the lack of land space and time associated with burial and the management of the gravesite. Instead, many opt for cremation.

WHY DO KOREAN PEOPLE THROW SALT WHEN YOU RETURN FROM A FUNERAL?

When you return home from a funeral, Korean people would throw salt on you at the door before you enter the home, to chase off the evil spirits that might have "tagged along" from the funeral. This superstitious practice is based on the belief that salt, which helps to keep food from spoiling, is associated with "purity" and "cleanliness," so throwing salt is a purifying ritual. In Korean pop culture, it's also used as a way to express a strong discontent and insult someone, like an unwelcoming guest. "Get him out of here and throw some salt!" is a popular expression.

JESA

WHY DO KOREAN PEOPLE OFFER FOOD TO THE PHOTOS OF THE ANCESTORS?

If you like watching heart-warming Korean family dramas like ***Neongkuljjae Gulleo-on Dangshin* 넝쿨째 굴러온 당신** (***My Husband Got a Family*, KBS 2, 2012**), where extended families of many generations live together under the same roof (which was typical until recently), there is this scene where everyone in the family gathered around a huge, low dining table on which a wide array of traditional Korean dishes and seasonal fruits were presented in front of the photos of the ancestors, followed by a series of rituals like burning incense, bowing, offering rice wine, and sticking a spoon upright in a rice bowl.

What you just saw is a traditional memorial ceremony for ancestors called ***jesa* 제사**. Technically speaking, ***jesa*** can refer to any type of memorial ceremony, but they are categorized by when they are held. Here is a lengthy list of rituals and their dates you can remember before-hand.

- FOR UP TO YOUR GRANDPARENTS OF THE PATERNAL SIDE.
- IF BOTH HAVE PASSED AWAY, A SINGLE JESA IS HELD FOR BOTH, ON THE DEATH ANNIVERSARY OF THE GRANDFATHER.

***Charye* 차례** – **Seollal 설날** (Korean Lunar New Year) and **Chuseok 추석** (Fall Harvest Festival, 15th day of the 8th month of the lunar calendar).

***Gijesa* 기제사** – On the night before or morning of the ancestor's death anniversary

***Sije* 시제** – Every season, for ancestors who are the fifth generation and beyond.

***Myoje* 묘제** – Memorial ceremony held at the gravesite

***Seongmyo* 성묘** – On **Hansik 한식** (April 5th) and **Chuseok**. It's a memorial ceremony performed at the gravesite of the ancestors. On top of the memorial ceremony, families tidy up the grave by cutting the weeds and mowing the grass.

SEE HOW IT'S DONE ON YouTube

Hansik* of The Day _ Korean Traditional Memorial Ritual, *Jesa
By Arirang Culture

ORDER OF THE CEREMONY

Truth be told, the rituals are quite complicated and even the most orthodox Confucian families have a difficult time remembering everything, not to mention the average Korean. But getting bogged down in the rules and having a headache is not what the ancestors want. What they would really want to see is everyone getting together, having a good time while remembering, and honoring the ones that came before them. In light of preserving the tradition, though, here is the typical order of the memorial ceremony.

Kangshin 강신 – "Inviting The Souls Of The Ancestors"

All attendees stand before the altar while the eldest male descendant, jeju, kneels down in front of the memorial altar. He burns three incense sticks and bows twice. (Sometimes the bowing is skipped). The jeju kneels again. Another person (usually the wife) gives the jeju an empty cup with a saucer and pours it (about 30% full). The jeju then takes the cup and makes a circle three times over the incense. The liquor is poured into a bowl filled with sand, called 모사 mosa, in three equal pours. The empty cup and a saucer are returned to the wife.The jeju makes two full bows. It's believed that the incense invites the souls of the ancestors from the above and the liquor invites those from the underground (which the sand is symbolic of).

Chamshin 참신 – "Greeting The Souls Of The Ancestors"

All attendees make full bows (twice for men and four times for women).

Choheon 초헌 – "First Offering Of Rice Wine"

The jeju makes the first offering of rice wine, followed by his wife. At the conclusion of the first ritual offering, the jeju makes two full bows and the wife makes four.

Aheon 아헌 – "Second Offering Of Rice Wine"

The second eldest male descendant within the family (the next eldest sons or sons-in-law) makes an offering of rice wine, following the same procedures.

Jongheon 종헌 - "Final Offering"

The offering of rice wine continues until no high-ranking male descendants are left.

Sapsi 삽시 - "Food Serving"

The meals are served to the ancestors by the jeju, by sticking a spoon upright in the middle of the rice bowl.

Yushik 유식 – "Recelvlng of the Offerings"

All attendees leave the room or turn away for a few minutes so that the souls of the ancestors can enjoy the offerings.

Cheolsang 철상 - "Removal of Table"

The table is cleared by first blowing out the candles and removing the dishes on the table, starting from the innermost. All the attendants make two full bows, sending the spirits off.

Eumbok 음복 - "Receiving Blessings"

Attendees share the food offerings removed from the table and partake in the feast, and it symbolizes the receiving of the blessings from the ancestors.

WHAT'S OFFERED ON THE TABLE?

When it comes to what goes on the table, there's no one right answer. It's different from region to region, and from family to family. With the change of times, what was not available in the past, such as the non-traditional Korean dishes and fruits like pizza and banana started to appear on the table, because the idea is that at the end of the day it's the deceased ancestors whom the memorial ceremony is held for, and if they liked them when they were alive, then why not serve them what they liked? Of course, Korean traditionalists would frown upon the setup. With that said, let's look at a typical table setting for a *Jesa* ceremony to see what it looks like.

Row 1 - Rice and soup, but on Seollal, ***tteokguk*** **떡국** (rice cake soup) is served instead. When serving liquor, it has to be clear (e.g., filtered rice wine). ***Songpyeon*** (half-moon shaped rice cake) takes the place of liquor and rice during **Chuseok**.

Row 2 - Various kinds of meat, pancakes, and fish. When you put the fish, keep the head facing east (right). Place the meat on the left side, and the fish on the right side.

Row 3 - Various soups. Place in the order of meat soup, tofu soup, and fish soup. Place soy sauce between them.

Row 4 - Vegetables, dried fish, and ***shikhye*** **식혜** (sweet rice drink). Place the dried fish on the left (west). *Shikhye* goes on the far right.

Row 5 - Place fruits, cookies, and desserts.

RESTRICTED FOODS

- Peaches because they expel ghosts & spirits.

- No fish ending with "*chi*" such as ***kkongchi* 꽁치** (mackerel) and ***galchi* 갈치** (cutlass fish) because it's believed that fish without scales are "cheap."

- Red beans, food with ***gochugaru* 고추가루** (red pepper powder) or garlic seasoning cannot be served because ghosts and spirits hate red color and garlic.

WHY ARE THE FOODS PLACED IN SPECIFIC ORDER? ARE THERE ANY RULES?

***Banseogaengdong* 반서갱동**: Rice on the west, soup on the east (opposite to the living).

***Jeokjeopgeojung* 적접거중**: Roast meat in the center.

***Eeodongyukseo* 어동육서**: Fish on the east and meat on the west.

***Dongdoseomi* 동두서미**: The head facing the east and the tail facing the west.

***Baebokbanghyang* 배복방향**: Dried fish with its back upward.

Sukseosaengdong* 숙서생동**: Cooked vegetables on the west and raw ***kimchi on the east.

***Hongdongbaekseo* 홍동백서**: Red fruits on the east and white fruits on the west.

Jwapouhye* 좌포우혜**: Dried fish at the left end and ***shikhye at the right end.

***Dongjoseoyul* 동조서율**: Dates on the east and the chestnuts on the west.

***Joyulishi* 조율이시**: Starting from the left, place dates, chestnuts, pears, and persimmons.

Although their origins are unclear, the above rules have been passed down as a custom by posterity, and some of the rules contradict each other. For example, if you place red dates on the left, following the ***joyulishi*** rule, you are violating ***hongdongbaekseo*** rule which dictates that red should go east (right). Are they not only complicated to follow? They often cause quarrels among family members.

WHAT ARE THE ANCESTRAL TABLETS?

***Shinwi* 신위** is one of the objects representing the presence of the dead, such as portraits or memorial tablets. Originally, it was made of wood, and normally it was not easy for most families to build a shrine. Therefore, ***jibang* 지방**, a disposable *shinwi*, was made before the rite. It contains the information of the name and official position of the deceased on a piece of paper and was burnt after the memorial ceremony. These days, portrait photos are a more popular choice.

WHY IS A FOLDING SCREEN SET UP DURING A JESA CEREMONY?

***Byeongpung* 병풍** is a folding screen with poetic calligraphy written across it which is set up facing north, as it's the direction for the dead. Not only does it cover other household objects like the TV during *jesa*, but it is symbolic of the presence of the dead because, in traditional funerals, the body of the deceased was put behind it.

WHY ARE ONLY WOMEN RESPONSIBLE FOR PREPARING FOR JESA?

While many look forward to the long holiday, it's a time many married Korean women fear - the never-ending kitchen labor, spending all day in the kitchen, making a large feast for *jesa* and *charye* held for their husbands' ancestors! It's because when a woman gets married in Korea, she becomes part of the husband's family, and the priority is always put on the husband's family matters. For example, visiting the home of the husband's parents is essential during the holidays, while that of her parents isn't. Inevitably, pent up emotions rise to the surface during the holidays - tensions between the in-laws and labor inequality are all contributing factors to the divorce rate that skyrockets after the holiday season. It's a Korean drama cliche where couples wrangle with each other in a car on their way back to Seoul from their visit to the husband's parent's home in the countryside.

HOW DO KOREANS WITH DIFFERENT RELIGIONS HANDLE JESA?

Korea is a free country where freedom of religion is guaranteed by the constitution. When it comes to *jesa*, Catholics (the Catholic Pope formally recognized it as a civil practice in 1939) and Buddhists practice the memorial ceremonies, while Protestants do not (as it could be viewed as "worshipping" other deities besides the Lord). So the Protestant members of a family are excused from partaking in the ritual.

WEDDINGS IN KOREA

- Traditional -

Foreign weddings, filled with exotic ceremonies and rituals, are quite a spectacle, but they can make you a little confused if you don't have knowledge of their cultural background. And when it comes to complexity, traditional Korean weddings are second to none. So let's learn about what Korean weddings were like in the past so they have more meaning.

PRE-WEDDING RITUALS

Traditional Korean weddings hold the essence of the Confucian values that center around ***hyo* 효**, "filial piety" – respecting one's parents, elders, and honoring the ancestors. For this reason, Koreans view weddings as a unison of two families and since marriages were taken sacredly, every aspect of it, from the initial discussion to finally tying the knot, entailed a series of elaborate procedures.

In the past, most marriages were arranged by the parents (hey, they will set up everything for you! It doesn't sound too bad, right?). The first step is called ***euihon* 의혼**, or "marriage discussion," this is when the parents of both families discuss the possibility of marriage, and it's often set up by a well-connected "matchmaker." And because elite families viewed marriage as a means to strategically develop or further strengthen their social status, various factors had to be considered during this process, including age, family customs, social status, academic achievements, wealth, as well as hereditary disorders. If everything checks out, then the groom's family sends a marriage proposal letter, and the bride's family replies with a permission letter.

Great! Now we can move on to set the date to seal the deal. The second step is called ***napchae* 납채**, or "date setting." In choosing the perfect date for this very special day, you might consider various divination methods such as observing the positioning of the stars, but for Koreans, *saju* plays an important role. As previously learned, *saju*, consisting of the "four pillars," which are four elements of birth are believed to determine one's fate and destiny. The year, month, day, and hour of the groom are written on a paper, wrapped carefully, and sent to a *saju* reader who will then analyze it to come up with the most auspicious date for wedding. Once done, the date is sent back to the groom's family.

Then the last step is called ***nappye* 납폐**, or "sending valuables'.' Once the date is selected, the groom's family sends to the bride a *ham* 함, a box containing wedding gifts prepared by the groom's family for his bride before the wedding. In the ham are many items, and some of the most important include the ***honseo* 혼서**, the ***chaedan* 채단**, and the ***yemul* 예물**. First, the *honseo* is "marriage papers/documents" that are given to the bride who is expected to keep them throughout the marriage. Upon death, they are placed together with her in the coffin. The *chaedan* is a set of red and blue cloths, representative of the traditional Yin/Yang philosophy. They are used to make wedding clothes. Another set of items is the *yemul*, a variety of gifts for the bride's family, and they typically include jewelry, clothes, and household items.

Traditional Korean weddings are held in the yard or the house of the bride to which the groom had to travel by horse on the wedding day. On this special day, ordinary people were permitted to wear luxurious clothes that only the upper class could wear. The bride and groom were allowed to don the costumes modeled after those of the royal court. The groom wore a black hat, and the bride covered her face with a veil until half the ceremony was over. On the head, she put on a ***jokduri* 족두리**, a beautiful Korean bridal crown decorated with embroidery and many accessories, with a ***binyeo* 비녀**, an ornamental hairpin to hold the hair bun in place.

ORDER OF CEREMONY

WATCH TRADITIONAL KOREAN WEDDING ON YouTube

"TRADITIONAL KOREAN WEDDING CEREMONY" BY ASIAN ART MUSEUM

Chinyeongrye 친영례: Bride's Family Greets The Groom

-The groom enters the yard where the wedding is held, led by ***gireokabi* 기럭아비**, who carries the wedding geese. He hands the geese to the groom.

Jeonanrye 전안례: Presentation of The Geese

-The groom places the wild geese on a table where his mother-in-law is sitting and bows twice.
-Mother-in-law accepts the wild geese and takes them into the house.

*The wild geese, replaced by wooden ones these days, represent many virtues a newlywed couple must possess.

- Love and loyalty - They mate for life and do not find another partner even if they lose one.- Harmony
- Even when flying in a group, they maintain hierarchy and order, thus creating harmony.

Gyobaerye 교배례: Bowing to Each Other

- Helpers wash the hands of the bride and groom.
- Facing each other while standing on the mat in the yard, they make full bows to each other, taking turns.

*Helpers on each side had to assist the bride because she had to sit cross-legged and stand up.
*Surprisingly, this was the first opportunity to see each other's faces because marriages were arranged by the parents, which means they could only hope their parents made the right choice!

Hapgeunrye 합근례: Drinking Together

- One of the helpers pours rice wine into a small cup for the groom, who then drinks it.- Another helper pours rice wine for the bride who only pretends to drink it.
- The groom's helpers then pour rice wine into the gourd dipper and the groom drinks it again.
- The bride's helper does the same in her gourd dipper.
- The groom and bride join together and make three separate full bows: one for their parents, one for their ancestors, and one for the guests.

*Drinking in a gourd dipper symbolizes marital harmony because the half-divided gourd has only one perfectly matching counterpart.

Seonghonrye 성혼례: Declaration of Marriage

- Bride and groom bows to both families and guests.
- The ceremony is concluded.

After the wedding ceremony, the groom takes his wife in a beautifully decorated palanquin called 꽃가마 kkotgama to his parents' house to live in.

WHAT ARE THE RED DOTS ON THE BRIDE'S FACE?

Yeonji* 연지** refers to red-colored cosmetics used by women, while ***gonji* 곤지** specifically refers to a red dot drawn on the forehead using it. Scholars are divided over the origin - Lee Ik and Lee Gyu-kyung, Confucian scholars in the late Joseon Dynasty, claimed that it was the custom of the Huns which was introduced to China and then spread to the Joseon Dynasty, while poet Choi Nam-sun asserted that it was the practice of the Mongols which was introduced to the Goryeo Dynasty. But whatever the origin, the bride wearing ***yeonji/gonji is part make-up and part shamanistic ritual - protecting the bride from the mischief of the evil spirits. But not all brides wore rouge makeup just because it was the wedding day. It was a custom that was only allowed for first marriages.

WHY WAS PEEPING INTO THE BRIDAL CHAMBER ON THEIR FIRST NIGHT ALLOWED?

What did Korean people turn to when there were no pay-per-views available to watch adult movies? They chose to peep into the bridal chamber of the newlyweds! After the newlyweds entered the freshly set up nest, neighbors and even relatives (et tu...?) gathered in front of the papered doors, poke holes using their fingers, and peep at what was going on inside. While it sounds all creepy and perverted, it was done with the couple's best interest at heart. During the Joseon Dynasty era, early marriage was a widespread custom, and children (boys around the age of 10 and girls in the early teens) weren't too young to tie the knot. And naturally, it caused many unforeseen problems (I mean, they are just kids). Among all, there was the issue of the scared bride running away on the wedding night, and in extreme cases, a secret lover would steal the bride from the unsuspecting little groom. To prevent this, the neighbors and relatives formed a "neighborhood watch" and kept vigil against the unfortunate events. The peeping, of course, must have been a way to make sure everything was going well inside – they knew their duty was over when the groom put out the candlelight. It's an old custom that's completely died out today.

- Modern -

These days, modern, or Western-style weddings with a Korean twist is the more popular choice among couples, mostly for the sake of simplicity and convenience. Compared to traditional weddings, it takes less time and most importantly, it's easier to find a venue because traditional weddings take place outside, making it vulnerable to unfriendly weather. Let's take a look at what modern Korean weddings look like.

PRE-WEDDING RITUALS

or

SANGGYEONRYE - THE IN-LAWS FACE-OFF!

You might have seen in Korean dramas where the soon-to-be-married couple and their parents gather at a nice restaurant over dinner. Known as ***sanggyeonrye* 상견례**, it is a formal meeting of the in-laws (usually just the couple and their parents, but can have other family members too), and is an opportunity for both families to get to know each other. As Koreans view weddings as a unison of two families, asking for permission from parents is still of the utmost importance. In Korean dramas (and in real life too), this is where conflicts arise most often – there's a power struggle between the two families, which happens when the parents of one side, or both, find the other, or each other's family "inadequate," be they their financial situation or social status. Also, because the parents provide monetary and material support to their children's wedding, there is a desire to exert as much influence on the marriage, causing a wedding engagement to be called off in extreme cases.

WATCH WHAT HAPPENS WHEN SANGGYEONRYE GOES WRONG!

YouTube

Abeojiga Isanghae 아버지가 이상해 (My Father Is Strange, KBS, 2017)

YEDAN, *YEMUL*, AND *HONSU*

Even if you passed *sanggyeonrye*, it's too early to let your guard down because there's another major hurdle – agreeing on how much to give, receive, and contribute. For Korean weddings, ***yemul* 예물** is the wedding gift for the bride, typically matching jewelry sets such as diamond rings, earrings, and necklaces while ***yedan* 예단**, originally meaning "silk gift for the groom's family," is the wedding gift for the groom's family, which are usually cash or other expensive items such as nice silverware and luxury goods like leather handbags. On top of that, the groom is expected to provide housing, while the bride is expected to provide household items such as the TV and refrigerator, known as ***honsu* 혼수**, or dowry. Most of the time, when these gifts from the bride fall short of the groom's parents' expectations, things can fall apart, resulting in major quarrels between the couple.

WHERE ARE MODERN KOREAN WEDDINGS HELD?

One good thing about going with the modern style Korean wedding is convenience! Partly because there are dedicated service providers who handle every aspect of the wedding, but the biggest reason is the Korean people's notion of ***bbali bbali* 빨리빨리** (quick, quick!) which values speed and efficiency. For this reason, the go-to venues for most weddings are wedding halls. While it's all convenient to have everything handled by professionals, it has its drawbacks too. The wedding venues are there to make money, and they try to squeeze in as many weddings as possible on a given day. Considering most weddings take place during the weekend, it's natural for them to maximize their earning opportunity by raising the turnover rate (typical wedding ceremony takes no longer than 90 minutes), which means that right around when your ceremony is wrapping, there are people already cleaning up and preparing for the next couple in the queue (party pooper!).

DRESS CODE

When it comes to what to wear, be conservative, and avoid wearing something that makes you stick out in the crowd, like bright colors like red and yellow. Some people advise avoiding white, especially female guests because it's the color reserved for the bride. Regarding the style, semi-formal (no jeans) is accepted these days. And as for whether guests can wear ***hanbok***, you don't have to because it's worn by the mother and the female relatives of the newlyweds.

CONGRATULATORY MONEY, GUESTBOOK, FOOD VOUCHER, AND PARKING PASS

Same as Korean funerals, you are expected to offer ***chukeuigeum* 축의금** (congratulatory money) as a gift, which would be used to cover the wedding expenses. Upon entrance, you will find two tables, one for the groom's side and another for the bride's side, where you will find people (usually their friends) collecting money envelopes, asking you to sign the guestbook, and handing out the parking pass along with the food voucher. As for the food voucher, there are two scenarios. One is a sit-down dining option, typically at upper-class hotels, where you are served a course of meals on a round table with other guests. Another is a buffet-style, which takes place at a separate dining place within the same building. As for gifting money, similar rules apply as Korean funerals. These days, the minimum is typically ₩50,000 KRW among not-so-close friends or acquaintances, and adjust the amount as you feel necessary. If you are quite close ₩70,000 KRW or ₩100,000 KRW is a safe range, and feel free to contribute more if deemed necessary. One thing to keep in mind is if you're bringing your significant other, it's advised to double the amount because the extra mouth means double the food expense for the marrying couple.

ORDER OF EVENTS

Opening Ceremony: The emcee (MC) of the event welcomes and gives thanks to the guests as they announce the beginning of the wedding. In some cases, they crack a joke to create a more lively atmosphere.

The Entrance of the Mothers: Mothers of both families enter, holding each other's hands. If one's parents are already deceased, divorced, or not able to enter for any physical reason, it can be omitted.

Candle Lighting: Mothers of both families light the candles. Afterward, they greet each other by exchanging bows and greet the guests. Introducing the Officiant: Introduce the officiant who will preside the wedding ceremony. If it is a wedding without an officiant, it is naturally omitted.

The Entrance of the Groom: The groom passes the "bridal path" and goes forward to greet the officiant first and then turns back to greet the guests.

The Entrance of The Bride: The bride comes in holding her father's hand. If the father of the bride is deceased or unable to enter with the bride, the groom may enter together at the same time.

Groom/Bride Bow Exchange: The bride and the groom bow to each other. Sometimes standing too close to each other when bowing causes a head-on collision, and causes some laughs!

Reading of The Marriage Vow: The officiant asks the bride and groom if they will swear to love forever. If it's a ceremony without an officiant, the bride and groom can read each other the letter of promises.

Reading of The Declaration of Marriage: The officiant reads the declaration following the marriage vows. If without an officiant, the emcee or, in general, the father of either side of the family does it. In the case of international marriages, it's often conducted in two languages.

The Officiant's Speech: The officiant gives a speech to the newly-born couple. Popular topics include life lessons, tips on married life, and words of blessing. The father of either side of the family can assume the role in a wedding ceremony without an officiant.

Chukga Singing (Congratulatory Song / Wedding Song): The friends of the couple sing for them. More often than not, it's the most entertaining part of the ceremony. Some choose to sing in a musical-like format and some even dance with the couple. Hiring a choir to sing a congratulatory song is a popular option for those not wanting any surprises.

Thanking Each Other's Parents: First, the couple goes to the bride's parents (sitting in a chair) and makes a full bow. Then the parents get up and hug the couple. The couple repeats the same to the groom's parents.

Thanking the Guests: The couple stands in the middle of the podium and thank the guests by making a half-bow, but the groom can make a big bow should he wish so. The parents of both families sometimes come to the podium together to thank the guests.

Groom/Bride Exiting and Flower Shower: The couple leaves together. Upon approaching the end of the "bridal path," the friends sprinkle the flower petals.

AFTER CEREMONY

GROUP PHOTO TIME!

Memories vanish but photos stay with you. For many guests at the wedding, the group photo time might be the most important part of the event because it's ironclad proof of your attendance. So after the wedding, guests hang around waiting for the group photo time. First, the family members are invited to the podium to take photos. Then, friends and colleagues all come up and take photos together. During this, the photographer would ask the guests to participate in creating dramatic photos for the couple, such as all clapping while the couple is kissing, or turning on the flashlights on their smartphones with the background lighting up as if a million fireflies are celebrating together.

Why Do Koreans Make A Fist When Taking A Picture? P. 244

PIROYEON 피로연 – AFTER PARTY/RECEPTION

After the wedding, guests will be guided to join in a separate room. These days, the wedding reception typically takes place at a banquet hall within the same building. Upon entrance, you will have to present the food voucher you previously received in the lobby after signing the guestbook to the receptionist. Here, there are two types of meals served – one is a sit-down, where a course of dishes is served to you, versus a buffet, where you will have to serve yourself. In some cases, especially younger couples, opt to have their separate after-party in place of a wedding reception. You do not need to offer a separate cash gift.

WHY DO KOREANS EAT NOODLES AT THE WEDDING?

Janchiguksu **잔치국수** ("party/banquet noodle") is one of the traditional Korean noodle dishes served at birthday parties as well as weddings because the long noodles symbolize longevity. It's been a popular menu choice for large scale events because it's easy to prepare in advance in large quantities. Just top it with garnishes and pour the soup and you are all set to enjoy the dish. Stemming from the tradition, asking a bachelor about when they will be serving noodles is an idiomatic expression of asking when he will get married.

PYEBAEK – DO YOU WANT MANY KIDS? THEN CATCH THE DATES AND CHESTNUTS!

GOTTA CATCH 'EM ALL! Nope, it's not Pokémon GO time, but it's something you will hear during the private family-only ***pyebaek* 폐백** ceremony which takes place after *piroyeon*, the wedding reception, after all guests leave. Originally, the ceremony was where the bride makes her first visit to her parents-in-laws and bows as a gesture of joining the groom's family (technically speaking, the correct term for the ceremony is ***hyungugorye* 현구고례**, and *pyebaek* means a set of valuables prepared for her in-laws as gifts during the ceremony, but it became more commonly known as *pyebaek* itself). Its' an important element from the traditional Korean wedding and modern Korean weddings also adopted it as a part of the wedding because it emphasizes the importance of having a harmonious family as well as respecting the elders. For the ceremony, the newlyweds make full bows to the parents, and the bride presents dates and chestnuts, a Korean representation of fertility, to the parents-in-law, who would then share the words of wisdom. Then the highlight of the event – throwing dates and chestnuts which the couple has to catch with the bride's long wedding skirt. It's said that how many you catch can predict how many kids you will have! Originally, the purpose of the ceremony was to introduce the new family member, the bride, to the family of the groom's side. In modern Korean weddings, the parents of the bride are often allowed to partake in the ceremony. The ceremony ends with the groom giving the bride a piggyback ride.

IBAJI FOOD - SHOW OFF THE COOKING SKILLS!

Perhaps a highlight for Gordon Ramsey, ***ibaji eumsik* 이바지 음식** (contribution food), is one of the wedding traditions that still remain in modern weddings. Featuring lavish home-cooked meals prepared using the bride's family's recipes with various seasonal and regional ingredients, it's a symbol of gratitude from the bride's parents for accepting their "inadequate child with many flaws" as a daughter-in-law, and a firm resolution to serve the in-law family with the utmost respect. At the same time, it was an opportunity to show off her mother's cooking skills. The foods are wrapped in silk cloth, carefully placed in bamboo baskets, and delivered to the groom's family on the wedding day.

WHO'S THE GUY WEARING A SQUID MASK?

[추억의영상] 90년대 함 사세요! (Traditional Korean Wedding Custom, 90s) IMF 직전, 오징어가면 함진아비 by Time traveler 시간여행자

WATCH ON YouTube

Remember the old tradition of the groom sending *ham* 함, a box containing wedding gifts, to the bride's family before the wedding? Well, it survived to our time, with slight changes to how it's done. Whereas it was sent by the servants in the past, the groom's relatives or close friends assume the role these days and become what's known as ***hamjinabi* 함진아비** (***ham***, not the SPAM ham,carrier). The ham carrier, along with his pack, makes a trip to the bride's house, wearing a dry squid mask (but can be painted with charcoal instead) because it's believed to ward off all evil spirits. Upon arrival, the ham carrier would shout **"*Ham Saseyo* 함 사세요!"** ("Buy the *ham*!") three times to summon the family members and friends of the bride. Then they will haggle over the "price" to pay for the ham, which is all part of the entertainment. The people from the bride's side will try to bring the ham home with minimal effort, and on the contrary, the ham carrier would maximize the "profit" by asking for a "payment" for each step he takes. Sometimes he might request the females from the bride's side to sing, on top of a "payment," just for some added fun. Aside from delivering the actual ham, it was a fun way to let the neighbors know about the wedding. Although it was a scene frequently observed until the 1990s, and in vintage Korean dramas, it's no longer easily seen due to people living mostly in apartments.

HOW DO KOREANS FIND THEIR BETTER HALF?

So we learned how Korean people get married, but that must have left many wondering – how do Korean people find their better half? Well, with the deluge of dating apps available, your next date is literally at your fingertips nowadays, but many still prefer the time-tested methods. They frequently appear in Korean dramas and movies, so knowing them will help you enjoy the situation fully.

SOGAETING 소개팅 - BLIND DATE

Sogae* 소개** means "introduction" and the word ***ting* 팅** comes from "meeting," so the literal meaning is a "meeting arranged through introduction (i.e., "arranged meet-up")," which is essentially a "blind date" set up by someone else, usually a mutual friend. There are two scenarios for a ***sogaeting to take place:

Scenario 1 (Target-specific): A boy named Tony stumbles upon a girl of his type named Jenna on social media, and learns that they have a mutual friend named Sarah. Tony sends Sarah a text message and asks her to set up a *sogaeting* with Jenna.

Scenario 2 (Broad-approach): Lauren is having coffee with her friend Sarah. Having recently broken up with her boyfriend, Lauren asks Sarah if there are any single friends available for a *sogaeting*. Ricky, who also broke up with his girlfriend a while ago, comes to Sarah's mind, so Sarah shows Lauren his pictures and Lauren finds him cute.

Either case, Sarah will ask what the other party thinks and if he/she agrees, it's a done deal! Sarah serves as the liaison and helps them exchange each other's contact info, and let the grown-ups handle the rest themselves.

MEETING - GROUP HANGOUT

Similar to *sogaeting*, but it's slightly different because it involves two groups, male participants and female participants, put together in a collaborative effort by a friend from the male side and a friend from the female side. It can have as little as four people (2 males vs. 2 females) but has no upper limit. With a large number of participants, you might imagine it as a dog-eat-dog battle-royale type of event, but it's more of a group hangout to get to know each other better and expand your network (but of course, there's no rule against falling in love at first sight, and sometimes people pair up right on the spot). And it's less pressurizing than a 1:1 *sogaeting* where you often find yourself trying too hard to impress your date. For this reason, it's usually set up at a pub where people can have "drinking games" and have fun all together – which may explain why Korea has so many "drinking games."

MATSEON 맞선 - ARRANGED DATE WITH A PROSPECTIVE MARRIAGE PARTNER

While the above two carry the banner of laissez-faire and free economy, ***matseon* 맞선**, or ***seon* 선**, is a more system-controlled form of dating because it's set up by the parents, relatives, and matchmaking companies for the goal of producing a marriage. For that reason, the main focus is to find a marriage partner who meets many criteria like education, occupation, and wealth, rather than an ideal type to date. It's a classic Korean drama cliché where the mother of a guy arranges a *matseon* without telling him, to separate him from his love who comes from a poor family because she is "inadequate" and fails to meet her standards.

SPECIAL DAYS FOR COUPLES IN KOREA

In the bubbly teenage Korean dramas like ***Hakgyo 2013* 학교 *2013* (*School 2013*, 2013, KBS)**, there are many "couple days" and "remembrance days" which the high school kids fuss over. Most of them are considered as marketing gimmicks disguised as a Valentine's Day spin-off, which explains why most of them fall on the 14th day of each month. Whatever the origin is, as long as they help to reconfirm the love of couples and give them happy memories, it seems like a fair trade.

JAN 14TH
DIARY DAY

A couple gives each other a diary as a gift, wishing for a great start of the new year.

HELLO DAY

Be the first person to say hello to your crush this day, and love will come true. Observed among teenagers.

FEB 14TH
VALENTINE'S DAY

A girl gives the boy chocolate and asks him out.

MAR 14TH
WHITE DAY

A boy gives the girl candy and asks her out. If you received a chocolate from a girl on Valentine's Day, you are expected to reciprocate.

APR 14TH
BLACK DAY

It's a consolation day for all the singles who didn't get chocolate during the days mentioned above. You dress up in black and eat *jjajangmyeon* 짜장면, black bean noodles, hoping it can lift the curse...

MAY 14TH
ROSE DAY

A couple exchanges roses as an expression of love.

JUN 14TH
KISS DAY

Should be self-explanatory.

JUL 14TH
SILVER DAY

A couple gives each other silver rings or silver products as gifts.

AUG 14TH
GREEN DAY

A couple takes a walk in the woods to bask in the fresh air and relieve stress.

SEP 14TH
PHOTO DAY

A couple takes pictures together.

OCT 14TH
WINE DAY

A couple drinks red wine together.

NOV 11TH
PEPERO DAY

A couple exchanges Pepero (cookie sticks dipped in chocolate), or you can give it to your crush and ask him/her out.

DEC 14TH
HUG DAY

A couple hugs each other.

WHY DO SAME-SEX PEOPLE HOLD HANDS?

In Korea, you will often find same-sex Koreans holding hands, even going arm-in-arm. Depending on where you come from, it might raise a red (or rainbow) flag, or might not mean anything at all. But for Koreans, they sure don't seem to care at all. For one, Korean people live in a very closely-knit society and have the characteristics of a collective culture deeply embedded in them. This contributes to more leniency towards personal space. But more importantly, it's largely because the notion of homosexuality is driven deep underground compared to other countries, and people just don't associate same-sex touching with homosexuality. Put together, being physically affectionate between the same-sex is completely natural to Korean people and no one would bat an eye, because nobody sees the connection with homosexuality. Rather, it's more of a display of friendship.

WHY DO KOREAN COUPLES WEAR THE SAME CLOTHES?

Want to call dibs on your significant other and let everyone know that he/she is taken? Well, there's no better way than wearing a pair of matching T-shirts! They can be identical in design, or something that displays a meaning only when put next to each other. Of course, there are other ways too – from couple smartphone cases and a couple diary, to couple shoes and couple rings (these are also worn on the fourth finger of the left hand, like marriage rings, so you can't automatically assume one's married just because they have it on there). Whatever you choose, it's a way of saying "We are together," although some find it too cringe-worthy.

WHY DO KOREAN CHILDREN GIVE CARNATIONS TO THEIR PARENTS ON PARENT'S DAY?

Parent's Day, designated May 8th every year, is a day to thank parents for their unconditional love and dedication. On this day, children make carnations at school and pin them on their parents' chests, while adult children give bouquets with gifts (cash is the number one choice picked by parents, by the way). So why carnations? This is closely related to the birth of Mother's Day. In 1868, three years after the end of the Civil War, the wounds of the war were deep, And a woman named Ann Maria Jarvis organized "Mothers' Friendship Day," a gathering of mothers to console and support each other. After Ann Jarvis passed away, her daughter Anna Jarvis organized gatherings to honor and remember the mothers. Carnations were the flowers her mother loved.

WHAT ARE KOREA'S OFFICIAL HOLIDAYS?

Shinjeong 신정- New Year's Day (Jan 1st of solar calendar)

Like many other countries, the first day of the Gregorian (solar) calendar is celebrated, and many Koreans visit the coast or the mountains to see the first sunrise of the year.

Seollal 설날 – Lunar New Year's Day (Jan 1st of lunar calendar)

It's a traditional Korean Lunar New Year's Day (Seollal) and is one of the most important holidays, much more significant than January 1st. Most people travel to their hometowns to visit their families. On this day, Koreans put on *hanbok* and bows to their elders, and eat *tteokguk* (rice cake soup) and *mandu guk* 만두국 (dumpling soup). They also play traditional games like *yutnori* 윷놀이 (traditional Korean board game), spinning tops, and flying kites.

Samiljeol 3.1절 - Independence Movement Day (Mar 1)

This is the day of commemorating the Declaration of Independence, which was proclaimed on March 1, 1919, against the Japanese occupation.

Eorininal 어린이날 - Children's Day (May 5)

This is the day all Korean kids wait for! Families celebrate with their kids, wishing them to grow up healthy and smart. They usually go out to amusement parks, zoos, or shopping malls (to buy gifts!)

Seokgatanshinil 석가탄신일 - Buddha's Birthday (8th day of 4th lunar month)

Korea traditionally has been a Buddhist country and the traces are found everywhere, especially in this holiday. It's the eighth day of the fourth lunar month, and you can see beautifully decorated temples across the country.

Hyeonchungil 현충일 - Memorial Day (June 6)

It's a very emotional day for Koreans as it commemorates and honors the fallen soldiers and civilians who lost their lives fighting for their country during the Korean War. Ceremonies are held at the National Cemetery in Seoul.

Gwangbokjeol 광복절 - Liberation Day (Aug 15)

Korea became free from the Japanese occupation on this day, when Japan surrendered to the allies in 1945, ending World War II.

Chuseok 추석 – Fall Harvest Festival (15th day of the 8th lunar month)

Along with Seollal, it's another very important traditional holiday – Koreans celebrate for a successful harvest year and families get together for memorial rituals called *charye*, for their ancestors.

Gaecheonjeol 개천절 - National Foundation Day (Oct 3)

According to the founding stories of Gojoseon 고조선, the first nation ever built on the Korean peninsula, the legendary God-King Dangun 단군, proclaimed the beginning of the nation. The founding date, or *gaecheonjeol* 개천절 (The opening day of Heaven) is celebrated at Chamseongdan Altar 참성단 on top of Manisan Mountain 마니산 in Ganghwado Island 강화도.

Hangul Day 한글날 (Oct 9)

It's when the publication of *Hunminjeongeum* 훈민정음 (The Proper Sounds for the Instruction of the People), the basis of Korean Alphabet, *hangul*, was proclaimed in 1446 by King Sejong The Great.

Christmas (Dec 25)

Korea has a large percentage of Christians, and Christmas is celebrated all over the country, where couples reaffirm their love and families get together for quality time.

WHY ARE THERE TWO NEW YEAR'S DAYS?

Are Koreans crazy about partying? Koreans celebrate the first day of the new year twice every year - Once on January 1 of the Solar (Gregorian) calendar, and once on January 1 of the Lunar calendar (usually between the third week of January and the middle of February). Let's find out why. The "Two New Year's Day" culture dates back to the Japanese colonial era. In 1910, Japan named the Solar New Year **Shinjeong 신정** (New New Year) and re-named the traditional Lunar New Year, **Seollal 설날**, to **Gujeong 구정** (Old New Year), as Japan persecuted Korean holiday customs and forced Japanese traditions on the Korean people (in Japan, the Lunar New Year was replaced by the Solar New Year in the late 1800s by **Emperor Meiji**). Furthermore, by labeling the Korean holiday "old," it downplayed the significance of the Korean tradition. Since then, Japan designated Shinjeong as the only national holiday and promoted it by stressing that celebrating two identical holidays is socially wasteful in many ways. Naturally, the traditional lunar New Year was pushed to the back seat. The Lunar New Year, which lost its status as a traditional holiday under the Japanese colonial rule, was not able to find its place until 75 years later. In 1985, it again became a national holiday under the name "Folklore Day." In 1989, the name was restored to Seollal, as a three-day holiday. The Lunar New Year might have disappeared if it weren't for the Korean people who were determined not to lose their traditions despite the oppression of Japanese colonial rule. Even after Seollal was officially recognized as Lunar New Year's Day, the Solar New Year also maintained its official holiday status as a three-day holiday. However, it was reduced to two days in 1991 and eventually became a one-day holiday in 1999.

WHY DO KOREANS EAT *TTEOKGUK* (RICE CAKE SOUP) ON NEW YEAR'S DAY?

***Tteokguk* 떡국** (rice cake soup) is a staple food for Seollal, the Korean Lunar New Year. According to historical documents, on this special day, *tteokguk* was served instead of rice for the ancestral memorial service known as ***charye* 차례**. Then why *tteokguk* among all other possible choices? Well, on New Year's Day, we bid farewell to the old and welcome in the new for a fresh start. For this reason, it contains the primitive religious belief of being clean and solemn, and ***garaetteok* 가래떡**, a long white cylindrical rice cake perfectly fit the bill. Also, the long shape symbolizes longevity, while the sliced pieces symbolize "prosperity" because of their similarity to the traditional Korean coins.

Tteokguk was enjoyed year-round by everyone, from the royal family and the aristocrats to the working class, but held a special status on Seollal. For this reason, the literature from the 1800s on the customs of the Joseon Dynasty recorded that people jokingly said, "The number of ***tteokguk*** bowls you've had so far is your age." But don't worry, even if you eat two or three bowls, you don't age more than a year.

SEBAE - MAKE THE NEW YEAR'S BOW (AND RECEIVE MONEY!)

On New Year's Day, men and women of all ages change into new clothes called ***seolbim*** **설빔** early in the morning and gather together to hold a memorial service for the deceased ancestors. Then, they bow to their grandparents first, and then, taking turns, the younger family members bow to the older family members to greet them for the first time in the New Year. This New Year's bow is called ***sebae*** **세배**. People visited the nearby neighbors' houses to give greetings for the New Year. It was customary for adults to serve alcohol and food to those who come to do *sebae*, but children were given a little money or *tteok* and fruits instead of alcohol. Nowadays, kids look forward to Seollal because they can earn pocket money from doing *sebae*, but if you're too young, it will probably go into your mom's pocket, who acts as your "money manager," happily of course. When bowing to the elderly, New Year's greetings such as, "May you be healthier in the New Year," and, "Happy New Year and live a long life," can be said. The elderly would return by giving words of blessings, such as, "I hope you get promoted in the new year," and, "I hope you achieve your wish in the new year."

WATCH HOW TO SEBAE ON YouTube

"JOHN AND MACK HOW TO SEBAE FT. GRANDMA"
BY ROCK KIDS

SEOLBIM - NEW YEAR, NEW YOU, IN NEW DRESS!

New Year's Day is a day to celebrate the new year with a new resolution. This determination was also expressed through a new dress called ***seolbim*** **설빔** worn on New Year's Day morning. Wearing *seolbim*, which was made by weaving and sewing material by hand, was a must-have ritual even in the days when the family was not well-off. Presenting themselves neat and tidy in new clothing was a way to pay respect to the ancestors as well as praying for the wishes of the New Year. The children's *seolbim* was particularly colorful. The boys wore a five-colored ***durumagi*** **두루마기**, and a traditional Korean overcoat including blue, red, yellow, white, and black, related to the energy of the traditional Five Elements (metal, wood, water, fire, earth). For girls, yellow ***jeogori*** **저고리**, the upper garment of Korean traditional clothes, and a flower-pink ***chima*** **치마**, skirt, were typical.

Traditional Korean Games

1. ***Tuho* 투호** - Throw sticks into a canister to win the match.
2. ***Yutnori* 윷놀이** - Korean board game. Players cast a set of four sticks to receive a set number of moves to bring home all four tokens before the opponent.

Korean Lucky Charms

3. ***Bokjumeoni* 복주머니** - "Fortune Bag"
4. ***Bokjori* 복조리** - "Fortune Strainer"

HWATU - WHAT IS THIS CARD GAME KOREANS PLAY?

Tazza : The High Roller 타짜 (2006)

Swapping cards? Try at your own risk because it will cost your hand should you get caught. ***Tazza : The High Roller* 타짜 (2006)**, is a movie about the world of gambling, which sometimes involves an ax, a hammer, and death threats. Anyone who ever played Texas Hold'em or ***Mahjong*** would quickly understand what's going on in the movie, but not the game itself in the movie. Often referred to as **고스톱 "go-stop,"** the formal term is ***hwatu*** **화투** "battle of flowers." This card game originated in Japan and is called ***hanafuda*** in Japanese. To be precise, *hwatu* is the name of the card set, and "go-stop" is the most popular type of game played with the cards. The reason why it's called "fight of flowers" is because there are pictures of flowers and plants on the cards, 12 decks of 4 cards, representing the 12 months of the year. Some say that *hwatu* was introduced from Japan during the Japanese Occupation (1910 - 1945), but it is estimated that *hwatu* was introduced to Korea in the late Joseon Period. The fact that the 1902 **Hwangseong Shinmun 황성신문** (newspaper) advertising section featured *hwatu* cards proves that it was already widely spread before the Japanese occupation. In fact, *hwatu* is one of the most popular types of table games in Korea, but negative views also exist because the image of illegal gambling is strongly linked. Rules vary from game to game, but if a certain score is accumulated before the opponent (usually 3-4 people play go-stop), you win, although you have the option to either "go" and continue to accumulate more points at the risk of allowing others to come from behind and losing the game or "stop" and take whatever you won. In Korea, you can see elderly people playing "go-stop" at funerals, but it's not for gambling. In the past, the consolers purposely talked in a loud voice to create a noisy and raucous atmosphere, to distract the mourning family from being lost in grief and help them focus on greeting and serving the visitors.

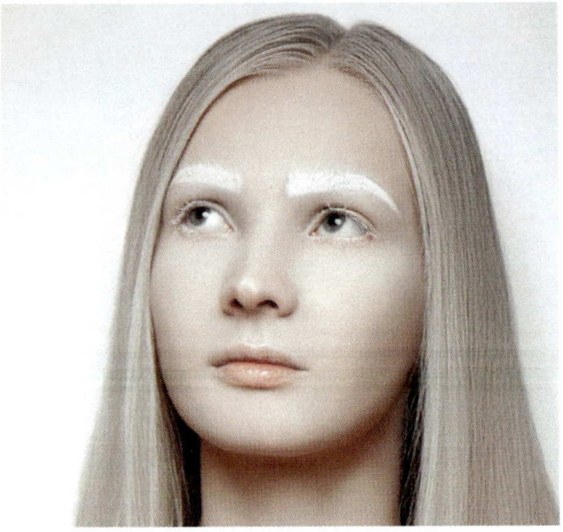

DON'T SLEEP ON NEW YEAR'S EVE OR YOUR EYEBROWS WILL TURN WHITE

In the past, Korean people didn't sleep on New Year's Eve, believing that sleeping will make one's eyebrows turn all white. For children who couldn't overcome the sleepiness were teased by the parents who put white flour on their eyebrows. This custom of staying up all night, called ***suse* 수세**, is believed to have originated to encourage people to work hard to prepare for the busy New Year's Day morning.

WHY WOULD KOREANS HIDE THEIR SHOES ON NEW YEAR'S EVE?

There is a ghost named ***yagwang* 야광** that comes down to where people live on New Year's Eve, tries on the children's shoes, and takes the ones that fit their feet. There was a superstitious belief that a child who lost his/her shoes would have bad luck all year round, so children would put their shoes upside down or hide them in their rooms before going to bed.

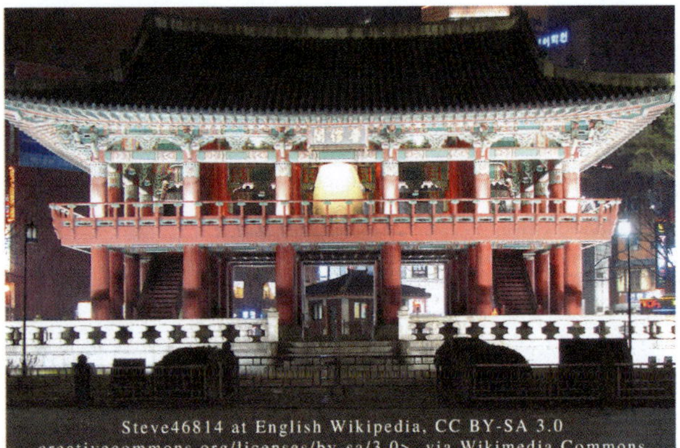

Steve46814 at English Wikipedia, CC BY-SA 3.0 creativecommons.org/licenses/by-sa/3.0>, via Wikimedia Commons

THE KOREAN NEW YEAR COUNTDOWN - BOSINGAK BELL-RINGING CEREMONY

It's believed to have originated from the Buddhist ceremony where the temple bell was struck 108 times on New Year's Eve, symbolic of removing the 108 defilements of humankind. The ceremony of striking of the bell at midnight, or ***jeyaeui jong* 제야의 종** ("the Watch-Night bell"), on the last day of the year, however, actually became a ritual during the Japanese Occupation. In 1928, the **Gyeongseong Broadcasting Station** aired the bell-striking on New Year's Day as a special program (the bell used at that time was borrowed from **Dongbonwonsa Temple**, a Japanese temple located below Namsan Mountain in Seoul). After Korea's liberation from Japan's colonial rule, the midnight ceremony began at the end of 1953 when ***Bosingak* Bell 보신각**, which was destroyed by the Korean War, was reconstructed. For the ceremony, the bell is struck 33 times, the same number used to announce the opening of the 4 gates at 5 A.M. during the Joseon Dynasty. It also meant wishing the Buddhist guardian deity for the nation's peace and prosperity. This event, similar to the countdown events around the world, is also popular among couples, but it might not be as exciting as you'd expect because there will be just too many people hoping to celebrate the special moment with their loved ones and you'd be lucky if you can have a glimpse of the bell. But no need to be disappointed yet - You can watch the bell-striking event, which is held regularly, on other days.

WHY DO SO MANY PEOPLE TRAVEL DURING CHUSEOK?

The holiday **Chuseok 추석**, literally meaning "Autumn Eve," and **Hangawi 한가위**, a native archaic Korean word meaning "the great middle (of Autumn)," falls on August 15th of the Lunar calendar, and is one of the biggest holidays in South Korea, along with Seollal. Originally, the purpose of Chuseok was to harvest some grain in advance after passing the crucial moments of farming to perform ancestral rites to pray for a good harvest. As the summer farming works were already over, and the weather was pleasant ahead of the big harvest in the fall, it was an ideal time for people to visit the ancestors' graves and enjoy the free time. Therefore, Chuseok is different from Thanksgiving Day, which is a ceremony of appreciation after finishing the harvest. With one or two days left before Chuseok, a huge number of Koreans return to their hometowns, leading to a huge traffic jam. It will be a time when downtown Seoul is empty due to the great migration. Finding a train ticket is extremely difficult, and if you choose to drive, it usually takes three to four times more than it usually does. But people endure the pain to be together with their family. After they barely arrive late at night, they stay up late talking to each other, and women are exhausted from the extra hour cooking and dish washing. On the morning of Chuseok, people get up early, prepare breakfast with the year's harvest, and hold the ancestral rite, *charye*. After breakfast, they visit and pay their respects at the ancestors' graves, which they had to visit and cut down the weeds beforehand. At night, they make a wish to the bright full moon (and make *songpyeon* together). Just a decade ago, the story above was a common sight in Korea. However, as times have changed, so has the way people spend Chuseok. Instead of heading home to visit their parents and relatives, many go on an overseas trip or rest at home alone.

Want a beautiful child? Then make a beautiful *songpyeon!* P. 70

WHY DO KOREAN PEOPLE BELIEVE THERE IS A RABBIT LIVING ON THE MOON?

People made a wish on the bright full moon on **Chuseok**, but until Apollo 11 landed on the moon, what (or who?) did Korean people in the old days think was living on the moon? Most Koreans imagined a rabbit was living on the moon, pounding something with a pestle in a mortar because the dark spots of the moon look just like that. The story, which originated from Chinese folk tales and spread to East Asia, has different things in the mortar. In Korea and Japan, the rabbit is believed to be making ***tteok*** and ***mochi*** (rice cake), and in China, it's making the elixir of life.

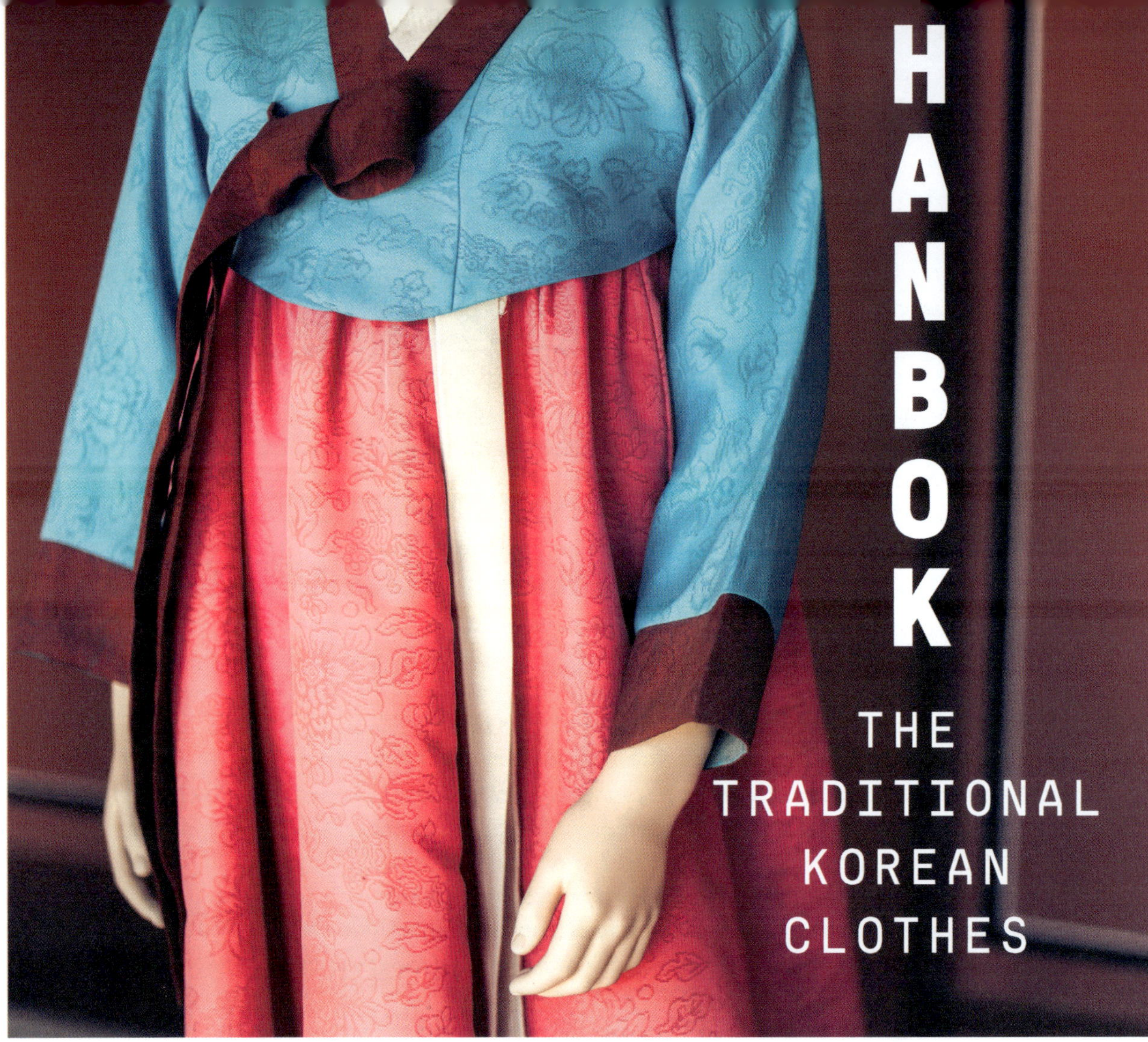

DO KOREANS WEAR KIMONO?

It's one of those questions that would make your Korean friends, who are proud of their 5000-years of rich history and culture, go, "Oh, no you didn't!" But to speak in defense of the foreign friends not familiar with Asian culture, kimono, Japanese word for "clothing," is perceived as a household name for "traditional Asian clothing," like Kleenex for facial tissue and Band-Aid for a bandage. Kimono just happens to be the most widely known term (i.e., first mover's advantage!). To answer the question, Koreans have their own unique traditional clothes called ***hanbok* 한복**, known for its harmonious beauty of straight lines and subtle curves. If you have a rough image of *hanbok*, it's probably through historical dramas (that's right, they were not Korean kimono). However, through nearly 5,000 years of history, Korea had many countries and diverse cultures, some of them influenced by other cultures (even now, the 60's fashion is drastically different from what's trendy now, although fashion goes round in circles). So, if you look at historical dramas that depict different times, you might be confused by the differences in the style (it's nothing to be ashamed of even if you didn't notice the differences because that means you were focusing on the story). Truth be told, it's actually quite hard for Koreans to tell, too. As for the origin, it's believed to have come from the ancient Scythian-Siberian culture of Northeast Asia, with its roots in one of the various costumes of nomadic people. There have been minor, sometimes major, changes throughout history, but basically they have common elements. The most important one is that it follows ***sangyuhago* 상유하고** ("upper garment/jacket goes on top and pants/skirt goes to the bottom") style, ideal for activities like horse riding and hunting.

THREE KINGDOMS PERIOD (57 BC ~ 668 AD)

7th century Tang Dynasty painting of envoys from the Three Kingdoms illustrates the different styles of clothes worn by the people of each kingdom.

While there were more ancient kingdoms before this period, we'll start from here due to the lack of historical records and relics from the ancient times. But more importantly the Three Kingdoms period is when the basic standardized style of *hanbok* was established. According to the historical paintings, relics, and records, the basic format for men was ***jeogori*** **저고리** (upper garment) and ***baji*** **바지** (trousers), and for women, it was ***jeogori*** and ***chima*** **치마** (skirt). They both put on ***durumagi/po*** **두루마기/포** (outer jacket/coat) on top. Also added were ***gwanmo*** **관모** (hat/headgear), ***dae*** **대** (belt), and various accessories depending on the class and status. One unique aspect of *hanbok* was that it must include pants, which even women wore as innerwear. Another characteristic is that it's worn in many layers, as many as 5-6 layers of tops and bottoms (Don't worry! Lighter and more breathable materials were used for summer *hanbok*, and *hanbok* clothes have easy-to-put-on-and-take-off open-front style). Moreover, *hanbok* is categorized into formal and casual clothes, which are further divided into men and women, adults and children, and seasonal. During the Three Kingdoms Period, textile manufacturing techniques vastly improved, capable of producing various types of silk and woolen fabrics.

야금모행 *Yageummohaeng* "A Secret Night Journey" by Shin Yun-bok depicts the Joseon-era Hanbok

Another important highlight of this era was class stratification, in which the clothes served as a means to represent different classes. The clothes of the privileged class were different from those of the ordinary people.

GOGURYEO PERIOD (37 BC ~ 668)

Pictures of the scale models from the Lotte World Folk Museum

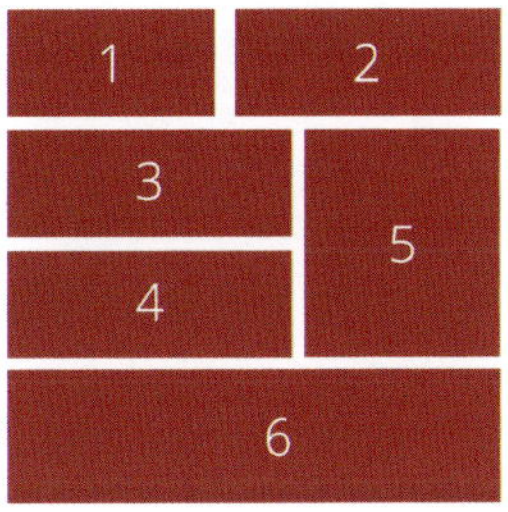

1. A mural from the 5th century CE Muyonchong (tomb) depicting a hunting scene.
2. A miniature scale model of a Goguryeo man hunting.
3. A mural from same tomb depicting several dancers performing "sleeve dance."
4. A mural from the Susanri tomb depicting a parade of women.
5. A miniature scale model reenactment of the procession scene painted on the walls of corridor on No.3 tomb in Anak. Shown in the picture are female servants.
6. From left - the clothes of a female aristocrat, male aristocrat, queen, king, lady-in-waiting, and chamberlain.

The **Goguryeo 고구려** people were located in the cold northern part of the country and always had to stay alert for possible Chinese invasions. This is reflected in the clothes worn by the Goguryeo people. The basic structure of Goguryeo men's clothes is separated into top and bottom, ideal for activities like shooting arrows, and the top *jeogori* had narrow sleeves, pants, and high-necked shoes that were suitable for horse riding. The woman's *jeogori* was long enough to cover the hips that a belt had to be worn and a skirt was worn over the inner pants. Men also wore a hat, ***gwanmo***. Both Goguryeo men and women wore ***po* 포**, an outer jacket/coat both for ceremonial occasions but also ordinary occasions. The male aristocrat wore a headgear called ***jeolpung* 절풍**, which was decorated with feathers, and earrings were worn, too. The female aristocrat wore long skirts and *jeogori*, which had a relaxed look with the sleeves stretched out. The lower-end of *jeogori* with embroidery on the high-end silk and a pleated skirt with various colors of cloth add to the overall refinement. Women wore skirts with a lot of pleats to mark their high status. The married commoner woman's hair was neatly tied, and the man wore a black hood. A belt around the waist was common in the Three Kingdoms Period, usually knotted at the front. Most commoner women wore pleated skirts made of hemp cloth or animal skins.

BAEKJE PERIOD (18 BC ~ 660)

It's not easy to know the style of **Baekje's 백제** costume in detail because there aren't many artifacts or records related to Baekje's costume, but according to the accounts found in the Book of Liang, a Chinese historical text, it's assumed to be almost the same as Goguryeo's. One unique aspect is that Baekje distinguished the ranks of government posts with their official hat, belt, and colors. *Gwanmo* was decorated with silver for high-rank officials, with purple, red, and blue garments that were separately used according to their ranks. The king wore a purple coat with wide sleeves, wide blue silk pants, a leather belt around his waist, black leather shoes, and a

1. **(From previous page) A scale model of a Baekje male commoner.**
2. **(From previous page) A scale model of a Baekje female commoner.**
3. **(From previous page) A scale model of a Baekje female aristocrat.**
4. **From left - the clothes of a government official, queen, king, and the Secretary of State.**

cone-shaped black silk headgear adorned with gold accessories on the sides. The queen wore a similar headgear, a *jeogori* (upper garment), and a *chima* (skirt), and a *durumagi* (outer coat) or a short-sleeved shirt on top of it. The royal family embellished the cloth with gold thread or gold foil and decorated it with high-quality ornaments, enhancing the royal authority. The commoners were not allowed to wear red clothes and used the blue inner bark of kudzu or hemp for cloth.

SILLA PERIOD (57 BC ~ 935)

Silla's 신라 clothing was similar to Goguryeo and Baekje until the unification of the Three Kingdoms. After the unification, the culture became more mature and luxurious (Silla was known as the "Golden Kingdom"). Also, the clothes of the **Tang Dynasty** came in and brought about many changes in style. Silla established a detailed class of status to establish the authority of the ruling class as the country became stronger. At that time, besides silk, woven hemp cloth rose to popularity, and the quality of the cloth was an indication of one's class. Belts, shoes, and even combs were different according to class. Both men and women wore *jeogori* (upper garment), *baji/chima* (pants/skirt), and *po* (outer coat).

The king and the royal family wore a gold crown *gwanmo* which was a symbol of absolute power. On top of a splendid *durumagi*, a gold belt full of ornaments, which was originally created for practical purposes, (such as carrying personal items, tools, and weapons) became a fashion accessory and were worn as such. The queen was sumptuously adorned with earrings and a necklace made of curved jades which show Silla's top-notch quality of workmanship and sophistication. The upper class mainly wore wide sleeves, wide pants, and the common people wore narrow sleeves and narrow pants.

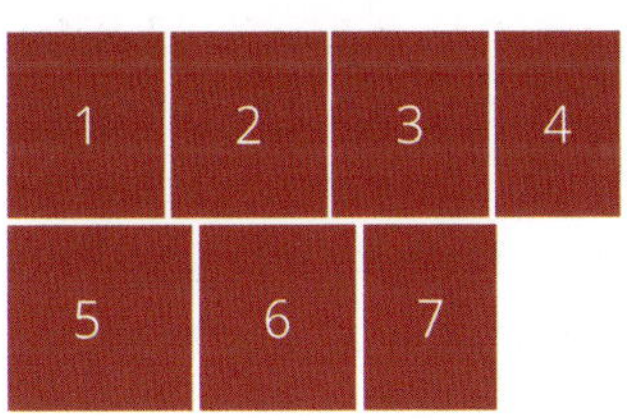

1. A scale model of a Silla commoner family.
2. A scale model of a Silla aristocrat family.
3.4.5. Scale models of Silla aristorcrats.
6. A scale model of a Unified Silla's Civil Official wearing a *bokdu* and *danryeong* and a female aristocrat.
7. A portrait of Queen Seondeok (Yu Hwang, 1990, Beobinsa Temple).

Unified Silla was greatly influenced by the **Tang Dynasty**, and a new style of clothing that didn't exist previously during the Three Kingdoms Period was introduced. Ceremonial dresses such as ***hwalot* 활옷**, ***wonsam* 원삼**, and ***dangeui* 당의** are such examples. Also, short-sleeved upper garment ***banbi* 반비** was introduced. Also, the government adopted the Tang Dynasty's uniform system for officials. Until the Three Kingdoms Period, each had its own official uniforms. During the reign of **Queen Jindeok 진덕여왕** of Silla, **Kim Chun-chu 김춘추** visited the Tang Dynasty of China as an envoy to meet with the Emperor Taizong of Tang and brought the official uniform system, including ***bokdu* 복두** headgear and ***danryeong* 단령**, circular-collar robe, and made it the official uniforms of all government officials. After that, from Goryeo to Joseon Dynasty, Chinese-style ceremonial robes were adopted and worn as a government uniform. According to ***Gyeonggukdaejeon* 경국대전**, a collection of codes of rules for the government, different colors were used according to one's rank. As a result of the cultural exchange with the Tang Dynasty, a new unique clothing style based on the traditional style was developed.

GORYEO PERIOD (918 ~ 1392)

The clothes of **Goryeo 고려** were inherited from the **Silla Dynasty** while absorbing and developing the styles of the Chinese Dynasties. The farmers and merchants wore white ramie and hemp clothing. Goryeo adopted the royal and official uniform system from the Song, Yuan, and Ming Dynasty (they put on a black hood and a white coat when off duty). The Mongols invaded Goryeo in 1231, and Goryeo later lost part of its territory to the Mongols who exploited, and interfered in domestic affairs (but Goryeo was not conquered nor did lose political independence), including forcing to embrace **Mongolian customs**, including their clothing style. As a result, they are still found in the form of Korean tradition.

Clockwise: Goryeo commoner family, Confucian scholar's clothes, Queen's ceremonial clothes, King's ceremonial clothes, *jokduri*, *otgoreum*.

Influenced by Mongolian costumes, the length of ***jeogori*** became shorter and the sleeves narrower, and ***otgoreum* 옷고름** (garment strap ribbon) replaced the waist strap. It was also a Mongolian custom for a bride to wear on her head ***jokduri* 족두리** (bridal crown) at a wedding. The Mongolian style was popular among the upper classes, while the commoners adhered to traditional costumes. Due to the active human and cultural exchanges between Goryeo and Yuan Dynasty, Mongolian customs were introduced to Goryeo, but Goryeo customs were also introduced to the Yuan Dynasty. Among the customs of Goryeo, clothing, shoes, and hats were popular, and the style was referred to as ***goryeoyang* 고려양** (a nascent form of ***Hallyu* 한류**, the Korean Wave?). During the 31st reign of **King Gongmin 공민왕**, the **Yuan Dynasty** collapsed and the **Ming Dynasty** of the Han tribe reigned over China. As a result, the Mongolian style gradually disappeared.

JOSEON PERIOD (1392 ~ 1897)

Hanbok of the Joseon Dynasty is closest to the image of *hanbok* that we have now, because chronologically it was the most recent Dynasty, with most data and records remaining. As a result, there are more Joseon Dynasty-era historical dramas than any other periods, adding to the familiarity. During this time, Confucianism was the governing philosophy, and hierarchical order was clearly shown through clothing.

In the early Joseon Dynasty, ***seuran* 스란** skirts (a decorative wrapping skirt with gold leaf patterns), which were almost similar to those of the Ming Dynasty, were popular but only the people with high social status could wear them. Since the mid-Joseon period, the back length on the men and women's clothes were generally long, coming down to the waist, but became shorter over time.

From left: A woman wearing a short, tight-fitting *jeogori* (jacket) and a plump *chima* (skirt) / A man in *durumagi* (traditional topcoat), A man in male *hanbok* consisting of *jeogori* (jacket) and *baji* (trousers), A woman wearing a jacket featuring the gorgeous-looking *jogakbo* (Korean traditional patchwork).

In the 18th century, *jeogori* was so short that it hardly covered the chest that the belt had to be worn high. The skirts were long and plentiful throughout the Joseon Dynasty, but they were especially long and wide in the 17th and 18th centuries, leading to a bell-shaped silhouette.In the 19th century, the area around the knees and ankles was expanded to make the overall look a triangular shape, and it's still widely used today.

After the mid-Joseon period, the Confucian ideology was further strengthened and more restrictions were put on women's clothes. Women used a kind of long hood called ***jangot* 장옷** or a pair of skirts called ***sseugaechima* 쓰개치마** to cover their faces when they went out. The commoners wore a *jeogori/chima/durumagi* combination, the basic style that came down from the Three Kingdoms Period.

Left: *jangot* / Right: *sseugaechima*
From paintings by Shin Yun-bok

Painting by Kim Hong-do illustrating the different clothes worn by different classes.

Painting by Chae Yong-shin

Heungseon Daewongun wearing *magoja*

The ***jeogori*** was long and relaxed, but after the Japanese Invasion of Korea in 1592, the ***hahusangbak* 하후상박** (slip top and puffy bottom) style, with a small, short *jeogori*, a puffy *chima*, appeared. In 1887, Regent **Heungseon Daewongun 흥선대원군**, who was kidnapped by the **Qing Dynasty**, returned from Manchuria wearing ***magua***, which was the jacket of the Qing Dynasty, and this became ***magoja* 마고자**, which was worn over *jeogori* and had buttons. Since the 1880s vests with pockets (influenced by the Western suits) became popular as it compensated for the shortcomings of *hanbok* which lacked them. As Western culture began to flood in, changes were brought about in clothing. People wore both *hanbok* and suits. Women's clothing also changed, and wearing seamless one-piece skirts called ***tongchima* 통치마** and white *jeogori* was the beginning of the modernized *hanbok*. As society changed, there was a movement to abolish wearing *jangeui* and *sseugaechima*, which women had to put on to cover their faces when they went out.

After the Korean War, *hanbok* and suits coexisted, but *hanbok* gradually lost its place due to rapid economic development and the influx of Western-style culture through the 1960s and 1970s. *Hanbok* has become special clothing worn only during the holidays, but it is hard to see it even during the holidays today. However, with the Korean Wave, foreign tourists are showing a greater interest in *hanbok*, combined with the efforts of the younger generation to revive and improve the traditional clothes, the future of *hanbok* doesn't look too gloomy.

Oh My Gat 갓!

WHAT ARE THE COOL HATS ANCIENT KOREANS WORE?

"Korea seems to be the land of hats: they are made in all kinds of shapes, and I have nowhere seen a greater variety, from the crown of gilded cardboard for the provincial governor to the modest headband of the peasant."

- Charles Varat, a French explorer charged with an ethnographic mission by the minister of Public Instruction. <Voyage en Corée> *Le Tour du Monde, LXIII*, 1892 Premier Semestre. Paris.

During the Joseon Dynasty, wearing a hat was an important part of the dress code, and a foreigner who visited Joseon described it as "the land of hats" because there were so many kinds of hats worn depending on one's status and situation. So, without further ado, let's take a trip to the world of hats from the Joseon Dynasty!

men

Painting by Shin Yun-bok

Chorip* 초립 -** A hat that was usually worn before ***heukrip became popular. Made of bamboo strips. Originally, it was worn by both the scholars and the common people, but in the late Joseon Dynasty, it was mostly worn by boys who weren't yet married but had a coming-of-age ceremony, as people started to wear *heukrip*.

Heukrip 흑립 – Literally means "black ***gat* 갓** (traditional Korean hat made of bamboo strips and horsehair)." It was designated as an official hat during the reign of **King Gongmin 공민왕** of Goryeo to break down the customs of the Yuan Dynasty and establish its own attire system, but it wasn't widely put in place until the late Joseon Dynasty. It was worn by *yangban* 양반 (noblemen) and *seonbi* 선비(scholars).

***Paeraengi* 패랭이** – A hat worn by the officials at post stations (they painted it black), and lower-class people like peddlers (they put a large cotton ball on it), and butchers. Made of bamboo strips.

Painting by Kwon Yong-jeong

***Hwiyang/Hwihang* 휘양/휘항** – A winter cap worn by men. It covers the head and shoulders. Made of leather, cloth, or cotton.

Painting by Kim Yang-gi

***Sungkyunkwan Scandal* 성균관스캔들 (2010, KBS 2)**

***Yugeon* 유건 -** Indoor hat of Sungkyunkwan Confucian scholars. Worn during studying or ancestral rites.

WHAT'S THE OLDEST UNIVERSITY IN KOREA?

Sungkyunkwan, founded at the beginning of the Joseon Dynasty in 1398 by royal decree to promote the scholarship in Confucianism, was the highest and foremost national educational institute. The current Sungkyunkwan University succeeded the original Sungkyunkwan, making it the oldest university in East Asia. The original Sungkyunkwan is located at the south end of the Humanities and Social Sciences Campus. Within the original campus, ***seokjeon daeje* 석전대제**, the ceremonial rite to honor Confucius and the Confucian sages of China and Korea are performed in the **Munmyo Shrine 문묘,** the primary temple of Confucius, twice a year in May and September.

Portraits of Kim Je-deok, Kim Man-jung, Yi Chae wearing *jeongjagwan, chungjeonggwan, dongpagwan*

***Jeongjagwan, Chungjeonggwan, Dongpagwan* 정자관, 충정관, 동파관** – Originally one of the hats of China. It's always worn in the house and is the symbol of *yangban* 양반, the noblemen.

Painting by Kim Deuk-sin

***Tanggeon* 탕건** – Originally worn only by government officials, it's more similar to a skullcap/hood than a full hat. It was mainly made of horsehair or leather, but cloth or bamboo was also used.

Painting by Sung Hyeop

Gamtu* 감투** – A hat similar to ***tanggeon. Worn by ordinary people who could afford it. Made with horsehair, leather, or cloth, and doesn't have a brim, making it easy to wear. This hat was worn by low-class people since the Goryeo Dynasty. It was used by commoners during the Joseon Dynasty.

Portrait of King Yeongjo

***Ikseongwan* 익선관** – The king of Joseon wore this hat when he wore his official uniform. It was introduced from the Ming Dynasty.

women

***Neoul* 너울** - Worn by the court or upper-class women to cover their faces when they go out.

Part of "The royal procession of King Jeongjo"

***Jisatgat* 지삿갓** – Made by weaving bamboo into a circle and applying *hanji* (traditional Korean paper) and oiling it. Used to prevent rain and sunshine. It's a hand-held rather than fixed on the hat with a ribbon.

Jeonmo* 전모**– It was worn by lower-class women such as ***gisaeng* 기생**. Made with *hanji*, just like ***jisatgat. Decorated with letters and various patterns (mainly butterflies and flowers).

Painting by Shin Yun-bok

"Go Out of the New Year" (1921)
by Elizabeth Keith

***Ayam* 아얌** - A cold cap for women. There is a long string shaped like a ***daenggi* 댕기** (pigtail ribbon) with a tassel in the center. Sometimes decorated with jewelry or gold.

***Nambawi* 남바위** – A winter cap used for both men and women A young child wears it for his/her ***doljanchi* 돌잔치** (first birthday party).

***Jobawi* 조바위** – A cold cap for women widely used from the aristocracy to the working class in the late Joseon. As *ayam* became less popular the long string at the back disappeared, and there were parts covering both sides instead.

Gache* 가체** is a head ornament/wig worn by women of high social class and ***gisaeng. It first appeared during the **Unified Silla Period**, and it's assumed to have been influenced by the Tang Dynasty. During the reign of **King Seongjong 성종** of the Joseon Dynasty, some were as tall as 30 cm (1 ft) because the larger and heavier they were, the more beautiful they were perceived. Consequently, many women suffered from neck pain, and some even broke their necks!

Painting by Shin Yun-bok

DID YOU KNOW ?

The roof of the Seoul Arts Center building is the shape of the 갓 *gat!*

GISAENG - MULTI-TALENTED FEMALE ENTERTAINERS

Hwang Jini **황진이 (2006, KBS)**

They could sing, dance, and recite poems. But most of all, they had a great store of knowledge that the upper-class enjoyed discussing current issues with them at banquets. Who were they? Renowned scholars of the time? Surprisingly, no, they were ***gisaeng/kisaeng*** **기생** - Korea's multi-talented female entertainers. Their origin is unclear but, according to some scholars, the victorious **Goryeo Dynasty** had to find a way to effectively manage the war prisoners they had as a result of the successful unification of the **Later Three Kingdoms**, and labelled male prisoners of war as "***no***" **노** and female prisoners as "***bi***" **비**. Among them, females who excelled in dance and music were selected separately by the state, who later established a female music band called ***goryeo yeoak*** **고려 여악**, and supplied them for the royal and Buddhist events. During the Joseon Dynasty, ***gisaengs*** were managed and supervised under the system set up by the state, and for that reason only those registered with the government could work. Once on the register, they could not escape from the status of ***cheonmin*** **천민** (the lowest class of people, the "untouchable"), which was passed down to their children. Gisaengs had to be educated and trained for years because they had to be good at singing, dancing, playing musical instruments, writing poems, as well as calligraphy and drawing. Not only that, they learned to speak and behave in a refined and cultured manner because their clientele were mostly upper-class people. Thus there was ***gyobang*** **교방**, a school for educating *gisaeng*s. The aspiring *gisaeng*s entered the school at an early age. At the end of the Joseon Dynasty, *gisaeng*s were divided into three groups: ***ilpae*** **일패**, ***ipae*** **이패**, and ***sampae*** **삼패** (1st, 2nd, and 3rd class). The *ilpae gisaeng*s were a group of highly educated and trained female talents and belonged to the government, so they were known as "*yangban* (aristocracy/noblemen) *gisaeng*." They were in charge of teaching and training new *gisaeng*s for three years. On the other hand, *ipae* and *sampae gisaeng*s were strictly prohibited from performing the dance and songs of *ilpae*. Unlike *ilpae gisaengs*, *ipae* and *sampae gisaeng*s were allowed in providing sexual services for their clientele. However, the system which categorized and distinguished the types and roles of *gisaeng* became blurry during the Japanese Occupation period, and there's been a tendency to regard them as "high-class courtesans" mainly focusing on sexual services which *ipae* and s*ampae gisaeng*s provided. As a result, the contributions they made to Joseon society have been easily overlooked. They were actually the only group of people who played the role of inheriting and transmitting female literary and traditional arts. Famed *gisaeng*s like **Hwang Jini 황진이** excelled in many fields and left numerous works such as ***sijo*** **시조**, traditional Korean poem, that are highly regarded as an important part of classical Korean literature.

TRADITIONAL KOREAN ENTERTAINMENT

Pansori: Korea's Authentic Musical Storytelling
BY Great Big Story

***Pansori* 판소리** – Korean Musical Storytelling. It is a type of solo opera in which a ***sorikkun* 소리꾼** (singer/vocalist) tells a story with gestures to the rhythm of ***gosu* 고수** (drummer). It was performed in a yard or concert hall, and for long stories, it could easily take over three hours.

Samulnori : The Korean Percussion Band
BY Arirang Culture

***Samulnori* 사물놀이** - meaning "play of 4 objects." It is a traditional type of music developed based on the rhythm of ***pungmulpae* 풍물패** (Korean traditional percussion band). The 4 instruments are ***kkwaengwari* 꽹과리** (small gong), ***jing* 징** (larger gong), ***janggu* 장구** (an hourglass-shaped drum), and ***buk* 북** (barrel drum).

Korean Folk Dance: Buchaechum
By Seonhwa Arts School

***Buchaechum* 부채춤 ("fan dance")** - It's the most representative group dance/performance of Korea, well known for the beautiful fans that captivate the audience with flashy dance moves. It was created by dancer Kim Baek-bong in 1954 who simplified and reinterpreted traditional Korean dances, such as the court dance, Korean Buddhist dance, and even the shamanistic rituals.

Bongsan Talchum Peformance
BY CBSaeji

***Talchum* 탈춤** - It's a traditional play performed while wearing a mask. At first, clowns performed at court events, but during the late Joseon Dynasty, it developed into a popular culture, satirizing the feudal status society and humorously depicting the hard life of the people. ***Hahoe Byeolsingut Talnori* 하회별신굿 탈놀이** (special ritual drama to the gods mask play) and ***Bongsan Talchum* 봉산탈춤** are among the more famous.

***Hahoe Tal* 하회탈** (mask) is a ritual and artistic mask handed down from around the late Goryeo Dynasty in Hahoe Village in Andong, Gyeongsangbuk-do. The material of the Hahoe masks is alder tree, and they are designated as National Treasure No. 121 in 1964. It's a valuable cultural heritage representing the faces of Koreans.

***Seopyeonje* 서편제 (1993)** is the story of a family of Korean *pansori* singers who are struggling to make a living in the modern world. Won the Berlin Fim Festival Honorary Golden Bear Award in 2005.

Nanta : Cookin' is a non-verbal performance that reinterprets traditional *samulnori* in a modern way which gained huge popularity through a world tour.

***Wangeui Namja* 왕의남자 (*The King and the Clown*, 2005)** - An acting troupe gets arrested for mocking their hedonistic king, and are given a chance to spare themselves under one condition - make the king laugh. The movie has traditional Korean play scenes including *talchum.*

WHY DO KOREANS TAKE OFF THEIR SHOES WHEN GOING INSIDE?

When you visit a Korean friend's house, you will immediately encounter, upon entering, a space which is set slightly lower than the floor. You see a lot of shoes here, and on the elevated threshold at the beginning of the floor, cotton slippers are neatly placed (but many houses don't have them). Using your smart brain, you analyze the situation and conclude that you need to take off your shoes! Upon entering the living room, you find your friends walking around in slippers, socks, and even barefoot. What's more, your foreign friends also joined the club. And the same is observed in the bathroom. The bathroom is also lower than the floor, and a pair of plastic slippers greets you. It must mean you should put them on when you use the bathroom. So, why such division and separation? To understand this concept, you have to learn about the traditional Korean heating system called ***ondol* 온돌**.

WHAT IS THE KOREAN HEATING SYSTEM - ONDOL?

The ***ondol* 온돌 / *gudeul* 구들** is a traditional Korean heating system that is widely believed to have originated about 2,500 years ago in **Bukokjeo 북옥저** (ancient Korean state which was located in Manchuria and the Russian Maritime Province of Siberia, later absorbed by **Goguryeo**). Given that Goguryeo (37 BC – 668 AD) inherited the lifestyles of the Bukokjeo people, and that ondol was also passed down to **Goryeo** and **Joseon** (spread most widely during the **17th-century Joseon period (1392 - 1897)**, connecting the origin of *ondol* with the Korean people shouldn't be a far stretch.

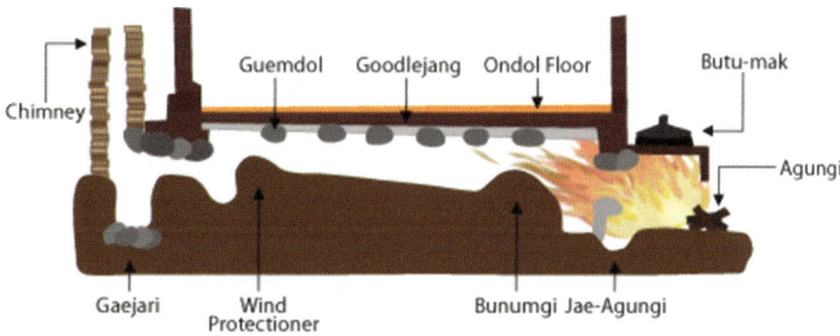

An illustration of the *ondol* system

It's similar in concept to a radiator that uses heat conduction, but the structure is different. When firewood is set on fire in the furnace called ***agungi* 아궁이** (which also doubles as a cooking station), the heat generated here heats up the wide stones laid under the ***jangpan* 장판** (oil/resin paper-covered floor) of the room known as ***gudeuljang* 구들장**, and the heat released by the hot stones makes the room warm.

In addition to heating by thermal conductivity, *ondol* combines radiant heating and convection heating, and the heat is maintained evenly from bottom to top and for a longer period compared to a fireplace or a radiator that generates heat from only one side.

And *ondol* is one of the most influential factors in the residential lifestyle of Koreans. Before the widespread use of ***ondol*** for residential use, Koreans had a drastically different lifestyle. Historical dramas set in **ancient Korea** to **early Goryeo period (918 - 1392)** such as **Seondeok Yeowang 선덕여왕 (*Queen Seondeok*, MBC, 2009)**, depict people sleeping in bed and sitting in chairs. But the widespread of ***ondol*** and the coziness it provided made Koreans prefer sitting on a cushion on the floor and sleeping on bedding laid out on the floor instead (go to a ***jjimjilbang* 찜질방** to see for yourself - once you lie on a cozy warm floor, you won't want to get up). *Ondol* is believed to have spread rapidly in the 17th century Joseon as a means to survive the cold winter. It led to a surge in demand for firewood, and historical records say that most of the mountains were bare towards the end of the Joseon Dynasty.

In addition, *ondol* has led to the development of a single-story residential architecture style in Korea. Most of the remaining ***hanok* 한옥** buildings in Korea are single-story, due to the enormous weight and construction costs of ondol system. It is said that there were many multi-story buildings in ordinary houses from **Goryeo** to the **early Joseon** period before the widespread of *ondol*. Even in Korea, where high-rise apartments are the norm today, Koreans just couldn't give up the coziness *ondol* provides. Combining tradition with modern technology, *ondol* has evolved into a system where water heated from boilers is fed into and circulates in the pipes buried under the flooring. Still, modern Korean apartments still reflect the traditional *hanok* lifestyle. As we learned previously, the widespread of *ondol* (floor-heating) in the late Joseon Dynasty and ***daecheongmaru*** (cooling floor) played an important role in making Koreans prefer the sitting-on-the-floor over the beds and chairs which also existed in the homes before that time. Naturally, keeping the floor clean was always a top priority. Also, a word of caution - Many Korean restaurants, especially the ones with rooms, would require you to take off your shoes and sit on the floor. So it's always a good idea to inspect your socks to see if they have a hole in them before going to a Korean restaurant to avoid a surprise.

WHY DO KOREANS SIT IN A YOGA POSE?

Sitting cross-legged on the floor is commonly called ***yangbandari* 양반다리** ("noblemen legs"). As the name suggests, it was mainly the posture taken by superiors and elders. Although females and younger people weren't completely prohibited from this posture in front of males or elders, they also chose to sit on their knees to show respect.

JJIMJILBANG - THE SAFE ONDOL HAVEN FOR THE WEARY AND BURDENED

"Come to me, all you who are weary and burdened, and I will give you rest." (Matthew 11:28)

Traditional *hanjeungmak* (sweat house) in the Joseon Dynasty era
Painting by Kim Jun-geun

If ***jjimjilbang* 찜질방**, the Korean spa was available in the olden days, it surely would have been the safe haven for the weary and burdened. The original form of *jjimjilbang* is considered to be a sweat room called ***hanjeungmak* 한증막** that had been in place since the Joseon Dynasty, which used the remaining heat in the kilns after baking charcoal or pottery.

The heated floors are inspired by the traditional Korean *ondol* system, which explains why Koreans love sitting on the floor. Today's *jjimjilbang*, which combines a bathhouse with a steam/sweat room first appeared in 1994, spread nationwide, and has evolved into a multi-purpose recreation center which offers not just rest but also entertainment.

Most *jjimjilbang*s operate 24 hours a day, with a dedicated sleeping area featuring comfy leather sofas, recliners, and couches. Some high-end facilities even offer mini caves for individual use! And with the relatively inexpensive cost, it's a decent alternative to traditional lodging. Not only that, but PC rooms are also available so you can keep current with your work.

Modern version of *hanjeungmak*

But the most awesome part about *jjimjilbang* is the restaurant/snack facilities! You can find a wide range of menu choices, from instant noodles and ***sundubu jjigae* 순두부 찌개** to ***kimchi bokkeumbap* 김치볶음밥** (kimchi fried rice) and chicken, but the "*jjimjilbang* specialty" is in the snack corner - cracking open some ***maekbanseok gyeran* 맥반석 계란** (eggs baked on elvan stone plates) or quenching your thirst after an intense sweating session with ***bingsu* 빙수** (shaved ice), ***sujeonggwa* 수정과** (cinnamon punch), and ice-cold ***shikhye* 식혜** (rice punch). They are enjoyed by everyone, Koreans and non-Koreans alike.

Boiled eggs and sikhye combo!

Green Tea *Bingsu*

TYPES OF SAUNA ROOMS AND THEIR SAID HEALTH BENEFITS

Disclaimer (THIS IS NOT MEDICAL/HEALTH ADVICE)

Jade Room
Constipation, Diarrhea, Indigestion, Meningitis, Menstrual Pain, Arthritis.

Herb Room
Nervousness, High Blood Pressure, Blood Circulation, Muscle Ache, Joint Pain.

Clay Room
Arthritis, Muscle Ache, Metabolism, Blood Circulation, Detoxification

Salt Room
Arthritis, Skin Rejuvenation, Blood Circulation

Germanium Room
Blood Circulation, Pain Relief, Muscle Ache, Joint Pain.

Most of the *jjimjilbang*s have sex-segregated and unisex sections. Obviously, the dressing and bathing rooms are separated, but most steam/sweat rooms and heated communal floors are unisex, though they vary from business to business. There are, however, single-sex only *jjimjilbang*s, so you might want to check before walking in.

UNIFORM

Once inside, you are to leave behind the clothes you were once in from the secular world and put on the uniform provided by the ***jjimjilbang***. Don't worry – it's not to strip you of your individuality but to prevent the facility from getting polluted and contaminated by the germs and viruses you might have carried from outside. Most of the time it wouldn't be your favorite color or style, but everyone else is in the same shoes.

WHAT IS THE KOREAN "LAMB HEAD TOWEL HAT"?

Made by rolling up both sides of a towel and wrapping around the head, the ***yangmeori* 양머리** "Lamb/Sheep Head" towel hat became popular after the main character Kim Sam-soon, wore it in a hit TV drama ***Nae Ireumeun Kim Sam-soon* 내 이름은 김삼순 *(My Name is Kim Sam-soon / My Lovely Sam Soon*, 2005, MBC)**. In ***jjimjilbang***, many people. regardless of age/sex. do it because it absorbs sweat and keeps the hair from going awry while adding some cuteness (you know how Koreans are obsessed with looks!).

Learn How To Make
The Korean Sheep Head Towel!
BY Seoulistic.com

WHY DO KOREANS SCRUB THEIR BODIES?

Throughout its life, a lobster sheds its shell up to 25 times, revealing a shiny new coat each time. Humans, lacking such ability, relied on other methods – Cleopatra enjoyed bathing in wine, and Yang Guifei in milk, to keep their skin supple and soft. Meanwhile, in Korea, ***ttaemiri* 때밀이** which literally means "body (dirt) scrubbing" has been a popular way to achieve the same result. In most Korean public baths and spa *jjimjilbang*, there are ***sesinsa* 세신사**, or "professional body cleansers" who will help you with the complete shedding process. First, soak your body in warm water for about 10 minutes and soften the dead skin cells. Then, entrust your body into the hands of the professional body cleansers, who are equipped with special scrubbing towels and gloves, better known as ***itaeri* towel 이태리 타월**. The pros will buff your body thoroughly, so all you need to do is just turn your body over and around per the guidance of the pros. When all done, you will be surprised to see a bunch of thin dark strings, similar to eraser shavings. They are the clumped dead skin cells of your body called ***ttae* 때**, meaning "body dirt." While some dermatologists claim that such an abrasive method could do more harm than good to your skin, but many people, including Amanda Seyfried and Miranda Kerr, swear by it because you can see instant results! I'm not sure if the same can be said for Conan O'Brien who tried *ttaemiri* in Los Angeles' Koreatown… It looks like poor Conan received some sort of medieval punishment…

Watch Conan O'Brien
Trying the Korean Body Scrub!
BY TeamCoCo

WHAT IS "ITALY TOWEL"?

Koreans have been using *itaeri* towel (Italy towel) since the late inventor Kim Pil-gon invented a durable towel using viscose rayon in the 1960s after two years of research. Before that, people used to wrap towels over a stone for buffing. The name "*itaeri*" comes from the fact that the weaving machine and dyes were made in Italy.

WHERE DID KOREANS LIVE IN THE PAST?

THE STORY OF *HANOK*

***Hanok* 한옥** is a term that refers to the traditional Korean houses made with eco-friendly materials such as soil, clay, timber, rocks, and rice straw, therefore these homes caused no harm to our body and of course, the nature surrounding them, reflecting the environmental factors of the Korean Peninsula as well as the lifestyle of the Korean people. One interesting fact about *hanok* houses is that the difference in social status can be inferred by looking at the shape of the roof of each house. If the roof is mostly made of clay and have a rice-straw-thatched roof, it's called ***chogajip* 초가집**, and commoners and some *yangban* 양반 (noblemen) with low income lived in it. On the other hand, when tiles called ***giwa* 기와** (made with baked soil) were placed on the roof of a house built mainly of wood and stones, it's called ***giwajip* 기와집**, and was inhabited by *yangban* and ***jungin* 중인**, the middle-class people. ***cheoma* 처마** (curvy edge of *hanok* roof) that soars high to the sky seems to represent their authority.

Clockwise from top-left: chogajip, giwa-tiled roof, cheoma, daecheongmaru

(*Daecheongmaru* Image licensed by KOGL-O, freely available for download at heritage.go.kr)

The *hanok* houses have different architectural styles depending on the climate and the characteristics of the Korean Peninsula. In the northern part of the country, where cold weather is frequent, the rooms are arranged in two rows with a low roof to block cold weather from outside while maintaining warmth. In the southern part of the country, however, rooms are aligned in one straight line with a high roof, to promote natural air circulation. Earlier, we learned that Koreans were able to make it through a cold winter thanks to the *ondol* system. Then how did they survive the scorching hot summer? In the days when there was no air conditioner, *hanok* houses had a special place called *daecheong* **대청**, which served as a natural cooling place. This space, also called ***daecheongmaru* 대청마루**, is a spacious wooden floor between rooms, where the ***cheoma*** not only keeps the *daecheongmaru* safe from the hot summer sun but by rising higher than other parts of the roof, it lifts the hot air upward, leaving *daecheongmaru* with a cool breeze. The beam, ***daedeulbo* 대들보** are the pillars supporting *hanok* houses, which is said to be safe from earthquakes because they are placed into a foundation stone, rather than the ground. It's also used as an expression that means "a very important person in the organization."

The doors and windows of *hanok* are filled with traditional Korean paper called ***hanji***, made of inner barks of mulberry. The *hanji* used on the doors and windows is called ***changhoji* 창호지**, and they block heat and wind while letting the light in. It's also interesting to compare the different types of patterns found on the doors and the windows of *hanok* houses.

Jangdokdae* 장독대** is an area outside the house dedicated to storing a series of jars called ***jangdok* 장독** (or ***onggi* 옹기 / *hangari* 항아리**), a Korean ethnic earthenware used to ferment or simply store preserved foods, such as ***kimchi, ***ganjang* 간장** (soy sauce), *doenjang* 된장 (bean paste) and *gochujang* (red pepper paste) or grains. The word ***dae*** means "place" or "support," so *jangdokdae* means "place for earthenware," and it's found near the kitchen. Sunshine and ventilation are key aspects of the location choice so that foods can be preserved well and kept fresh, often lasting more than several years. The similar storage area in the royal palaces was called ***yeomgo* 염고** and was supervised by a court lady called ***janggomama* 장고마마**.

***Jang* - Korean Sauce And Soup Base P. 61**

HOW DO KOREAN GUYS STAY COOL? 죽부인 JUKBUIN THE "BAMBOO WIFE"

Literally meaning "bamboo wife," ***Jukbuin* 죽부인** is a type of body pillow that was introduced from the Tang Dynasty of China. Made of thinly split bamboo trees that are hand-woven into a form similar to a sandbag. When used as a sleeping companion, the open structure provides the body with maximum exposure to cooling breezes. It was an essential item during the hot summer days in Korea. Although it was just a body pillow made of bamboo trees, it was taboo for a son to use what his father used, and when his father died, it was burned along with his clothes.

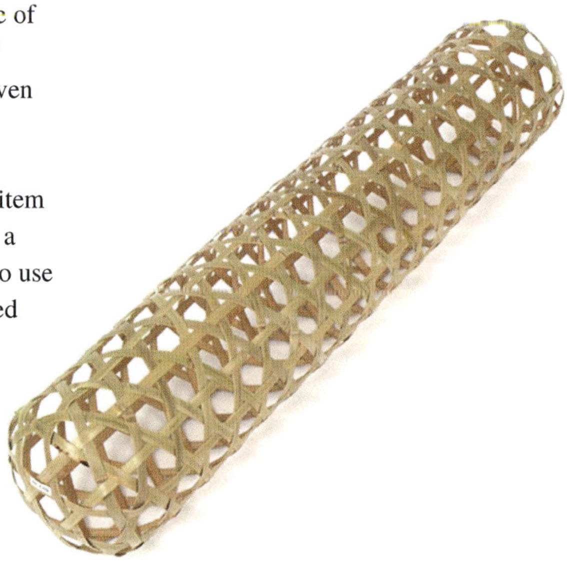

WHAT ARE THE HUGE KOREAN TOTEM POLES IN FOLK VILLAGES? THE GUARDIANS OF KOREAN VILLAGES!

Hi there! Don't we look familiar? That's right! You might have seen us in Korean historical dramas, standing tall at the entrance of a village, making scary faces! Made of wood, we are village guardians, keeping demons and evil spirits at bay. At the same time, we double as boundary markers at the edge of a village.Usually, we're adorned with engravings describing the characteristics of the carved figures on the front of the poles.

"Male" ***jangseungs* 장승** usually bear engravings in ***hangul*** or ***hanja*** that reads ***cheonhadaejanggun* 천하대장군 天下大將軍** (Great General of All Under Heaven) and are decorated with headpieces worn by Korean aristocrats and scholars. "Female" ***jangseungs***, on the other hand, wear less elaborate headpieces and bear engravings reading ***jihayeojanggun* 지하여장군 地下女將軍** (Female General of the Underworld).

Despite our efforts to look pretty, an American Protestant missionary, Homer Bezaleel Hulbert, described us as "Village Devil Posts" in 'The Passing of Korea' (1906).

Knowing our backstory, how do we look to you now? When you visit Korea, don't be intimidated by our scary looks because we're friendly and love tourists!

WHY DO KOREAN APARTMENTS LOOK LIKE MATCHBOXES?

In the 1960s, in line with the urban development policy, a large number of people flocked to the capital city of Seoul, and accommodating them became a major issue. Apartments, which had the advantage of providing a maximum amount of housing in limited land space, were the ideal choice. The construction of an enormous number of apartments took place under the government initiative. As a result, apartments now account for most of the housing types of Koreans, and even in rural areas these days. One thing to point out is that the concept of an apartment is more similar to that of a condominium in the U.S. because they are owned properties. The structure and space of Korean apartments reflect the traditional residential lifestyles found in hanok. The interior floor plan of the Korean-style apartment, which has a spacious living room and kitchen, through which the rooms are connected, is a modern interpretation of the courtyard and daecheongmaru of hanok. However, many criticize the large apartment complexes for being ugly boxy buildings painted in dull colors and looking just like matchboxes. Citizens feel it mars the beauty of the city, while some say despite their unappealing looks, the apartments are still a symbol of the society.

JEONSE – WHY WOULD KOREAN LANDLORDS LET THEIR TENANTS STAY FOR FREE?

***Jeonse* 전세**, which can be translated as "key money deposit," can be a very strange concept for foreigners who are used to the culture of either owning or paying monthly rent for their home. For a *jeonse* contract, instead of paying monthly rent, the tenant pays a certain amount (usually 7-80% of the selling price) for the contracted period (e.g., two or three years). Then the landlord can make a profit by investing it or using it where it's needed (then it's effectively the same as getting an interest-free loan). The part that amazes the foreigners is that upon the expiration of the contract, the landlord must return the entire amount to the tenant! Because of this, many foreigners unfamiliar with the concept wonder, "Why lend the house for free?" In Korean dramas, it's also used as a device to express the sorrow of poor families who have no money to buy a house and have to keep moving at the end of each *jeonse* contract.

WHO FOUNDED KOREA?

Portrait of Dangun, Encyclopedia of Korean Culture (encykorea.aks.ac.kr), The Academy of Korean Studies

According to the founding legend recorded in the ***Samguk Yusa* 삼국유사** (record of history and legends), the Lord of Heaven, **Hwanin 환인,** had a son, **Hwanung 환웅**, who descended to **Taebaek Mountain 태백산** (modern day Baekdu Mountain 백두산 area which is the highest in the Korean peninsula) and founded the city of **Shinsi 신시**. Then a tiger and a bear came to Hwanung and asked how they could become humans and they were told that if they went into a cave and lived there for 100 days while only eating mugwort and garlic **Hwanung** will transform them into human beings. Both accepted the challenge, but about halfway through the 100 days the tiger gave up and ran out of the cave. The bear, on the other hand, successfully restrained herself and became a beautiful woman called **Ungnyeo 웅녀, 熊女**. Hwanung married Ungnyeo, and she gave birth to **Dangun 단군**, who became the founding father of **Gojoseon 고조선** in 2333 BC. Today, the said legend is interpreted by scholars as a symbolic representation of a marriage with a member of a bear-worshiping tribe, rather than a literal bear-turned-human woman. The founding date, or **Gaecheonjeol 개천절** ("The Heaven Opening Day") is celebrated as a national holiday in Korea (October 3rd).

WHAT WAS THE NATIONAL MOTTO OF GOJOSEON?

홍익인간

hongik ingan

"Broadly Benefit Humanity (Devotion to Human Welfare)"

HOW OLD IS KOREA?

According to traditional Korean calendar system ***dangungiwon* 단군기원** or ***dangi* 단기**, year 1 starts on the founding date of the first Korean kingdom **Gojoseon** (2333 BC, which means 2333 years before the Gregorian calendar was used as the global standard today). So by adding the Gregorian year, you get the current *dangi* year. For example, the year 2020 in the U.S. would be translated as the year 4353 in *dangi*. For Korean people, this number is a symbol of pride, as it means that the ancestors of the Korean people have kept their long history and tradition for 5,000 years.

Dangun Founding Legend-Inspired Dramas with Fantasy Elements
Asdal Yeondaegi 아스달 연대기 (*Arthdal Chronicles*, 2019, tvN)
Taewang Sashingi 태왕 사신기 (*The Legend*, 2007, MBC)

WHAT IS THE THREE KINGDOMS PERIOD?

A classification of the period (57 BC to 668 AD) of Korean history established on the ancient Korean Peninsula with **Goguryeo** in the north, **Baekje** in the midwest, and **Silla** in the southeast and other minor states.

The map of history of Korea in 476, the moment of greatest territorial expansion of Goguryeo.

7th century Tang Dynasty painting of envoys from the Three Kingdoms of Korea: Baekje, Goguryeo, and Silla illustrates the different styles of clothes.

Three Kingdoms Period (57 BC ~ 668)

57 BC Bak Hyeokgeose founds Silla

37 BC Jumong founds Goguryeo

18 BC Onjo founds Baekje

372 Under Sosurim, Goguryeo imports Buddhism from Former Qin of China.

384 Chimnyu of Baekje officially adopts Buddhism.

392 Gwanggaeto the Great of Goguryeo begins his reign, expanding Goguryeo into a major regional power.

433 Baekje and Silla form an alliance against Goguryeo's aggression.

527 Silla formally adopts Buddhism / Martyrdom of Ichadon

553 Silla attacks Baekje, breaking the alliance.

598 Sui Dynasty attacks Goguryeo and Goguryeo-Sui War begins

612 Goguryeo repulses second Sui invasion at the Salsu.

614 Sui Dynasty defeated.

645 First campaign in the Goguryeo–Tang War.

648 Silla establishes alliance with Tang.

660 Baekje falls to the Silla-Tang forces.

668 Goguryeo falls to the Silla-Tang forces.

Unified Silla (676 ~ 935)

676 Silla repels Chinese alliance forces from Korean peninsula, completes unification of much of the Three Kingdoms.

698 The founding of Balhae by former Goguryeo general Dae Joyeong.

751 Silla, at its cultural peak, constructs Seokguram.

828 Jang Bogo establishes Cheonghaejin, a major center of trade with China, Japan, and Vietnam.

918 Founding of Goryeo by Taejo of Goryeo.

935 Silla formally surrenders to Goryeo, and Goryeo controls the Korean peninsula.

A mural from the 5th century CE Muyonchong (tomb) depicting a hunting scene.

Why Do Koreans Dominate Archery? P. 244

GOGURYEO, THE LARGEST DYNASTY IN KOREAN HISTORY (37 BC ~ 668)

Goguryeo 고구려 is said to have been founded by **Jumong 주몽** in 37 BCE and was the largest of the Three Kingdoms, which became a full-fledged aristocratic state during the reign of **King Sosurim 소수림왕**, who promulgated various laws and decrees that helped to centralize royal authority. Like other ancient Korean kingdoms, **Buddhism** was the cultural backbone, while **Confucian** education was emphasized as a means of regulating/managing the social order. Today, some of the ruins and tombs, which became **UNESCO World Heritage sites** in 2004, can be found in the far southern Jilin province in China, the territories which the Kingdom covered.

Jumong / Dongmyeongseongwang 주몽 / 동명성왕

Birth name is **Jumong 주몽**, which literally means "Holy King of the East," was the founding monarch of the **Goguryeo** Kingdom, the northernmost of the Three Kingdoms of Korea. According to the founding legends, he was the son of **Haemosu 해모수** and **Lady Yuhwa 유화부인**, who was the daughter of the god of the **Amnok River 압록강**. **Lady Yuwha** was impregnated by sunlight and gave birth to an egg, and from the egg hatched a baby boy. Jumong was known for his exceptional skill at archery, and in 37 BCE, he became the first king of **Goguryeo** and reunited all of the five tribes of **Jolbon 졸본. Soseono 소서노,** who was a daughter of a Jolbon chief, and his second wife, gave birth to his son, **Onjo 온조**, who later established the kingdom of **Baekje**. The kingdom of Goguryeo evolved into a great regional territory with considerable power and influence and stood for 705 years and was ruled in total by 28 consecutive emperors. Today, the descendants of **Jumong** still bear his family name "Go."

Gwanggaeto the Great 광개토대왕

Gwanggaeto the Great (birth name: **Go Damdeok 고담덕**), was the nineteenth monarch of **Goguryeo** Kingdom. Under Gwanggaeto, Goguryeo rose as a powerful dynasty in East Asia, making enormous advances and conquests into western Manchuria against **Khitan** tribes; inner Mongolia and the Maritime Province of Russia as well as the Han River valley in central Korea to control over two-thirds of the Korean Peninsula. He also defeated **Baekje**, which was then the most powerful kingdom of Korea. His accomplishments are recorded on the **Gwanggaeto Stele**, erected in 414 at the supposed site of his tomb in Jian, present-day China-North Korea border, and is still standing tall as the largest engraved stele in the world.

The Gwanggaeto Stele, standing tall at 7 meters (23 ft.) high.

Standard portrait of Gwanggaeto the Great by Lee Jong Sang (National Museum of Modern and Contemporary Art Seoul) Licensed by CC BY-SA 4.0 (creativecommons.org/licenses/by/4.0/)

Battle of Salsu 살수대첩 (612)

Recorded as one of the most brutal battles in world history, it was an enormous victory by **Goguryeo** over the **Sui Dynasty** of China. Led by General **Eulji Mundeok 을지문덕**, the Sui army was lured into the **Salsu River**, where the Goguryeo soldiers were preparing an attack by cutting off the flow of water with a dam in advance, and when the unsuspecting Sui troops were halfway across, they opened it. Thousands drowned and the surviving troops were killed by the Goguryeo cavalry. Over 300,000 Sui troops died while only 2,700 troops were lost on Guguryeo's side. This defeat had a major impact on the Sui Dynasty, causing them to collapse from within, leading to an eventual fall.

BAEKJE
THE CULTURAL POWERHOUSE (18 BC ~ 660)

Baekje 백제 is said to have been founded by legendary leader **Onjo** in 18 BC in the **Gwangju 광주** area. Around the 3rd century AD, it became a fully-developed kingdom. During the reign of **King Goi 고이왕**, and during the reign of **King Geunchogo 근초고왕**, it ruled a significant portion of central Korea, including the whole Han River basin. Buddhism and Confucianism were the two pillars of the kingdom, and a large number of eminent scholars were produced. One of the most famous and distinctive artworks of the era is a Buddha statue that has a subtle and mysterious smile, known as the "**Baekje Smile**."

Gilt Bronze Buddha (National Museum of Korea) Licensed by KOGL Type 1 (https://www.kogl.or.kr/info/licenseType1.do)

King Onjo 온조

Onjo, the son of **Jumong** and **Soseono** of the **Goguryeo** Kingdom, was the founding monarch of **Baekje** which was located in the western part of the Korean Peninsula. According to the ***Samguksagi* 삼국사기** (a historical record of the Three Kingdoms of Korea), he was the ancestor of all Baekje kings. He was the younger brother of **Yuri 유리**, who became Goguryeo's second king, and younger brother of **Biryu 비류** who built a small state in **Michuhol 미추홀**. When Biryu died, his people joined **Sipje 십제**, which Onjo later renamed to Baekje. Onjo was able to successfully manage and stifle sporadic rebellions from other tribes, and reigned for 46 years, laying the foundations for a powerful dynasty that would last for 678 years.

Great Gilt-bronze Incense Burner 백제금동대향로

Measuring 64 centimeters (25 inches) high and 19 centimeters (7.4 inches) in diameter, it weighs almost 12 kilograms (26.5 lbs). This three-dimensional artifact, estimated to have been made in the 6th century, features realistic ornaments of the dragon and phoenix (symbol of yin and yang) and is believed to have been used for ancestral rites or other important ceremonies.

Great Gilt-bronze Incense Burner (National Museum of Korea) Licensed by KOGL Type 1 (https://www.kogl.or.kr/info/licenseType1.do)

Gyeongju Bulguksa Temple from the Silla Kingdom

SILLA, THE GOLDEN KINGDOM (57 BC ~ 935)

Silla 신라, believed to have been founded by **Bak Hyeokgeose 박혁거세** in 57 BC, developed into a full-fledged kingdom as a result of the establishment of the hereditary monarchy of the Kim family. During this time, Buddhism was adopted as the national religion and flourished. The traces? Magnificent Buddha sculptures and temples can be found everywhere in **Gyeongju 경주**, where the Kingdom's capital was located. The people of Silla, especially the aristocrats, were fond of extravagant luxury. Among all, gold ornaments, such as gold crowns, belts, and various jewelry show how dexterous and artsy they were! No wonder they are called "**The Golden Kingdom**."

Bak Hyeokgeose 박혁거세

He was the founding monarch of **Silla** and the progenitor of all **Bak (Park)** clans in Korea. According to the ***Samgukyusa* 삼국유사** (a collection of legends, folktales and historical accounts relating to the Three Kingdoms of Korea), leaders of chiefdoms (believed to have been refugees from Gojoseon) got together to discuss selecting a king and forming a kingdom, and at that moment in the forest, a strange light shone from the sky, and where a white horse bowed down, there was a large egg from which a boy came out of. After getting bathed, his body radiated and animals jumped with joy. The people revered him and made him king of the state named **Seorabeol 서라벌** when he became 13-years-old. He married **Lady Aryeong 알영부인**, who is said to have been born from the ribs of a dragon. The Park clans are the third-largest group in Korea today.

Seokguram Grotto 석굴암

The Seokguram Grotto 석굴암 (man-made cave) is part of the **Bulguksa Temple 불국사** complex on **Toham Mountain 토함산,** in **Gyeongju 경주**, South Korea. This awe-inspiring grotto, National Treasure No. 24, was added to the UNESCO World Heritage in 1995, along with the Bulguksa Temple complex. The grotto is situated to overlook **the East Sea** and rests 750 meters (2460 ft) above sea level. It's said to have been built by **Kim Daeseong 김대성** and originally called **Seokbulsa 석불사** (Stone Buddha Temple) whose construction first took place in 742 when he resigned his position in the king's court in 751 during the reign of **King Gyeongdeok 경덕왕** of **Silla**, which is considered as the cultural peak of the Kingdom. According to a legend, Kim dedicated the Grotto to his parents from a previous life and the Temple to his parents in his present life. The construction was finished in 774, and is acknowledged as one of the finest Buddhist sculptures in the world, and is currently one of the best known cultural destinations in South Korea.

Golden Crowns Found in Cheonmachong

This scintillating gold crown, excavated from **Cheonmachong 천마총** (Tomb No. 155, also known as "The Heavenly Horse Tomb" due to the mural of the flying horse) in 1973, is believed to have belonged to **King Soji 소지왕** or **King Jijeung 지증왕**. The crown is 32.5 centimeters (12.8 inches) in height, and three prongs are forming the Chinese character 山 "mountain" on the front of the crown. On the back, there are two prongs in the shape of a deer antler. There are also two dangling gold chains, hanging from the end of the headband, shaped as leaves. After getting designated as the 188th National Treasure of Korea, it's currently housed in Gyeongju National Museum.

Cheomseongdae 첨성대

National Treasure No. 31, **Cheomseongdae** is a Silla-era observatory located in Gyeongju. Said to have been built during the reign of **Queen Seondeok 선덕여왕** of Silla in the mid-7th century, it's the oldest existing astronomical observatory in the world and it maintains its original form without reconstruction or restoration. The use of Cheomseongdae was said to be astronomical observations, but recently different views have emerged because unlike most astronomical observatories, it was built on flat ground, and it was too narrow for people to go in and out. Therefore, some speculate that the structure may have played an astrological role in predicting the fortune of the Dynasty or served as an altar for religious ceremonies. It's still standing tall at 9.17 meters (30 ft) and 4.93 meters (16 ft) in diameter.

Martyrdom of Ichadon 이차돈

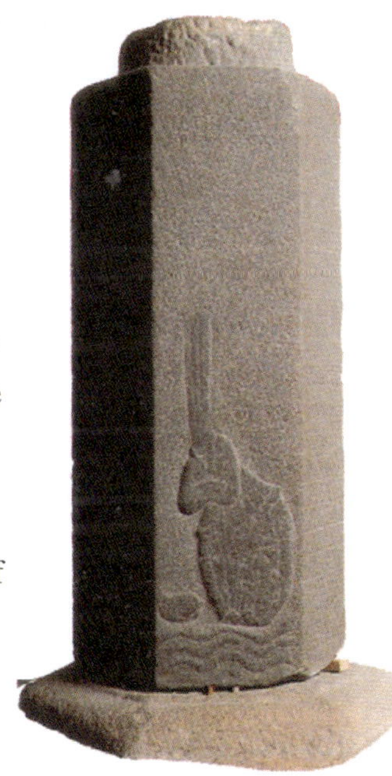

Ichadon 이차돈 (501-527) was a Buddhist monk and advisor to the Silla's **King Beopheung 법흥왕**, who desired to promulgate Buddhism as the state religion, but was facing opposition from the court officials. Ichadon devised a strategy to overcome the opposition. Convincing the king to make such a proclamation using the royal seal, Ichadon told the king to deny having made such a proclamation, and Ichadon would confess and accept the punishment of execution for forgery. He prophesied to the king that at his execution a miracle would convince the opposing court faction. His scheme went as planned, and when he was executed, the earth shook, the sun darkened, beautiful flowers rained from the sky, and white blood instead of red blood sprayed 100 feet in the air from his beheaded corpse. The omen was accepted as a manifestation of heaven's approval, making Buddhism the state religion in 527 CE. His body was then taken to the sacred **Geumgang Mountains 금강산** and buried there with respect. His martyrdom led to the construction of **Heungryunsa Monastery 흥륜사**, Silla's first state-sponsored temple.

Gilt-bronze Maitreya in Meditation

Better known as ***bangasayusang*** **반가사유상** (National Treasure of Korea No. 83) It's believed to be a statue of the Maitreya, the future Buddha, in a semi-seated contemplative pose, commonly referred to as the "Contemplative Bodhisattva" or Gilt-Bronze Seated Maitreya. Recognized as one of the finest Buddhist sculptures ever produced, it's housed in the National Museum of Korea as one of the most popular exhibits. The bodhisattva, sitting on a stool with his right leg crossed over his left knee, makes a thoughtful expression with his finger resting subtly on his face. The pose symbolizes an event occurred during Buddha's life before his renouncement as a prince: While observing farmers on the fields, he awakened to the cyclical nature of human suffering, and the artwork depicts the posture at this moment of awakening.

Gilt-bronze Maitreya in Meditation (National Museum of Korea)
Licensed by KOGL Type 1 (https://www.kogl.or.kr/info/licenseType1.do)

The Smile of Silla Roof-End Tile

This roof-end tile, (***sumakse*** **수막세**), which attaches to a curved tile at the edges of a roof/wall, has a smiling human face better known as "**The Smile of Silla**." Contrary to other cultures where scary faces are used (e.g., goblins), the people of Silla instead used friendly smiles to soothe all bad spirits and send them back to where they originally came from. It was the inspiration behind the logo of the Korean company **LG**.

LG

Who Are The *Chaebols*? P. 91

Hwarang: The Poet Warrior Youth 화랑 (KBS, 2016)

Hwarang

Hwarang* 화랑** was a mental and physical training and education organization composed of the youth of the Silla Dynasty. It was established to recruit talented people (usually children of kings and nobles, but there were no class restrictions), and the members, called ***nangdo* 낭도** were united under the leadership of the leader, *hwarang*. Among the group's goals, the main role was to select talented people and have them appointed to key positions in Silla. At the same time, military training was of utmost importance. In fact, Silla in the 6th and 7th centuries, when *hwarang* was founded, continued war with neighboring countries, and national security was very unstable. For this reason, the *nangdo*s served as a reserve force and participated in battles as soldiers. **화랑도 *hwarangdo, the ideology of *hwarang* was to serve the nation solely through individual discipline, and it was considered an honor to die in battle.

WHO UNIFIED THE THREE KINGDOMS?

The Three Kingdoms Period was a tempestuous time when three powerful kingdoms were holding each other in check and competing with each other. Over a long period, there were numerous battles and wars, both large and small, sometimes with a coalition with foreign forces to invade each other. In 648, **Silla** formed an alliance with the **Chinese Tang Dynasty** and **Baekjae** was the first of the three Kingdoms to fall in 660. In 668, **Goguryeo** fell to the **Silla-Tang forces**. When Silla repelled the Tang forces from the Korean Peninsula in 676, it finally completed the unification of the Three Kingdoms and became known as the **Unified Silla**. **King Munmu the Great 문무대왕** was the first ruler of the expanded Dynasty, which lasted for another 260 years.

GORYEO, THE GOLDEN AGE OF KOREAN BUDDHISM (918 ~ 1388)

918 Founding of Goryeo by Taejo.

1033 Goryeo builds the Cheonri Jangseong (lit. "Thousand Li Wall"), a massive wall running along the northern border.

1145 Kim Bu-sik compiles the Samguk Sagi, Korea's oldest extant history text.

1231 The Mongol invasions of Korea begin.

1234 Choi Yun-ui's Sangjeong Gogeum Yemun is published, world's first metal-block printed text.

1251 Goryeo completes the Tripitaka Koreana, the most comprehensive and oldest intact version of the Buddhist canon in Chinese script.

1270 Goryeo signs a peace treaty with the Mongols, beginning an 80-year period of Yuan overlordship. The Sambyeolcho Rebellion lasts for three more years.

1285 Il-yeon compiles the Samguk Yusa, record of history and legends.

1388 General Yi Seonggye, ordered to engage China in a border dispute, turns his troops against the Goryeo court.

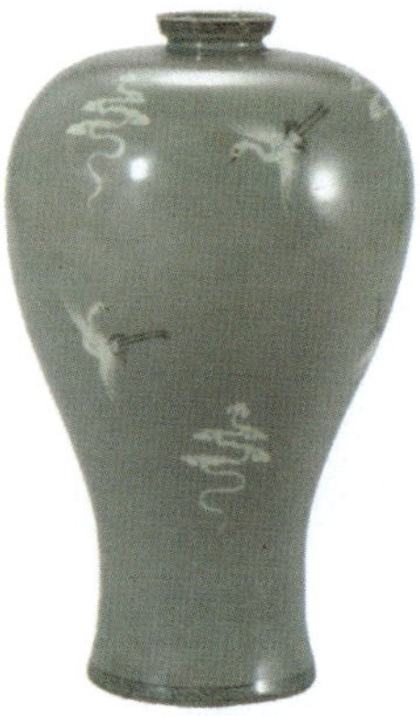

Maebyeong (plum bottle) decorated with cranes and clouds (National Museum of Korea) Licensed by KOGL Type 1 (www.kogl.or.kr/info/licenseType1.do)

Silla, which unified the Three Kingdoms and established itself as a powerful kingdom, began to crack in the 9th century due to internal strife. As a result, Baekje and Goguryeo, which had been destroyed, were revived under the names referred to as **Hubaekje 후백제 (Later Baekje)** and **Hugoguryeo 후고구려 (Later Goguryeo)**. Eventually, in 918, **King Taejo 태조** established **Goryeo 고려** and absorbed them (Later Baekje and Later Goguryeo) to create a new unified dynasty. During the Goryeo Dynasty, Buddhism reached its zenith. It was designated as a state religion and more than 70 temples were located in the capital, enough to be called the "Golden Age of Korean Buddhism." Among many, the **Tripitaka Koreana** in **Haeinsa Temple 해인사** is a great cultural achievement, which was created with the hope of using the power of Buddha to fight against the war of invasion by the Khitan people.

Taejo of Goryeo 태조

Taejo 태조 (reigned. 918-943, birth name **Wang Geon 왕건**), was the founder and first king of the Goryeo Kingdom which unified and ruled ancient Three Kingdoms of Korea from 918 to 1392. The posthumous title, Taejo means "Great Founder," and he laid the foundation stones for his Dynasty which witnessed an unprecedented flourishing of Korean culture. The Unified Silla Kingdom (668-935) ruled over the Korean Peninsula for nearly three centuries but started to decline as rebellions broke out frequently from the peasantry and the aristocracy. During the time, **Gyeon Hwon 견훤**, a peasant leader, rose to power amid the political turmoil in 892 and revived the old Baekje kingdom. A little later in 901, **Gung Ye 궁예**, an aristocratic Buddhist monk leader who was supported by his first minister and general Wang Geon, proclaimed a new Goguryeo state. Wang Geon succeeded Gung Ye, who was killed by the hands of his people due to his fanatical tyranny, in 918. Wang Geon attacked Later Baekje, founded by Gyeon Hwon, and the declining Silla. In 935, Silla finally surrendered and Wang Geon unified the kingdoms once again, under a new name, 고려 Goryeo (High and Beautiful), whose name implies that it's the successor of the previous kingdom, Goguryeo. He kept a large portion of the Silla institutions of government and distributed lands and high government positions to former Baekje and Silla elites. He also continued the endorsement of Buddhism and Confucianism.

WHAT DOES KOREA MEAN?

During the Goryeo Dynasty commerce flourished (commercial and natural trades alongside cultural exchanges were very active) with merchants coming from as far as the Middle East. From then on, the national name of Goryeo became widely known and it continued to become the "Korea" of today.

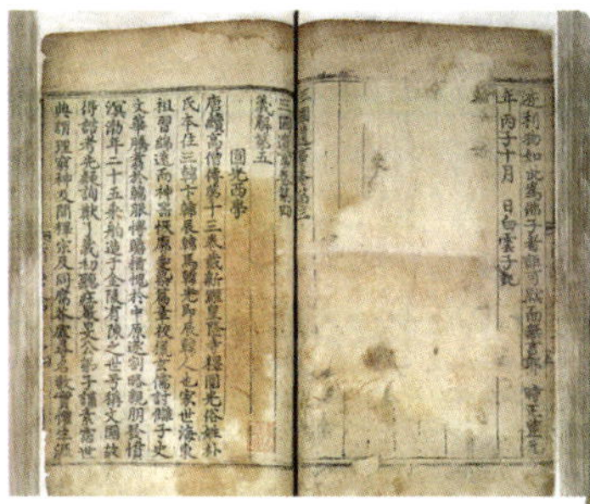

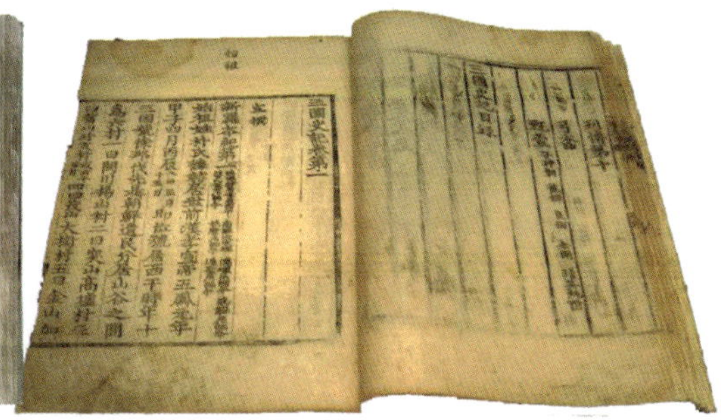

Samguksagi 삼국사기 and Samgukyusa 삼국유사

The ***Samguk Sagi***, literally meaning "History of the Three Kingdoms," is a collection of historical records of **the Three Kingdoms.** It's the oldest surviving chronicle of Korean history, and the compilation project was ordered by **King Injong 인종** of Goryeo and was undertaken by the government official and historian **Kim Busik 김부식** and a team of junior scholars. The purpose of the project, which was completed in 1145, was to create a complete compilation of Korean history, whose different versions were scattered among the Three Kingdoms and lost due to the continued wars. At the same time, by incorporating in the text the Korean exemplars of Confucian virtues, it also served as an educational resource, which is considered to have helped establish Korean nationalism and identity. The ***Samguk Yusa* 삼국유사**, literally meaning "Memorabilia of the Three Kingdoms," is a compilation of the history and legends of Korea, starting all the way from the founding of the very first nation, **Gojoseon**, all the way up to the Three Kingdoms Period. Written by the Buddhist Monk **Il Yeon 일연**, it differs from the *Samguk Sagi* as it covers various areas of history, with a focus on Buddhist legends and the folk tales of the Silla Dynasty, with a relatively smaller coverage on the other two kingdoms. Despite its limits, it remains an invaluable historical source and a component of Korean literature.

Mongol Invasions and Sambyeolcho 삼별초

From 1231, Goryeo was sporadically but continuously invaded by the Mongol Empire (1206~1388), who devastated a significant portion of the lands of Goryeo and its population throughout a series of invasions which lasted for nearly three decades (1231~1259). To escape from the attacks, the Goryeo government, controlled by the military regime led by the 최 Choi family, decided to give up the land and flee to **Ganghwado Island 강화도,** where the **Mongolian horse riders** were unable to land on. Naturally, it became a resistance base against the Mongol invasion. Unfortunately, Goryeo faced frequent rebellions from its own people, and struggled internally, due to the fragile foundation of the government. In 1258, a large rebellion broke out and resulted in the establishment of **Dongnyeong Prefectures 동녕부** by the Mongols. Meanwhile, the ***sambyeolcho* 삼별초** (Three Elite Patrols'), was organized by the **Choi clan** to maintain order and security on the island base by performing roles as police and combat forces. Even after the Goryeo kingdom fell to the hands of the Mongols, they continued to fight back tenaciously, moving bases multiples times, including **Jindo 진도** and **Jejudo 제주도 Island**.

"Haeinsa Temple, Tripitaka Koreana"
Arian Zwegers at flickr.com/photos/azwegers
licensed under CC BY 2.0 (creativecommons.org/licenses/by/2.0/)

Copy of a Tripitaka Koreana woodblock.
Image by Steve46814 licensed under CC-BY-3.0 via Wikimedia Commons
(creativecommons.org/licenses/by/3.0/)

Palman Daejanggyeong / Tripitaka Koreana 팔만대장경

The ***Palman Daejanggyeong* 팔만대장경** or **Tripiṭaka Koreana**("Eighty-Thousand Tripiṭaka") is a compilation of the Buddhist scriptures, carved onto 81,258 wooden printing blocks in the 13th century. According to the records, the work began in 1011 during the **Goryeo–Khitan War** and was completed in 1087. During the wartime, Goryeo believed the act of carving the scriptures onto the woodblocks would bring about a divine intervention (i.e., Buddha's help), which would help the kingdom persevere through the difficult times. The original Tripitaka Koreana contained around 6,000 volumes, but they were destroyed by fire during the Mongol invasions of Korea in 1232. Seeking divine assistance once again with fighting the Mongols, **King Gojong 고종** ordered the revision and re-creation of the Tripiṭaka, and the carving began in 1237 and was completed 12 years later, and the result is the world's most comprehensive and oldest intact version of Buddhist canon in *hanja* (Chinese Characters incorporated into the Korean language) script. Surprisingly, of the 52,330,152 characters carved, there are no known errors or errata found. Each woodblock is 24 centimeters(9.4 inches) high and 70 centimeters (27.5 inches) long, as thick as 4 centimeters (1.6 inches). With over 1,496 titles and 6,568 volumes, they weigh 280 tons total (that's 140 elephants piled together!). The most amazing part is they still remain in pristine condition – no warping/deformation despite its creation 750 years ago, thanks to the special treatment the craftsmen incorporated. The production of the Tripiṭaka Koreana is a symbol of national commitment and desire to fight off the invaders. For that reason, it was designated as Korea's National Treasure in 1962 and was inscribed in the **UNESCO Memory of the World Register** in 2007. Currently, it's stored in **Haeinsa 해인사**, a Buddhist temple in South Gyeongsang Province, in South Korea.

Period Dramas Based On The History of Goguryeo

Gwanggaetotaewang 광개토태왕 (*Gwanggaeto, The Great Conqueror*, 2011, KBS1) *Jumong* 주몽 (2006, MBC)
Daejoyoung 대조영 (2006, KBS1)

Period Drama Based On The History of Baekje

Seodongyo 서동요 (2005, SBS) *Geunchogowang* 근초고왕 (*The King of Legend* 2010, KBS1)

Period Drama Based On The History of Silla

Seondeokyeowang 선덕여왕 (*Queen Seondeok* 2009, MBC) *Daewangeui Kkum* 대왕의 꿈 (*Dream of the Emperor* 2013, KBS 1)

Gyengbokgung Palace

JOSEON - THE LAND OF THE MORNING CALM (1392 - 1897)

Joseon Dynasty was founded by General **Yi Seong-gye 이성계** who brought the collapse to the Goryeo Dynasty through a military coup. Joseon Dynasty embraced Neo-Confucianism as national ideology, and Confucian culture, which still affects much of the lives of modern-day Koreans, was able to fully blossom during this period. It lasted over 500 years, from 1392 to 1897, leaving numerous cultural heritages including the creation of ***hangul* 한글** the Korean alphabet until it was taken over by the Japanese Imperialists. Currently, the five grand royal palaces of the Joseon Dynasty remain in downtown Seoul.

1392 Yi Seonggye is crowned king, officially beginning the Joseon Dynasty.

1396 Capital moved to Hanyang. (modern day Seoul)

1402 The use of paper currency is initiated.

1446 The Hangul alphabet, created 3 years earlier, is promulgated by King Sejong the Great.

1592 The Japanese invasion of Korea begins under the command of Toyotomi Hideyoshi. Admiral Yi Sun-Sin employs the Turtle ship to repel Japanese naval forces.

1653 Dutch ship, with Captain Hendrick Hamel, gets wrecked on Jejudo Island.

1791 Persecution of Catholicism begins.

1864 Gojong ascends the throne with his father, Daewongun, as Regent.

1866 French Campaign against Korea.

1871 United States expedition to Korea.

1876 Kim Okgyun leads the Gapsin coup. In 3 days, Chinese forces are able to overwhelm the Progressives and their Japanese supporters.

1884 Donghak Rebellion prompts the First Sino-Japanese War and Gabo Reforms.

1895 China recognizes Korean independence in the Treaty of Shimonoseki. Empress Myeongseong was murdered by Japanese assassins.

1896 King Gojong flees to the Russian legation in Korea (Seoul).

Taejo / Yi Seong-gye 태조 / 이성계

Taejo 태조, birth name **Yi Seong-gye 이성계** (1335 - 1408), was the founder and the first king of the Joseon Dynasty, reigning from 1392 to 1398, and was the main figure in overthrowing the Goryeo Dynasty. By the late 14th century, the Goryeo Dynasty was beginning to fall apart, with its foundations collapsing from years of war against the Mongol Empire. During the time, General Yi Seong-gye gained power and was respected for pushing the Mongol remnants off the kingdom and repelling Japanese pirates. When the newly rising Ming Dynasty demanded the return of a significant portion of Goryeo's northern territory, Goryeo was split into two factions – anti-Ming who argued to fight back and those who sought peace. Yi, the latter, however, was chosen to lead the invasion. At **Wihwado Island 위화도** on the **Amnok River 압록강**, he decided to revolt and withdrew the troops, and headed back to the capital. The military coup succeeded, and he dethroned the King. He first put a puppet king, but later exiled him, and ascended the throne, and began the Joseon Dynasty.

Yukryongi nareusha 육룡이 나르샤
(*Six Flying Dragons*, 2015, SBS)

K-Drama series about
Yi Seong-gye's Military Coup &
The Beginning of the Joseon Dynasty

Yi Sun-Shin 이순신 - The Legendary Korean War Hero

Yi Sun-shin (Yi Sun-sin) 이순신 (1545 – 1598) was a Korean naval commander/admiral and is arguably the most beloved and revered figure in the entire Korean history. Famed for his incredible victories against the Japanese navy during the ***Imjin Waeran* 임진왜란 (Imjin War - Japanese invasion of Joseon 1592 – 1598)**, as well as his exemplary moral conduct on and off the battlefield. His title of ***Samdo Sugun Tongjesa* 삼도수군통제사** (Naval Commander of the Three Provinces) was the title for the commander of the Korean navy until 1896. Yi Sun-shin's most remarkable military achievement, which has been made into a movie as well, occurred at the Battle of **Myeongnyang 명량**, where the Joseon navy was outnumbered by 133 warships to 13, and forced into a last stand. But without losing a single ship, he led the navy to repel the Japanese force, destroying and impairing 31 of the 133 enemy warships. Behind the incredible victory was the construction of armored warship, ***Geobukseon* 거북선** ("turtle ship"), whose original design was suggested during the reign of **King Taejong 태종**. Using his creative mind, the armored ship was brought back to life and played a crucial role in defeating the Japanese. On the verge of completely expelling the Japanese force, he was mortally wounded by an enemy bullet at the Battle of **Noryang 노량** on December 16, 1598. During his last moments, he ordered the subordinates to not announce his death. After death, he was rewarded with various honors from the royal court, including a posthumous title of **Chungmugong 충무공** (Duke of Loyalty and Warfare).

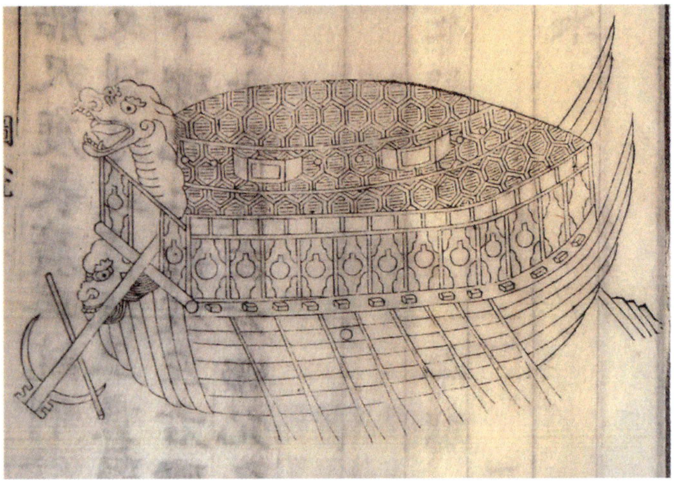

16th century Korean turtle ship in a depiction dating to 1795.
The woodblock print is based on a contemporary, late 18th century model.

Epic Battle Scenes!

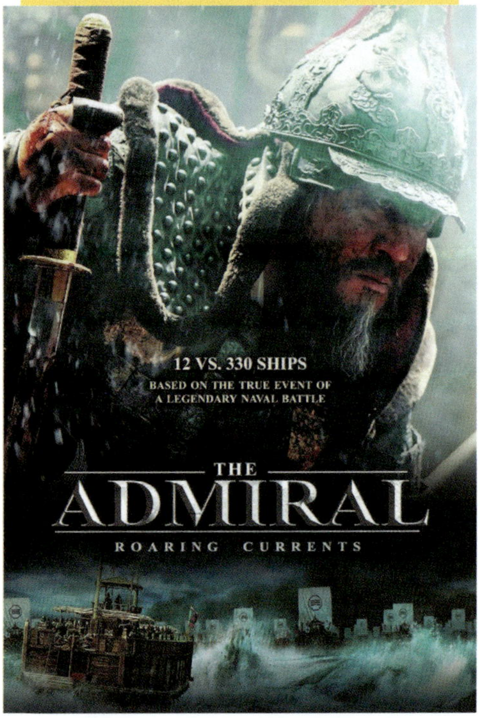

Myeongryang 명량
(*The Admiral : Roaring Currents*, 2014)

Admiral Yi Sun-sin remains a venerated hero among Koreans, and you can find his face and the turtle ship on the **100 Korean Won** and **5 Korean Won coins** today. You can also find his statue at the **Gwanghwamun Square**. Standing 17 meters (56 ft) tall with a sword in his hand is the bronze statue of the legendary war hero, Admiral Yi Sun-shin.

YI SOON SHIN - WARRIOR AND DEFENDER

The Story of Yi Soon-shin has been made into a cartoon series by Onrie Kompan Productions

A miniature *Geobukseon*, the armored "turtle" warship, along with a pair of war drums are also found underneath. The statue was erected in 1968, after **President Park Chung Hee** ordered to "build a statue of a figure most feared and admired by the Japanese." The floor fountain is named "12.23 Fountain," symbolic of the 12 ships he fought to repel the Japanese invaders and 23 victories he achieved.

WHO ARE THE PEOPLE ON THE KOREAN CURRENCY NOTES?

Toegye Yi Hwang 퇴계이황 (1501-1570) was a leading thinker, educator, painter, and Neo-Confucianist scholar of Joseon. The painting on the back of the ₩1,000-won note is ***Gyesangjeonggeodo* 계상정거도,** a work by **Gyeomjae Jeongseon 겸재 정선**, a master of landscape painting. The painting, created in 1746, depicts the surrounding landscape of **Dosan Seodang 도산서당**, where Toegye Yi Hwang stayed during his lifetime.

Yulgok Yi I 율곡이이 (1536 - 1584) was a prominent Confucian scholar of the Joseon Dynasty. If Toegye fully understood Neo-Confucianism, Yi I successfully indigenized it. On the back of the ₩5,000-won note is ***Chochungdo* 초충도** (painting of grass and insects) painted by **Sin Saimdang 신사임당**, his mother. It was originally painted on eight folding screens, and on the note are a "Watermelon and Grasshopper" and a "Cockscomb and Frog."

King Sejong The Great 세종대왕 (1397-1450) is one of the most beloved and respected figures in Korea. Known as the King of humanity, he tried to develop and improve all the daily aspects of his people, including education, history, geography, politics, economy, agriculture, medicine, music, and religion. To predict nature to prevent damage to farming, King Sejong worked hard with scientists such as Jang Yeong-sil, Park Yeon, and Jeong Cho to create a device called ***Honcheonui* 혼천의**, which was able to measure the location of the sun, moon, and the five planets, and it is featured on the back of the ₩10,000-won note.

Sin Saimdang 신사임당 (1504 - 1551) was a genius painter and a poet of the early Joseon period. As the mother of **Yulgok Yi I**, she was revered as a model for a good wife and a wise mother. Sin Saimdang loved ***Sagunja* 사군자**, or the "Four Gracious Plants (plum, orchid, chrysanthemum, and bamboo)."The painting on the back of the note, called Wolmaedo 월매도 is not a painting by Sin Saimdang, but it is said to be the most famous and outstanding painting of plum blossoms painted during the mid-Joseon period.

HWACHA – JOSEON'S MULTIPLE ROCKET LAUNCHER!

***Hwacha* 화차** was a Joseon Dynasty weapon that could fire hundreds of rocket-powered arrows or iron-headed arrows out of a gun barrel at the same time!

***Shingijeon* 신기전 (*The Divine Weapon*, 2008)**

Watch it in action on YouTube!

HWACHA – The Super Rocket Pod (Mythbusters Ep. 110)

WHY WERE KOREANS CALLED "WHITE-CLOTHES PEOPLE"?

Oppert, a Jewish businessman from Germany, wrote during his visit to Joseon in a book titled ***Ein verschlossenes land, reisen nach Corea***, that, "Men and women, their clothes are white," and Laguerie, a Far East correspondent from France, also wrote, "Everyone is dressed in white." (1832) Koreans often enjoy using the word ***baekeuiminjok* 백의민족**, which literally means "white-clothes people (white-clad people)" when referring to themselves. But the fact that such an expression isn't found in old historical records makes it likely that it wasn't a long-held tradition and that the nickname comes from how Koreans were viewed in the eyes of the foreigners who visited Korea during the late Joseon Dynasty when the popularity of white clothes rose significantly. Quite convincing! Then why did Koreans enjoy wearing white clothes? There are many theories about the reason, but opinions are divided. First, there is a theory that Koreans have long been fond of wearing white as a symbol of worshiping the sun. The second theory is an economic reason. Clothes with colors (court costumes were colorful and commoners also wore colorful costumes when there were special events such as weddings) were relatively expensive, so commoners could not afford them, and white would naturally have been worn by the majority of the population. During the Japanese occupation, it became a symbol of the anti-Japanese resistance movement when the Japanese encouraged Koreans to wear colored clothes instead of white clothes, and Koreans saw it as an attempt to suppress national spirit.

Royal Palaces OF THE JOSEON DYNASTY

GYEONGBOKGUNG - "Palace Greatly Blessed by Heaven"

1 2
3

1. **Geunjeongjeon 근정전** was the throne hall where the king formally granted audiences to his officials, gave declarations of national importance, and greeted foreign envoys and ambassadors

2. **Gyeonghoeru 경회루** was a pavilion used to hold important state banquets. The present building was constructed in 1867 (during the reign of King Gojong) on an island of an artificial lake that is 128 m (420 ft) wide and 113 m (370 ft) across.

3. **Hyangwonjeong 향원정** is a two-story hexagonal pavilion built on an artificial island of a lake.

With **Mount Bugak 북악산** as a backdrop and **Yukjogeori** 육조거리 ("Street of Six Ministries" (today's Sejong-no 세종로) just outside the main entrance to the palace **Gwanghwamun Gate 광화문**, **Gyeongbokgung 경복궁** was built in 1395 (three years after the foundation of the Joseon Dynasty), in the heart of the Dynasty's capital, **Hanyang 한양** (today's Seoul) and served as the Dynasty's main palace. Sadly, it was reduced to ashes during the Japanese invasion of 1592, and was left abandoned until 1867. Today, the restored complex consists of 330 buildings, forming a labyrinthine configuration, in which the walls separate offices for the king and state officials called **Oejeon 외전** (outer court) from living quarters for the royal family and gardens called **Naejeon** 내전 (inner court). Added to the extensive complex were other palaces of various sizes, including **Junggung** 중궁 (the Queen's residence) and **Donggung 동궁** (the Crown Prince's residence).

In the early 20th century during the Japanese Occupation (1910 - 1945), Gyeongbokgung, the symbol of national sovereignty, was demolished and the ownership of the land was transferred to the Japanese Governor-General in 1911. In 1915, a significant portion of the buildings were torn down for an exhibition. Following the event, the Japanese built the Government-General building on the site.

The South Korean government has been making continuous efforts to restore Gyeongbokgung since 1990. The Government-General building was demolished in 1996 under the command of **President Kim Young-sam 김영삼**. **Heungnyemun Gate 흥례문** and **Gwanghwamun Gate 광화문** have also been reconstructed in their original locations. The inner court and Donggung, the Crown Prince's residence, have also been restored recently.

Gwanghwamun, meaning "spreading light," is the main and largest gate of Gyeongbokgung. First constructed in 1395, it served as a landmark and symbol of the capital **Hanyang**, but it went through recurring accounts of destruction and disrepair. It was destroyed by fire during the Japanese invasion in 1592 and was left in ruins until 1867 when it was finally restored along with the rest of Gyeongbokgung Palace. It was again deconstructed and moved to a different location by the Japanese during the Japanese Occupation so that a massive Japanese Government-General building could be built on the site. After getting completely destroyed during the Korean War, it was once again restored and relocated near the original location in 1969 and is one of the most popular spots among tourists.

On the wall outside of **Jagyeongjeon 자경전**, you can find ***Shipjangsaeng* 십장생**. Meaning "Ten Symbols of Longevity," it's a traditional Korean pattern consisting of the sun, mountain, rock, water, cloud, pine tree, elixir plant, turtle, crane, and deer. Each symbol stands for longevity, but when used together it strengthens their original meaning.

Wall outside of Jagyeongjeon in Gyeongbokgung

해치 ***haechi***, or 해태 ***haetae***, is a legendary creature in Chinese and Korean mythology that's believed to be able to distinguish good from evil and keep justice. Since ancient times, the *haechi* have been regarded as auspicious animals that prevent fires and disasters, which is why you can find their statues at the entrance of the palaces. The Seoul Metropolitan Government selected *haechi* as the city's icon in May 2008. Since then, the Seoul Metropolitan Government has placed *haechi* statues in various parts of the city, including **Gwanghwamun Square**. Why don't you look around Seoul's historic attractions and find them all?

CHANGDEOKGUNG - "Palace of Prospering Virtue"

Injeongjeon 인정전, meaning "hall of benevolent ruling", was the throne hall of Palace and the most representative and dignified building of the palace. It was used for major state affairs.

Huwon 후원 ("rear garden") is a beautiful garden which incorporates a lotus pond. It was originally constructed for the use of the royal family and palace women.

***Irworobongdo* 일월오봉도**, meaning "The Painting of The Sun, The Moon and Five Mountain Peaks," Irworobongdo is a painting on a folding screen that sits behind the king's throne. It depicts the Sun on one side and the Moon on the other, with five mountain peaks and water below them, and it was buried with the king when he died. It's said that the painting is complete only when the king is seated before it.

***Eojwa* 어좌**, or "The Phoenix Throne" is the throne of the hereditary monarchs of Korea. The phoenix has a long association with Korean royalty.

Changdeokgung 창덕궁 is also known as **Donggwol** 동궐 (Eastern Palace) because of its location which sits to the east of the main palace, Gyeongbokgung. Changdeokgung was home to the Joseon government, as well as a beloved residence of numerous kings of the Joseon Dynasty. For this reason, it was the longest-serving royal residential palace. Its unique beauty comes from the fact that it flawlessly blends into its surrounding nature and landscape, and **Huwon 후원**, the palace's rear garden, and the only rear garden of any Korean palace, is the essence of Korean landscaping, occupying about 60% of the palace. Luckily, Changdeokgung Palace is well-preserved compared to other palaces that were damaged and destroyed throughout history and many of its original features still remain intact. It was added to the **UNESCO World Heritage List** in 1997.

CHANGGYEONGGUNG - "Palace of Magnificent Joy"

Chundangji 춘당지 ("Spring Pond". Joseon kings who resided in the Palace tilled the soil with plows drawn by an ox. This symbolic ceremony was a tradition of wishing for a good harvest while promoting agriculture and share the arduous labor the farmers had to endure.

Changgyeonggung 창경궁 was built in the mid-15th century by **King Sejong 세종** for his father, **Taejong 태종**. Originally named **Suganggung 수강궁**, it received the current name after a renovation and expansion project that took place in 1483. Like other palaces, many of its structures were destroyed as a result of the multiple invasions by Japan. It was reconstructed by successive Kings, but a significant portion was once again torn down by the Japanese during **the Japanese Occupation**, to make room for a modern park for the Japanese Empire. On the site, the Japanese built a zoo, a botanical garden, and a museum. After getting destroyed during the **Korean War**, the zoo was restocked but was eventually relocated to present-day **Seoul Grand Park**.

***Samdo* 삼도 ("Three Paths")**
Inside the palace, paths are divided into three sections. The central path, widest and highest among them, is the royal path, called **eodo** 어도, which was used exclusively by the kings. The east path was used by civil servants and the west path by military officials.

***Pumgyeseok* 품계석 ("Rank Stones")**
Two rows of rank stones, indicate the position of court officials during ceremonies.

***deumeu* 드므 / *deumu* 드무**
Around the corners of the hall, there are bronze water jars with water filled up to the brim (they are kept empty today). While they serve practical purposes of putting out fires, their main purpose was to ward off the evil spirits of fire because the reflection on the water inside the jars would startle them. Interestingly, during the winter, they would keep fire around the jars to prevent them from freezing. This is a great example of harmony between shamanistic traditions and scientific reasoning of the time.

WHAT ARE THE MINI STATUES ON THE KOREAN PALACE ROOF?

Look up to the roofs of Korean palaces and at the peak of the roof you will find mysterious statues called ***japsang* 잡상**, which are always placed in an odd number (the most a palace can have is 11). Their purpose goes back to the Korean shamanic religion and they are intended to chase away evil spirits and misfortune, similar to that of gargoyles in the Western culture, as well as to show the dignity and grandeur of a building. The tradition is considered to have been a result of the Chinese influence during the Joseon Dynasty, as evidenced by the fact that the first few *japsang* statues on a roof are believed to be the characters and the deities of Earth from the Chinese classic ***Journey to the West***.

DEOKSUGUNG- "Palace of Virtuous Longevity"

Seokjojeon 석조전 is a Western-style building and was the last residential quarter of King Gojong

Deoksugung 덕수궁 is different from other Korean palaces in style for containing a harmonious mixture of medieval and modern style architecture. For example - you will find a **Western-style garden** and a modern seal engraved on a fountain. Originally, Deoksugung was not a palace, but when the 14th king of the Joseon Dynasty, **King Seonjo 선조**, returned from evacuation during the Japanese invasion in 1592, all palaces were severely damaged, and Deoksugung was chosen as a temporary residence for the royal family. The 15th king, **King Gwanghaegun 광해군**, renamed it to **Gyeonggunung 경운궁**, and formalized it as a royal palace, and **Emperor Gojong 고종** of the **Korean Empire** (also the 26th king of the Joseon Dynasty), stayed here and expanded it. During the Joseon Dynasty, the royal guard was responsible for opening and closing the palace gate as well as patrolling and you can see the reenactment taking place today when you visit.

(Left) **Jeonggwanheon 정관헌**, a building used for rest and entertainment.

(Above) The symbol of a deer keeping a herb of eternal youth, ***bulocho* 불로초**.

ROYAL GUARD CHANGING CEREMONY

Sumunjang gyodaeuisik* 수문장 교대의식** (The Chief Gate-keeper Changing Ceremony). The royal guard system, which started when 예종 King Yejong, the 8th king of the Joseon Dynasty who came to the throne in 1469, was conceptually the same as the national defense, as it was used as a means to strengthen the royal authority and maintain stability. The royal guard system was structured when the gate guard system and its rules were institutionalized and incorporated in ***Gyeonggukdaejeon 경국대전 (National Code) during the reign of **King Seongjong 성종**, the 9th king. The changing ceremony of the royal guard in front of the **Daehanmun Gate 대한문** started in 1906 when the gate was designated as the main gate to the Palace.

The Order of the Changing Ceremony

1) Entrance of the officials and announcement of the ceremony
2) Delivery of the passcode and passcode response
3) First drumbeat (passing the case with the keys)
4) Second drumbeat (checking the authenticity of the token and identification of the plate which represents the chief gatekeeper, ***sumunjang* 수문장**)
5) Third drumbeat (implementation of the shift)
6) Closing announcement

The ***yonggo*** 용고 ("dragon drum"), is a barrel drum with tacked heads decorated with painted dragon designs, used in the military wind-and-percussion music called ***daechwita*** 대취타.

GYEONGHUIGUNG - "Palace of Joy and Harmony"

The construction of **Gyeonghuigung 경희궁** began in 1617 during the reign of **King Gwanghaegun 광해군**, the 15th king of the Joseon Dynasty, and was completed in 1620. It was originally called **Gyeongdeokgung 경덕궁** because Gyeongdeok was the posthumous epithet of **Wonjong 원종**, who was named king after his death. In the latter Joseon Dynasty period, Gyeonghuigung served as the secondary palace for the king, and as it was situated on the west side of Seoul, it was also called **Seogwol 서궐** (West Palace). The secondary palace is usually the palace where the King moves to in times of emergency. From **King Injo 인조** to **King Cheoljong 철종**, about 10 kings of the Joseon Dynasty stayed here.

Before losing most of its complex to two devastating fires in the 19th century, it was of a considerable size, with an arched bridge connecting it to **Deoksugung**. During the Japanese Occupation, the remaining was dismantled to make space for **Gyeongseong Middle School 경성중학교**, which was a school for Japanese citizens. Reconstruction efforts began in the late 1990s as part of a government project, but due to urban growth and decades of neglect, the government was only able to reconstruct around 1/3 of the former Palace.

Imperial Family of The Korean Empire (Daehan Maeil Sinbo, Seoul Shinmun)

THE KOREAN EMPIRE - DREAMING OF A MODERN STATE (1897 ~ 1910)

Daehanjeguk 대한제국 (The Great Han Empire), or the Korean Empire, was the new name which the 26th King of the Joseon Dynasty, and the first Emperor of the Empire, **King Gojong 고종** renamed the Joseon Dynasty from on October 12th, 1897. In the turbulent late 19th century East Asia, the Korean Empire proclaimed itself as an independent country and promoted modernization in various fields such as the military, economy, land system, and education through the **Gwangmu Reformation 광무개혁**, but was eventually annexed by the Japanese Empire and collapsed in 1910.

1897 Proclamation of the Empire - King Gojong returns after 1 year of refugee at the Russian Legation.

1905 Korea-Japan Treaty of 1905 gives Japan complete power for Korea's foreign affairs and placed all trade through Korean ports under Japanese supervision.

1907 June - The Hague Secret Emissary Affair

July - Emperor Gojong abdicated by the Japanese Imperialists, and Gojong's son Sunjong succeeded to the throne.

1909 Ito Hirobumi (Japanese Resident-General of Korea) assassinated by Korean general and independence activist An Jung-geun.

1910 The Japan-Korea Treaty of 1910 started the annexation of the Korean Empire by Imperial Japan.

Emperor Gojong 고종 황제

Gojong, the **Gwangmu Emperor 광무대제** (1852 – 1919), was the 26th and final king of the Joseon Dynasty. During his reign, he was influenced by **Empress Myeongseong 명성황후 (Queen Min)**, and unlike his father **Heungseon Daewongun 흥선대원군,** who maintained a closed-door/national-isolation policy, he adopted an open-door foreign policy. He signed a Treaty of Amity and Trade with the US in 1882, although it was done in hopes of gaining protection from Imperial Japan, China, and Russia. While the conflict among three neighboring powerhouses was rising, Gojong proclaimed Korea an empire in 1897, and became the first Emperor, and the Joseon Dynasty ended at the same time. In an effort to maintain Korean sovereignty, he played and leveraged on the power struggle among the rivals, effectively preventing each of them from having total control over Korea. His efforts finally came to an end after the **Russo-Japanese War (1904–05)**.

Seokjojeon 석조전 in the Deoksugung Palace 덕수궁, the last residential quarter of King Gojong

Empress Myeongseong 명성황후

A portrait of Empress Myeongseong by a Japanese illustrator

Empress Myeongseong 명성황후 (1851 - 1895) was the first official wife of **King Gojong 고종**, the 26th king of Joseon and the first emperor of the Korean Empire. The government of Meiji Japan was ambitious with overseas expansion and saw her as an obstacle, putting efforts to remove her but failed. After the first **Sino-Japanese War** which ended with Japan's victory, Joseon came under the Japanese influence. As a result, the Empress argued for stronger ties between Korea and Russia as a means to block Japanese influence. The efforts to remove her from the political arena, orchestrated through failed rebellions prompted by **Heungseon Daewongun** (an influential regent working with the Japanese), compelled her to take a harsher stand against Japanese influence. The Japanese government sent a group of ***ronins*** (assassins) and assassinated the Empress. This horrendous incident ignited outrage among other foreign powers, and the Joseon people's **anti-Japanese sentiment** soared.

Eulsa Treaty 을사조약

Victorious Japan forced Emperor Gwangmu (King Gojong) to accept pro-Japanese advisors to the royal court, which in turn, led him to sign the Protectorate Treaty of 1905, more commonly known as **Eulsa Joyak 을사조약 (Eulsa Treaty)** between Korea and Japan. As a result, Korea lost its status and rights as an independent sovereign nation.

The Hague Secret Emissary Affair

Emperor Gwangmu (King Gojong) secretly sent representatives (**Yi Jun 이준, Yi Sang-seol 이상설** and **Yi Wi-jong 이위종**) more commonly known as "Hague Secret Emissary Affair," to the **Hague Peace Convention** in 1907, to assert the Korean sovereignty and to declare the invalidity of Japanese diplomatic maneuvers, including the **Eulsa Treaty of 1905**. At the convention, the representatives asserted the Emperor's rights to rule Korea independent of Japan. Sadly, the emissaries were not allowed by the nations to take part in the conference. Eventually, though, they managed to hold interviews with newspapers and spoke out about the unfairness being done by the Japanese. As a result, the enraged Japanese forced Emperor Gwangmu to abdicate and his son **Sunjong 순종** was put to the throne and ruled for just three years before the Korean Empire got annexed by Japan in 1910.

Yi Wan-yong 이완용 The Worst Traitor in Korean History

이완용 Yi Wan-yong (1858 - 1926), also known as **Ye Wanyong**, is one of the **Five Eulsa (Japan-Korea Protectorate Treaty of 1905) Traitors** and is considered the worst traitor who sold his country out to Japan. He threatened King Gojong to sign the Eulsa Treaty and changed the State Council of Joseon to the cabinet system of which he became the Prime Minister. After the Hague Secret Emissary Affair, he held King Gojong accountable and forced him to step down, and crowned King Sunjong. As the Prime Minister, he signed a **Korea-Japan annexation**.

A story of "Righteous Army (civilian militia)" during the Korean Empire period.

Mr. Sunshine (2018, tvN)

Deokhye Ongju 덕혜옹주 (*The Last Princess* 2018)

A story of Princess Deokhye who was taken to Japan as a hostage

For memorial of establishing Provisional Government of the Republic of Korea October 11, 1919

JAPANESE OCCUPATION - SAD HISTORY (1910 ~ 1945)

The period from 1910, when the **Korean Empire** was annexed by Japan, to 1945 when it was liberated, is one of the saddest and most painful periods in Korean history. After the annexation, Japan set up the Government-General of Joseon and systematically suppressed Koreans with administrative, legislative, judicial, and military forces in their hands, and persistently tried to plant their spirit and culture. Korean names were forcibly changed to Japanese names, and the mandatory use of the Japanese language by students, alongside the abolition of Korean language courses in all schools, were intended to thoroughly "Japanize" Koreans. Cultural property looting and economic exploitation were also frequent. This evil deed reached its peak through the **Pacific War** and **World War II**. The **Japanese imperialists** committed countless crimes against humanity, including forced labor, military sexual slavery brothels, and horrific experiments on the living bodies of the Korean people. While some argue that the Japanese colonial government's urban planning had a positive impact on the modernization of Seoul, they also acknowledge that the purpose was strictly exploitation, on the pretext of "development" and this indelible scar is why many Koreans still have anti-Japanese sentiment.

1916 The final wave of Uibyeong rebels is defeated by Japanese forces.

1919 Spurred by the sudden and mysterious death of Gojong, March 1st Movement, organized by Yu Gwan Sun and other independence activisits, began. Declaration of Korean Independence. Nationwide peaceful demonstrations are crushed by Japanese military and police forces after two months. Governor-General Hasegawa resigns.

The establishment of The Provisional Government of the Republic of Korea in Shanghai.

1920 Battle of Cheongsanri, Korean independence Army, led by Kim Jwa-jin, victory.

1932 Korean independence activist Lee Bong Chang fails in his attempt to assassinate Emperor Hirohito in Tokyo.

Korean independence activist Yun Bong Gil bombs Japanese Military gathering in Shanghai.

1945 The Empire of Japan surrenders to the Allies. According to the terms of Potsdam Declaration, Korea becomes independent.

Korean Independence Fighters

Ahn Jung-geun 안중근 (1879 – 1910) was an independence activist and a martyr at the end of the Korean Empire. He assassinated **Prince Ito Hirobumi**, the main culprit of the invasion, and former Resident-General of Joseon, at **Harbin Railway Station** in Manchuria. **The Order of Merit for National Foundation** was posthumously awarded.

Kim Gu 김구 (1876 ~ 1949) was an independence activist and politician of the **Provisional Government of Korea** during the Japanese Occupation. After Korea's liberation from Japan's colonial rule, he tried to establish an independent and unified government but was assassinated by **Ahn Doo-hee 안두희** in 1949. ***Baekbeomilji* 백범일지**, a diary written during his career in the provisional government, remains a valuable historical record.

Yun Bong-gil 윤봉길 (1908 ~ 1932) was an independence activist during the Japanese Occupation. In 1932, he threw a **bomb** at an event venue in Hongkou Park in Shanghai which was celebrating the **Japanese Emperor's birthday and victory in the war**, causing significant damage to Japanese colonial leaders. Along with Ahn Jung-geun's attack on Ito Hirobumi in Harbin, this is considered one of the greatest achievements of the Korean independence movement.

Ahn Chang-ho 안창호 (1878 ~ 1938) was an independence activist and educator at the end of the Korean Empire and during the Japanese occupation. He led educational activities to foster national competence and independence movements to regain the sovereignty of Korea. He established the **New People's Association**, **Daeseong School 대성학교**, and **Young Korean Academy**. His pen-name is **Dosan 도산**, which is also **the name of a park in Seoul** established to commemorate his achievement and legacy.

A movie inspired by the activities of the Korean Independence Fighters.

Amsal 암살 (Assassination, 2015)

But I See Koreans Speaking Fluent Japanese In Movies. How Is This Possible? P. 30

March 1st Movement & Ryu Gwan-sun 유관순

Demonstration for independence in the Park.
The Koreans are seen shouting "Mansei" with their hands up in the air. Not a single man is armed.

[Red Cross pamphlet on March 1st Movement]

Hanggeo: Yugwansun Iyagi
항거: 유관순 이야기
(A Resistance, 2019)

Ryu Gwan-sun 유관순 (alternative spelling **Yu Gwan-sun**, 1902 – 1920), was an organizer of the March 1st Movement, one of the earliest public displays of Korean resistance during the Japanese Occupation, is a symbol of Korea's fight for independence against imperial Japan. The event was a peaceful protest where thousands of Koreans gathered to cry out "***Daehan Doklip Manse*" 대한독립만세** ("Long Live Korean Independence"), while waving thousands of Korean flags. It went on for hours until the Japanese military police started firing at the unarmed protesters. Sadly, 19 people died, including Ryu's parents. After getting arrested, she was severely tortured and interrogated, but never gave away the whereabouts of her collaborators. She later died in jail from the after-effects of torture.

WHO WERE THE "COMFORT WOMEN"?

It refers to the military sexual slavery system set up and operated by the Japanese military, which led to numerous crimes such as wartime rape and sexual abuse, committed against the women in colonies and occupied territories. It was done under the connivance and with the direct involvement of the Japanese government - during World War II, the Japanese government had to find a way to satisfy the sexual desires of their soldiers, and they set up illegal military brothels, recruited and managed women from colonies and occupied areas, including China, Taiwan, Malaysia, Vietnam, Indonesia, and even the Netherlands. The term ***wianbu* 위안부** (*ianfu* in Japanese) literally means "comfort women," and was a euphemism used by the Japanese military. The so-called recruitment process had problems. Many of them were forcibly conscripted while many others were defrauded by a broker who guaranteed them a factory job. They were locked up against their will and sexually exploited and are still suffering from the trauma of that time. Each of the affected countries is demanding an open and sustained apology from Japan. Korean civic organizations have been installing what's known as the "Statue of Peace" ***sonyeosang* 소녀상** ("statue of a girl") around the world to raise awareness of the atrocity and console the victims.

WHY DO KOREANS LIKE THE ROSE OF SHARON SO MUCH?

Emblem of South Korea and the National Assembly

"Three thousand li (unit of measurement for length) of splendid rivers and mountains, filled with ***mugunghwa***." As can be seen from a passage from Korea's national anthem, Koreans have loved and cherished *mugunghwa*, also known as the "Rose of Sharon." The flower, which literally means "Flower of infinitude/eternity," is named so because the continuous blooming and fading were seen as such. Moreover, Korean people identified themselves with the flower and regarded it as a symbol of the Korean national spirit, that has survived unabated despite numerous hardships and struggles. For this reason, **Namgoong Eok 남궁억**, the president of **Hwangseong Newspaper 황성신문** and independence activist during the Japanese Occupation, established the **Mogok School** in September 1919 and made efforts to spread *mugunghwa* to the entire country. Although *mugunghwa* has never been officially designated as the national flower of Korea by law, it's customarily recognized as the national flower of Korea and is used as a symbol of the nation.

WHY ARE KOREANS SO FURIOUS OVER THE JAPANESE "RISING SUN" FLAG?

Imagine wearing a T-shirt with a big print of the Nazi **Hakenkreuz** striding through the streets of Jerusalem. Even if you are the biggest thrill-seeker in the world who enjoys living dangerously, this isn't something you wouldn't dare to do because it's the symbol of racism and all the inhumane atrocities the Nazi's had done during the Holocaust. But did you know that in Korea, like Hakenkreuz, there is something Koreans are furious about? Yes, it's the "**Rising Sun Flag**" of Japan. To the eyes of foreigners not familiar with the Asian people's pain and suffering during the Japanese colonial era, it might look like a cool variation of the Japanese flag, one of the reasons why it's widely used on items like T-shirts and cell phone cases. But for the Asian people affected by the Japanese colonial era, it simply isn't a trendy image. This is because the flag was recognized as an imperial flag as it appeared as a symbol of the Japanese military in the Pacific War, which involved and exploited many Asian countries on the pretext of protecting Asia against Western forces. Many foreign celebrities, stars, as well as companies and organizations, inadvertently wore clothes or introduced products with the Rising Sun Flag and apologized after receiving complaints from Koreans. Not only that, but many popular Korean idol stars have also come under fire for wearing clothes or using products that have the design. However, some scholars point out that there is a misunderstanding about the Rising Sun Flag - it was a flag that has long been used by the Japanese military, and does not only symbolize Japanese imperialism. Technically, it's the current Japanese flag that was used as the national flag during that heinous time, and it's factually incorrect to place the Rising Sun Flag in the same position as the Hakenkreuz for that reason. While scholars should discuss whether to treat the Nazi Hakenkreuz and the Rising Sun Flag the same way, it's important to understand that they are equal in that they bring painful memories to the affected countries and their people.

WHAT IS DOKDO AND WHAT'S ALL THE FUSS ABOUT IT?

Along with the Japanese Rising Sun Flag, another sensitive and important issue to Koreans, and a symbol of Korea-Japan conflict, is an island called **Dokdo 독도**. Dokdo, made up of two islets **Dongdo 동도** (East Island) and **Seodo 서도** (West Island), is a pair of volcanic islets located off the east coast of South Korea, next to the larger **Ulleungdo Island 울릉도**, and right in between the **Korean Peninsula** and the Japanese Archipelago. As the nickname "a lonely island" suggests, it's the easternmost territory belonging to South Korea. But as irony would have it, it's far from being "lonely," because Japan has been tenaciously claiming sovereignty over the islands. Japan claims that Dokdo (**Takeshima** is the Japanese name) was a terra nullius (nobody's land) before the Japanese annexation of Korea (1910), meaning that Korea never had control of the island. Therefore, when they discovered and used it as a temporary lighthouse during the Russo-Japanese War, Japan was the first to incorporate it as its territory. Hence, Japan claims that South Korea is illegally occupying Japanese territory now. However, in 1905, Japan forcibly seized Dokdo, then part of Joseon (1392-1910). After the end of World War II, Japan, as one of the defeated countries, was forced to return all territory seized under imperialism to the rightful owners. Nevertheless, Japan still insists that Dokdo is Japan's territory – they even changed their original argument from claiming that no country possessed Dokdo before they occupation in 1905 to new assertions in 1953 that Japanese diplomatic documents marked Dokdo as Japan's indigenous territory.

Even Japan's public documents such as 'The Tottori-han's Submission' (1693) and 'The Dajokan Order' (1877) emphasize that Dokdo is not part of Japan. These documents directly contradict Japan's current claim that Dokdo was an unclaimed territory. Moreover, Supreme Commander for the Allied Powers Index Number (SCAPIN) 677 in 1946, a memorandum that sealed the range of territories that would be changed after the end of the Second World War, excluded Dokdo from its administrative and governmental district. These documents add to the evidence that Dokdo is not under the dominance of Japan and that such fact has been globally acknowledged, even by Japan.

Official documents from Korea and Japan along with international statements from events such as the Potsdam and Cairo conferences reflect the Japanese government's unjust claim on Dokdo. Despite the evidence, the Japanese government still denies Korea's claim to Dokdo. Japan's current assertions on Dokdo can be explained as [a] threat to Korea's sovereignty and a repetition of the imperialism that triggered World War II in the past." (maywespeak.com/)

The Korean government's position on the island is firm. "Dokdo Island is not a subject for territorial dispute. Dokdo is an integral part of Korean territory, historically, geographically and under international law. No territorial dispute exists regarding Dokdo, and therefore Dokdo is not a matter to be dealt with through diplomatic negotiations or judicial settlement. The government of the Republic of Korea exercises Korea's irrefutable territorial sovereignty over Dokdo."
(dokdo.mofa.go.kr/eng/dokdo/government_position.jsp)

Why is Dokdo important? First of all, Dokdo is sitting in the middle of the **East Sea**, a repository of a vast amount of **natural resources**. In particular, it's estimated that there are about 600 million tons of solidified methane hydrate, which could generate 10 trillion won (about 8 billion USD) in profits over the next 30 years. But there is a very special reason why Koreans have a strong emotional attachment to the "lonely island." It's because the pain of having the country taken over by the Japanese Imperialists still lingers in everyone's minds. Dokdo was the **first part of Korean territory to be incorporated into the territory of Japan** in 1905, just a little before the Japanese Occupation began. Thus, for Koreans, loving Dokdo is a pledge not to repeat the **pain and shame of the past**, and a **symbol of patriotism**. Koreans have been residing in Dokdo since March 1965. As of March 2017, 25 people (24 households) are registered as residents. There are about 40 Dokdo guards, 3 Dokdo lighthouse keepers, with 2 working in the Dokdo management office.

WHAT'S THE NATIONAL ANTHEM OF KOREA?

During the Japanese Occupation and before the founding of the Republic of Korea, Korea didn't have an official national anthem, and they made a makeshift national anthem, where they set the song's lyrics to the tunes of a Scottish folk song, "Auld Lang Syne." Later in 1935, the lyrics were set to the melody composed by **Ahn Eak-tai** (alternative spelling, **Ahn Ik-Tae**) **안익태,** and was adopted as the national anthem of the Provisional Government of Korea, which existed from 1919 to 1948. **Aegukga 애국가**, literally meaning "The Patriotic Song," has four verses, but on most occasions, only the first one is performed at public events.

Verse 1: 동해 물과 백두산이 마르고 닳도록 하느님이 보우하사 우리나라 만세.
(Until that day when Mt. Baekdu is worn away and the East Sea's waters run dry,
May God protect and preserve our country!)

Refrain: 무궁화 삼천리 화려강산 대한 사람, 대한으로 길이 보전하세.
(Hibiscus and three thousand *ri* (Korean unit of measurement) full of splendid mountains and rivers;
Great Koreans, to the Great Korean way, stay always true!)

Verse 2: 남산 위에 저 소나무 철갑을 두른 듯 바람서리 불변함은 우리 기상일세.
(As the pine atop Namsan Peak stands firm, unchanged through wind and frost, as if wrapped in armor, so shall our resilient spirit.) / **Refrain**

Verse 3: 가을 하늘 공활한데 높고 구름 없이 밝은 달은 우리 가슴 일편단심일세.
(The autumn skies are void and vast, high and cloudless;
the bright moon is like our heart, undivided and true.) / **Refrain**

Verse 4: 이 기상과 이 맘으로 충성을 다하여 괴로우나 즐거우나 나라 사랑하세.
(With this spirit and this mind, let us give all loyalty, in suffering or joy, to love our nation.) / **Refrain**

Translation from wikipedia.org/wiki/Aegukga

2019 New version National Anthem of Korea
By 에레멜lmlxiabeize

WHY IS KOREA DIVIDED?

When the trembling voice of the Japanese Emperor Michinomiya Hirohito declared Japan's complete surrender over the radio on Aug 15th, 1945, World War II, the most destructive war in human history, finally came to an end. At the same time, the 35 years of pain and suffering brought upon the Korean people as a result of the Japanese Occupation (1910 - 1945) was also over. Korea was finally liberated. But the joy didn't last long. Fundamental shifts in global politics and ideological split among the Koreans led to the division of Korea into two occupation zones - the U.S. administering the southern half and the Soviet Union the northern half of the 38th parallel. Over the next three years, 1945-1948, a communist regime supported by the Soviet Union was set in the northern part of Korea above the 38th

1945. 08. 15 Japan surrenders following the WWII defeat. As a result, the Japanese occupation ended and Korea was liberated.

Fundamental shifts in global politics and ideology leads to the division of Korea into two occupation zones - the US administering the southern half and the Soviet Union the northern half of the 38th parallel.

1945. 06. 25 At the dawn of June 25, 1950, North Korean forces began the sudden invasion of South Korea, triggering the Korean War

1945. 06. 27 President Harry Truman deploys troops, hoping to stop the spread of Communism to South Korea.

1950. 10 The Communist China, which bordered North Korea, starts to worry about protecting themselves, and sends a massive amount of troops, making important victories that pushed the UN troops back acorss the 38th parallel.

1951.07.10 With the battling at a stalemate, peace talks began, but it will take two years for the opposite sides to reach an agreement.

1953.07.27 Armistice agreement ends a 3-year-long brutal war between two Koreas.

1954.04 US and Chinese representatives meet to discuss the terms to reunite Korea but fail to reach an agreement, leaving Korea divided.

Montage of images from the Korean War. Clockwise from top: U.S. Marines retreating during the Battle of the Chosin Reservoir, U.N. landing at Incheon, Korean refugees in front of an American M-26 tank, U.S. Marines, led by First Lieutenant Baldomero Lopez, landing at Incheon, and an American F-86 Sabre fighter jet.

parallel, while a democratic government was set up and supported by the **United States** below the 38th parallel. The Korean Peninsula became the chessboard on which the intense **Cold War** power struggle between the U.S. and the Soviet Union was played.

In 1948, a United Nations-sponsored vote was held to let the people of Korea decide their own future, but all the efforts went for naught when North Korea refused to participate. South Korea took the initiative and said checkmate by forming its own provisional democratic government, with Harvard and Princeton educated Dr. **Syngman Rhee** as the first South Korean president. North Korea quickly reacted by forming their own socialist government led by a former communist guerrilla **Kim Il-sung**. This historical moment was the last time Korea was ever together as one.

At the dawn of June 25th, 1950, North Korean forces began a sudden invasion of South Korea with the operation code name **폭풍** ***pokpung*** (Storm), triggering the Korean War. Immediately after the blitz, **President Harry Truman** deployed the U.S. troops, hoping to stop the spread of Communism to South Korea, but it wasn't enough to stop North Korea who was backed by the Soviet Union's full military support and carefully planned to invade the South. South Korea was not only over-powered but also caught off-guard. North Korea was able to seize the capital city of the South, **Seoul**, just three days after the outbreak of the war. Then the North kept on marching, all the way down to **Busan**, the final defense line of the South.

Just when South Korea was on the verge of falling to the hands of the communists, tables turned when the United Nations forces, under the command of **General Douglas MacArthur**, launched a series of massive counterattacks, starting with the "**Incheon Landing Operation (Operation Chromite)**" on September 15th. As a result, the forces were able to reach the North's capital city of Pyongyang on October 10th and all the way up to the northernmost **Amnok River**. They were just a few kilometers away from victory. But in mid-November, Kim Il-Sung of North Korea, on the brink of defeat, sent a series of urgent letters to **Mao Zedong**, the **Chairman of the People's Republic of China** for reinforcement. Mao responded by sending a massive (over 300,000 soldiers) force of the Chinese army known as the "**People's Volunteer Army**." With the intervention, the tide turned again. The Chinese army found out that the weakness of the South - U.S. army traveled only by road, the UN forces' superior air power wasn't a big threat during nighttime, and most importantly, the South Korean force was the weakest link. The Chinese army bypassed the roads and took the mountain route, attacked the Korean troops at night to block the supply route, and cut off the retreat. As a result, the South Korea-UN forces were pushed back, giving up Seoul on January 4th, but reclaimed it on March 15th. With the battling at a stalemate, peace talks began on July 10th, 1951, but it would take two years for both sides to reach an agreement. Finally, on July 27th, 1953, armistice agreement was signed and it ended a 3-year-long brutal war between two Koreas. A year later, the representatives from the U.S. and China met to discuss the terms on uniting the two but failed to reach an agreement, leaving the Korean Peninsula **divided in half at the 38th parallel**.

Some of the Best Korean War-Inspired Movies

***Incheon Sangrykjakjeon* 인선상륙작전**
(Operation Chromite, 2016)

***Taegeukgl Hwlnulllmyeo* 대극기 휘날리머**
(The Brotherhood of War, 2004)

***Welcome To Dongmukgol* 웰컴투동막골, 2005**

thank you

to all the fallen heroes from around the world who lost their lives for the freedom of the Republic of Korea.

1960	April Revolution overthrows the autocratic Rhee administration. Rhee resigns and goes into exile. Yun Bo Seon becomes the President.
1961	General Park Chung Hee, overthrows the government through a military coup and becomes President.
1962	Start of the Five-year plans of South Korea.
1964	South Korea joins Vietnam War.
1970	Start of the government-operated New Community Movement.
1976	The Axe Murder Incident in Panmunjom, Joint Security Area, triggers the North Korean leader Kim Il-sung's first official apology to the South.
1977	South Korea celebrates 10 billion dollars gained by exports.
1979	President Park Chung Hee is assassinated by chief of KCIA (Korean Central Intelligence Agency), Kim Jaegyu.
1980	General Chun Doo Hwan gets military power through a coup and becomes the President. Gwangju Uprising. Martial Law is declared throughout the nation.
1987	June Democracy Movement overthrows the autocratic Chun regime. The ruling party of Fifth epublic, Democratic Justice Party, declares democratic elections.
1988	24th Summer Olympic Games held in Seoul.
1991	North Korea and South Korea join the United Nations (UN).
1992	South Korea's first satellite, KITSAT-1, 우리별 Uribyol is successfully launched.
1993	Test of Rodong-1, a single stage, mobile liquid propellant medium range ballistic missile by North Korea.
1994	Kim Jong Il takes control of North Korea upon the death of his father Kim Il-Sung. Start of the Arduous March.
1999	North Korea promises to freeze long-range missile tests.
2000	The first summit between North Korean leader Kim Jong Il and South Korean President Kim Dae Jung is held.
2002	The 2002 FIFA World Cup jointly held by Korea & Japan. North Korea pledges to extend moratorium on missile tests beyond 2003.
2006	Test of Taepodong-2 missile.
2007	The second summit is held, with Roh Moo-hyun (South) and Kim Jong Il (North) representing each side. North Korea fires short-range missile into the East Sea.
2010	North Korea launches missile and attacks Korean Pohang class corvette, ROKS Cheonan. In November, North Korean army rains artillery fire on Yeonpyeongdo island.
2011	Kim Jong Il dies, Kim Jong un takes over as the Supreme Leader of North Korea.

Rhee Syngman 이승만

Rhee Syngman 이승만 (March 26th, 1875 – July 19th, 1965), was the **first president of South Korea**. In his early years, he was forced to live in exile in Hawaii and Shanghai because of the nationalist activities he participated in against Japan during the Japanese Occupation. While in the U.S., he studied at George Washington University, Harvard, and Princeton University. Rhee originally served (1920 - 1925) as president of the **Korean Provisional Government in Shanghai**, until he was expelled by **Kim Ku**. From 1934 until 1944, he zealously campaigned in New York and Washington D.C., to win international support for **Korean independence**. Capitalizing on his closeness and familiarity with the United States, Rhee soon built up a mass political organization. As a result, Rhee was able to be elected as the first president of South Korea in 1948 and was re-elected for three consecutive terms following that. His presidency remains controversial among historians today because of his authoritarian government but is also highly regarded for his achievements as a strong anti-Communist, and for leading South Korea through the Korean War. His presidency ended in resignation following the **April Revolution**. He died in exile in Hawaii.

APRIL REVOLUTION

The April Revolution was a **large-scale uprising** led by labor and student groups, triggered by the discovery in **Masan Harbor** of the body of a high school student **Kim Ju-yul**, killed by a tear-gas shell during his participation in demonstrations against a fixed election by then ruling party of Korea in March 1960. As a result, a series of protests led to the eventual resignation of the Rhee administration and the transition to the Second Republic of South Korea.

Park Chung Hee 박정희

Park Chung Hee 박정희 (November 1917 – 26 October 1979) was a South Korean politician and general who served as the president of South Korea from 1963 to 1979, after seizing power through a **military coup** he led in 1961. Before he took over the control and became president, he was a military leader in the South Korean army and served as the chairman of the Supreme Council for National Reconstruction (1961 – 1963). Park's successful coup ended the interim government (Second Republic) and started the Third Republic. During his reign, he declared martial law and amended the constitution into a highly authoritarian form, termed the **Yushin 유신 (reformation) Constitution**. Park led a series of monumental campaigns that transformed the devastated nation into an economic powerhouse, which is better known today as the "**Miracle on The Han River**." Despite the economic success, there was a political discourse among the people in the office, and Park was assassinated by **Kim Jae-gyu**, the then director of the **Korean Central Intelligence Agency (KCIA)**. After his death, South Korea's economic growth continued thanks to the strong foundations established under his leadership, but some also criticize that they were achieved at the expense of civil liberties.

WHO ARE THE "KIM DYNASTY"?

From Left: Kim Il-Sung, Kim Jong-Il, Kim Jong-Un

The "**Kim Dynasty**" is a tongue-in-cheek expression that refers to the absolute power of the **North Korean leadership**, which has been passed down for three generations, termed so because it's something you'd see in the dynastic era. Ever since he was named the first leader of the provisional communist government set up in the North by the Soviet Union after the division of Korea in 1945, he never gave up his ambition to unify Korea under a communist government.

As a result, he started the Korean War and committed numerous atrocities against the South, including military provocations and terrorist attacks on civilians. Domestically, he showed outstanding ability in political maneuvering. He further consolidated his absolute power through the reign of terror and ruthlessly purging political opponents who threatened his throne. Through ***Juche Sasang* 주체사상** "Juche Ideology," which adopted and modified the communist ideology to be in line with North Korea's situation, the North Korean society developed a cult of individuality and worshipped him by calling ***suryongnim* 수령님** ("Great Leader"). When he suddenly died in 1994, his body was embalmed and placed in a public mausoleum at the **Kumsusan Palace of the Sun 금수산 태양궁전** as has been the case with many other idolized communist leaders.

As a result of Kim Il-sung's death, his son Kim Jong-il was named leader after him, and was revered as ***widaehan yongdoja* 위대한 영도자** ("Great Leader"). Kim Jong-ile was determined (or does it run in the family?) to carry on the late father's grand ambition to communize the South with force, and made numerous provocations such as terrorist attacks against the South Korean civilians (a Korean Air Flight 858 exploded in mid-air by a bomb set up by 2 North Korean spies), launching missiles, as well as developing nuclear missiles.

After Kim Jong-il's unexpected death was announced in 2011, his son Kim Jong-un, took over power and was immediately revered as a ***choego yongdoja* 최고 영도자** ("Supreme Leader"). And because he studied in Switzerland as a child and experienced capitalism and freedom, people expected that he would lead North Korea to eventually open up, but instead, he chose the path of ruthless dictatorship like his ancestors. As of 2019, North Korea is recognized as a "de facto nuclear power" by the international community, which the three-generation regime has been using as a tactic to maintain its existence. In 2018, Kim Jong-un had an Inter-Korea summit with South Korea's **President Moon Jae-in** to discuss the official ending of the Korean War. The same year a U.S.-North Korea summit with President Donald Trump took place to discuss the possibility of completely abandoning nuclear weapons in return for massive economic aid while guaranteeing the existence of the Kim Jong-un regime. Permanent peace on the Korean Peninsula seemed to be within reach, but due to the wide disagreements on the terms, no tangible results have come from the negotiation at this time.

WHAT IS THE "BAEKDU BLOODLINE"?

***Bakedu heyoltong* 백두혈통** ("Baekdu Bloodline.") The term "**Baekdu**" comes from **Baekdusan** 백두산 ("Mount Baekdu,") a sacred, and the tallest mountain, on the Korean Peninsula, which North Korea claims to be the base of **Kim Il-sung**'s anti-Japanese activities, as well as the birthplace of **Kim Jong-il**. However, critics claim that these words were entirely made up by Kim Il-sung's son, Kim Jong-il, to justify the succession of power within the family. In 2013 the Ten Principles for the Establishment of a Monolithic Ideological System proclaimed,"The supreme leader in North Korea can only be of Baekdu Bloodline," and **Kim Jong-un**'s power is expected to remain for a considerable amount of time.

DID YOU KNOW THAT KOREA IS STILL AT WAR?

Although the Korean Armistice Agreement was signed on July 27th, 1953, no peace treaty was signed, which means technically, South and North Korea are still at war. In 2018, the leaders of South and North Korea met at the **Demilitarized Zone (DMZ)** to discuss the matter.

WHY DO KOREAN MALES HAVE TO GO TO THE MILITARY?

All Korean males, including your favorite K-Pop idol ***oppa***, who have reached the age of 18, and meet a certain level of physical, mental, and academic requirements, are required to serve in the military for a minimum of 18 months (more for Navy and Air Force). The timing of enlistment may be deferred for reasons permitted by the law. Also, if you win an international competition/sports competition (such as the Olympics and music competition) or a certain level of prize set forth by the law, you are exempted from military service (but you will still be required to receive basic military training for four weeks). If it's difficult to serve in the military for various reasons, alternative service can be performed, such as public service personnel or working at a designated enterprise selected by the Commissioner of the Military Manpower.

How much do soldiers get paid? As of 2020, a newly joined private will receive ₩408,100 won (about $380 USD) a month, which is 50% of the minimum wage set by the law. While in the military, anyone, including entertainers, can't engage in commercial activities such as appearing on TV or performing at concerts, and it causes significant damage to those who are at their prime (of course it does the same to any other Korean males, for that matter). Fans of globally renowned K-Pop bands have petitioned to consider applying the exemption rule to treat their achievements the same as having won a prize at an international music competition and thus elevated the country's reputation but to no avail.

The mandatory military service also creates a number of social issues. Some of the rich and the powerful were called on the carpet for using dishonest methods to have their sons exempted from military enlistment.

WHAT IS DMZ? THE SCARIEST PLACE ON EARTH!

The Demilitarized Zone in Korea

Three ROK soldiers watching the border at Panmunjeom in the DMZ between North and South Korea.

DMZ viewed from the North

What is the scariest place you can think of? A haunted house? That's cute. According to Bill Clinton, the **Demilitarized Zone (DMZ)** is the scariest place on earth. The DMZ is a 4 km-long (up 2 km north and down 2 km south from the **Military Demarcation Line** (**MDL**) neutral zone created as a result of the armistice agreement in 1953 and is the most heavily-guarded border on Earth. While military activities of any type are strictly prohibited here, this is where one of the Earth's most intense confrontations is taking place, even at this very moment. The descendants of the sworn enemies - North Korean soldiers, South Korean soldiers, and the United Nations forces, are watching each other around the clock, separated by a massive minefield and barbed wire fences. The tension and stress are so enormous that a single mistake could easily trigger a shootout and lead to a full-blown war. Anyone standing here would agree with what Bill Clinton said.

***Gongdong Gyeongbi Guyeok JSA* 공동경비구역**
(*Joint Security Area*, 2000)

JOINT SECURITY AREA – SLEEPING WITH THE ENEMY

Called the "**Military Armistice Commission Joint Security Area (JSA)**," or "**판문점 Panmunjom**," it's an area located along the Military Demarcation Line in the Demilitarized Zone. It was set up at the headquarters of the Military Armistice Commission in October 1953 to facilitate the smooth operation of the meeting by the U.N. Forces, the Chinese People's Assistance Force, and the North Korean military during the cease-fire. And this is where the armistice agreement was signed (the original location at that time is a little different from now because it was located slightly above the MDL). Inside the Joint Security Area, there are about 10 buildings, including the main hall of the Military Armistice Commission, the **Panmungak 판문각** on the North Korean side, and the **Jayueuijip 자유의집** ("House of Freedom"), on the U.N. side. Initially, the area was jointly guarded by the U.N. and North Korean forces. In 1976, after an ax-murder incident by the North Korean military, the North areas are guarded by the North's military and the UN areas guarded by the U.N. forces (since 2014, South Korea is in charge of guarding the area). **The 2019 Koreas–United States DMZ Summit** was also held at the House of Freedom. The JSA is probably the most symbolic place of Korea's division where Koreans are put in different military uniforms due to ideological differences and point a gun at each other. It's possible to visit the JSA through a group tour, but for those who can't, I highly recommend watching this amazing movie titled ***Gongdong Gyeongbi Guyeok JSA* 공동경비구역 (*Joint Security Area*, 2000)** as an alternative.

CAN NORTH KOREANS AND SOUTH KOREANS UNDERSTAND EACH OTHER?

Yes and no. Basically, both South and North Korea speak Korean with minor differences. Because they have identical grammar rules, including word order and sentence composition, they are not considered two different languages, but instead different types of Korean dialects from each other's point of view, with differences in intonation, pronunciation, but above all, the use of words. For example, the South Korean language actively accepts foreign words and uses them as they are, while the North Korean language uses foreign words in "pure Korean." Of course, many of the same Korean words also use different terms. The difference further diverges when using professional lingo, and communication can become difficult as if they were speaking two different languages. In sum, South Koreans and North Koreans can communicate, but it can get difficult from time to time.

	SOUTH KOREA	**NORTH KOREA**
Tunnel	터널 Tunnel	차굴 *chagul* "Car Tunnel"
Front Light	헤드라이트 Headlight	앞등 *apdeung* "Front Light"
Mother-in-Law	시어머니 *shieomeoni*	아고 *ago*

LOST IN TRANSLATION

WHAT ARE SOME KOREAN DIALECTS?

Gyeongsang-do 경상도 dialect is tonal, which means the intonation or pitch in which a sound is spoken affects the meaning. Also, many sentences are spoken in a literary style and end with "*~da*" "**~다**," "*no*" "**~노**," and "*na*" "**~나**."

Chungcheong-do 충청도 dialect is perceived to be slower than other dialects, even in emergency situations. But it actually sounds like that because the end of the sentence is drawn out. Also, sentences end with "*~yeo*" "**~여**," "*~gyeo*" "**~겨**," and "*~yu*" "**~유**." For example, "*haesseoyo*" "“**했어요**" ("I did") is "*haesseoyu-*" "**했어유**," with the end drawn out.

Jeolla-do 전라도 dialect has a variety of accent-heavy rejoinders, such as "*atta*" "**아따**," (boy/gee!) and "*chammallo*" "**참말로**," (really/seriously). Also, many sentences end with "*ranke*" "**~랑께**," and "*bureo*" "**~부러**."

Jeju-do 제주도 dialect is the most unique one compared to others, as Jeju Island is separated from the inland by the sea. One of the examples is the structure of an interrogative sentence. "*-haetsseo?*" "-했어?" "did you do it?" is "*haen*?" "**~핸**?" in Jeju dialect. ***Eoseo oseyo*** "**어서오세요**" "Welcome," is ***honjeo opseo***" "**혼저옵서**" in Jeju dialect.

WHY DO KOREANS SAY "I GO" SO MUCH?

Why do Korean people say "**I go**" even when they are not going anywhere? What you hear is ***aigo/aigu*** **아이고/아이고** , which is an interjection for "oops" or "oh, man," which can be used to show frustration, embarrassment, and surprise, like when you drop something or see someone hit their pinky toe on the furniture! It can also be used when you are scolding someone. For example, "***Aigoo***! Did you catch a cold? Didn't I tell you to bundle up?"

DOUBLE CHECK!
KOREAN YES/NO DOESN'T ALWAYS MEAN YES/NO!

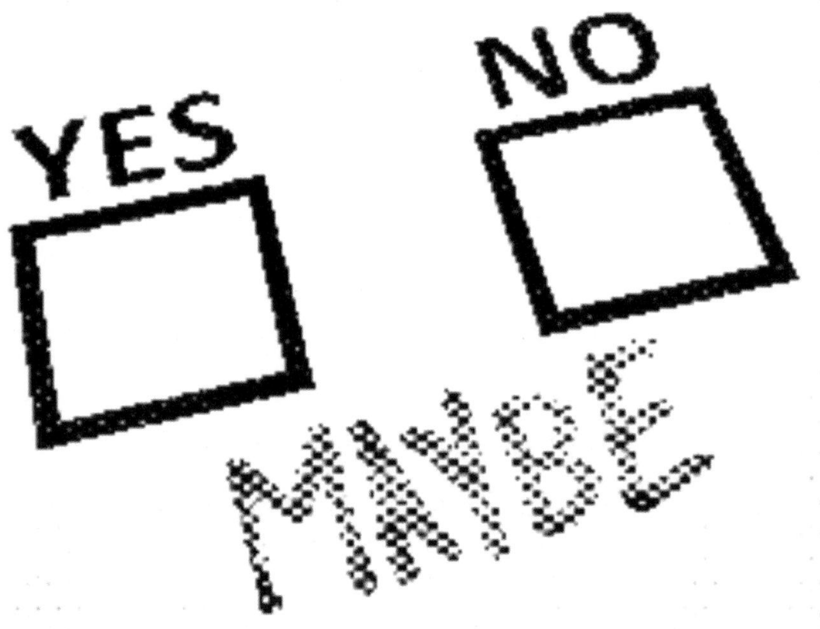

English Teacher: "You didn't do your homework?"
Korean Student: "No, teacher."
English Teacher: "What? You're going to fail the class then."
Korean Student: "Why? I did my homework."
English Teacher: "You just said you didn't do your homework."
Korean Student: "No teacher, I said I did my homework."
English Teacher: Okay, let's take a roll. Cheol-su? Isn't Cheol-su here?
Korean Student: Yes, teacher.
English Teacher: Well, I don't see him? Where is he?
Korean Student: I said Cheol-su is not here, teacher!

Do you see what's going on here? In the first case above, what the Korean student meant was "No, I did do my homework, teacher, and in the second example the implied answer was, "Yes, Cheol-su isn't here, teacher." As you can see, the Korean student has negated the sentence as a whole, while the English teacher was focusing on the action. So when you talk to a Korean speaker in English, it's best to double-check. Isn't this confusing? Yes? No? Is that the Korean Yes or No?

"PUSAN" AND "BUSAN" AND "CHANG" AND "JANG" WHY THE DIFFERENT SPELLINGS FOR THE SAME NAME?

PUSAN International Film Festival

17th BUSAN International Film Festival 4-13 October, 2012

Until 2011, the **Pusan International Film Festival** (**PIFF**) was held in **Busan**, rather than **Pusan**. At first glance, it seems like Pusan and Busan are two different places, with similar-sounding names. But in reality, they are exactly the same place, with a slightly different spelling. Why the disparity? The root cause of this issue is that there have been two romanization systems for the Korean language. The old one was called "**McCune-Reischauer System**," used between the period of 1984 and 2000, which used K for Korean consonants ㄱ, T for ㄷ, P for ㅍ, and CH for ㅈ. The current "**Revised Romanization System**" uses G for ㄱ, D for ㄷ, B for ㅍ, and J for ㅈ, because many linguists argued that it describes the sound more precisely. When Pusan International Festival first started in 1996, Pusan was the proper way, and until 2011 when the event committee decided to change the official name in accordance with the revised system, the disparity persisted. More examples – in old Korean books written in English, you can find ***gimchi*** in place of ***kimchi***, and for Korean last names, Jang was spelled Chang, Jo as Cho, and so on. The confusion coming from the coexistence of two different systems has been causing a major headache for foreigners traveling to Korea (you'd be appalled if you were relying on an outdated tour book for Pusan only to find out that there's no such place!), but things are getting better as the old system is phasing out.

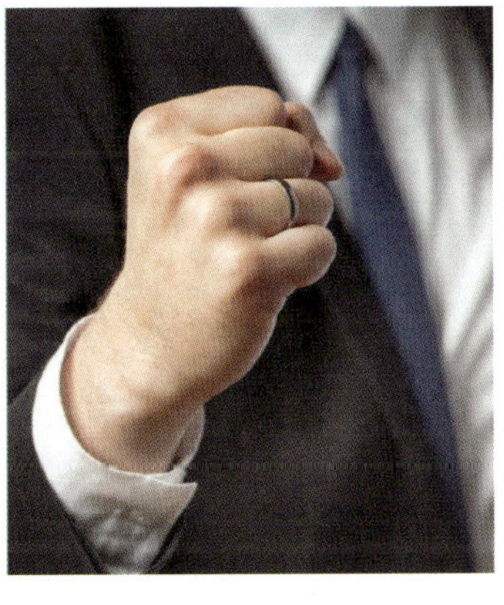

WHY DO KOREANS MAKE A FIST WHEN TAKING A PICTURE?

I hate to sound like a broken record, but remember? Koreans are the people with a "can-do" spirit, and ***hwaiting*** **화이팅** (Fighting/Let's go!) is an expression frequently used in everyday conversation. This fist-making gesture is the symbol of resolution and determination because there's nothing like saying *hwaiting*, to promote harmony and unity among the Korean people.

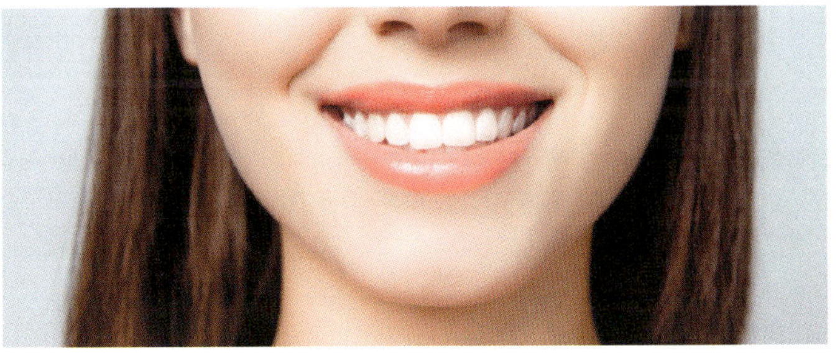

YOU SAY CHEESE? KOREANS SAY *KIMCHI*!

Of course, saying *kimchi* is another popular option because it makes the corners of your mouth turn up and smile, same as saying cheese or whisky (or whiskey, for your Irish readers).

WHY ARE KOREANS ALWAYS IN A HURRY?

When asked about the most impressive characteristics of Koreans, foreigners always pick ***bbali bbali* 빨리빨리** ("*quickly, quickly*") as their number one answer. Besides ***hwaiting* 화이팅**, the expression of the Korean "can-do" spirit, *ppali ppali* is the "Let's get it done fast" spirit, which shows the efficiency-oriented nature of the Korean people. Some say that's what made it possible for the nation to recover so quickly from the scars of war, but it has its downside too. Because it puts speed over everything else, taking a shortcut by bending rules and not sticking to the manual was common and often overlooked. As a result, it led to poor quality work and some man-made disasters that took the lives of many innocent people. But Koreans learned quickly from their mistakes and such practices are starting to fade away as the compliance with workplace rules is strictly enforced and monitored today. Now, let's look at some of the positive aspects which the *ppali ppali* spirit contributed to.

WHY ARE KOREAN DELIVERIES SO FAST?

CHINESE DELIVERY AND THE ICONIC "STEEL CONTAINER"

Koreans had been enjoying food delivery from way before Smartphones appeared. Among the most popular was **Chinese food delivery**, with the iconic ***cheolgabang* 철가방** "steel container," a delivery container used by Chinese restaurants. Whether you're picnicking at Hangang or at a PC Bang, there's nothing to worry - this *cheolgabang* man will find you.

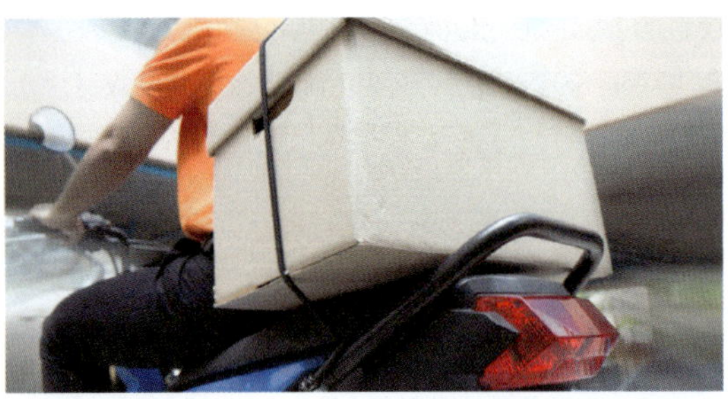

QUICK SERVICE!

We are talking about the possibility of flying drones delivering your stuff, but in Korea, there is quick service! It's a private courier service, who safely and quickly deliver anything from documents to a large container box - they will get the job done, in less than an hour, tops!

TAEKBAE – 1 DAY SHIPPING

Korean ***taekbae* 택배** (parcel service) is extremely reliable and fast. Place an order today, and you can expect your *taekbae* package to arrive at your door smiling the next day.

SUPER FAST INTERNET

According to the survey reports by the Internet speed-testing agencies Akamia, OOKLA, Cable, Korea has one of the fastest Internet, being the only country with an average speed of over 25Mbps in 2017.

WHY DO KOREANS LOVE INTERNET EXPLORER?

Just up until the early 2010s, Internet Explorer (IE) was pretty much the only browser used in Korea. For this reason, many web sites, including e-government systems, banking, and a majority of online games were developed for the IE, using non-standard codes and Active X which had died out long ago. As a result, some of those outdated pages are still causing compatibility issues and give Korean people (and foreigners!) a major headache.

WHAT IS "OFFICIAL ID CERTIFICATE" FOR ONLINE USE IN KOREA?

Known as ***gongin injeungseo* 공인인증서** "Official ID Certificate," it's a type of digital ID-card used for various online activities including online banking and shopping. While it sounds like an awesome way to prevent digital fraud, there are many hoops to jump through to get it. Also maintaining it (has to be renewed each year with a fee), and using it (sometimes you have to install the visiting site's proprietary software) are quite pesky, too.

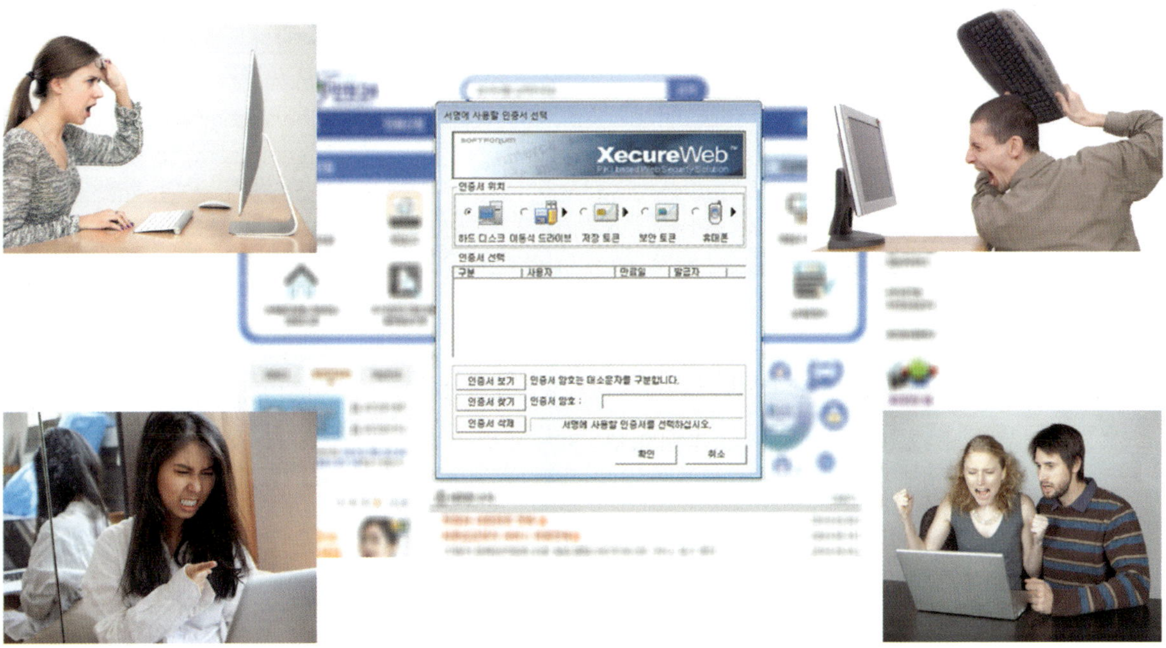

GOOGLE IT? YOU MEAN LOOK IT UP ON NAVER?

NAVER

Google is a household name for an Internet search engine in the US, but if you say "Google it," then people will most likely whip out their smartphone and open the green app called Naver and make a search query in the green box.

WHY DO KOREANS SAY THEY ARE A NATION OF "PURE BLOODED KOREANS"?

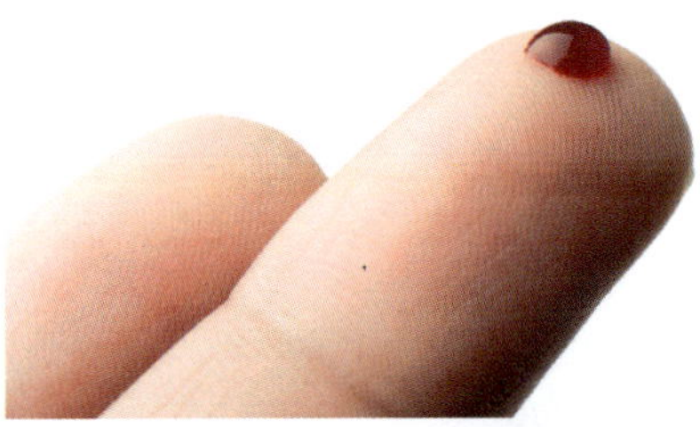

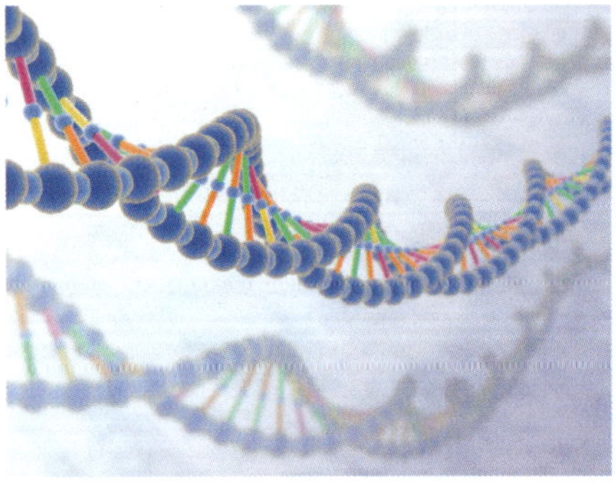

The phrase, "Korea is a single-race/homogeneous nation," is something that Koreans have learned through the curriculum, and it's an idea that's so deeply embedded that no one would feel the need to give it a second thought. Since the country's first nation, **Gojoseon 고조선**, Koreans have lived as the main members of the nation, calling themselves ***Baedal Minjok* 배달 민족** ("The *Baedal* People"), where *Baedal* refers to "ancient Korea," speaking same language, sharing the same history and cultural background, unlike other countries made up of many different ethnic groups. So this idea of "single-race/homogeneous nation" has also been interpreted as "pure-blooded." So are Koreans really "**pure-blooded**," and made up of only Koreans? The latest DNA findings by Professor Kim Wook of Dankook University's Department of Bioscience say something different about this commonly held myth. According to research, Koreans have the genotypes common in **Mongolians** and **Eastern** and **Southern Siberians**, as well as the genotypes common in **Southeast Asians** and **Southern** and **Northern Chinese people**. And Koreans were most genetically similar to the Manchurian people in Northeastern China, and partially similar to the **Chinese Miao** people and **Southeast Asians** such as **Vietnam**. This shows that the Korean people are largely a mixed race between the **Northern** and **Southern regions** (which is actually not surprising, considering that Korea was invaded near 1,000 times throughout history). Then why did this myth emerge? These concepts, sometimes seen as insular and nationalistic, was a national philosophy that held the Korean people together like a coagulant during the foreign invasions and the Japanese Occupation. Historians say that it should be thought of as a "cultural lineage" which people on the Korean Peninsula share, rather than a concept of "bloodline." Recently, the immigrant population in Korea has been rapidly increasing, giving birth to multicultural families. And many argue that race shouldn't be about the looks but the culture which one identifies with, therefore they should also be considered as part of the "single Korean race" if they are absorbed into Korean culture and embrace the Korean lifestyle.

WHY DO KOREANS HOLD THEIR NECK WHEN THEY GET OFF THEIR CARS FROM A MINOR FENDER-BENDER?

Young-mi, a college girl, zones out behind the wheel for a fraction of a second and bonk! It's a fender bender. It can't be too bad, it was more like a little push! She gets out of the car to assess the damage and luckily there's not even a hint of a scratch on the bumper - no need to call the police or insurance company! But guess what? The ***ajusshi* 아저씨** from the other car gets out, holding the back of his neck, with his face contorted with pain! Wait a minute… You can't be serious, right? And the *ajusshi* insists that he goes to a hospital and gets treated for a while. No matter how big or small the accident is, it's a cliché scene in Korean dramas. Of course, the neck is the most vulnerable part of the body susceptible to damage in a car accident, but why the oversell in the little harmless "contact" between two cars? These people, known as "**nylon** (a type of synthetic fiber, carries the negative connotation of being "fake") **patients**," seek to receive a large amount of settlement money from the insurance company of the driver at fault by faking their injuries. Doing so is taking advantage of the legal loophole - if a medical certificate is issued by a (corroborating) medical institution, the driver at fault will be responsible even if it's suspected of insurance fraud, and it's more likely to happen to female drivers.

DAERIGISA - DRUNK? DON'T DRIVE AND CALL THE "DRIVER FOR HIRE"

It goes without saying that drinking and driving is a very dangerous act. But in Korea, you don't have to worry because there is a service that allows you to hire a driver who drives on your behalf when you drink alcohol. ***daerigisa* 대리기사**, "driver-for-hire," is a very convenient service that comes to your location and drives to a requested location through a phone call or smartphone application. It's a popular after-work side job especially in this time of gig economy. Of course, many retired people find it a valid source of income, despite having to work in the wee hours and deal with the mean drunks.

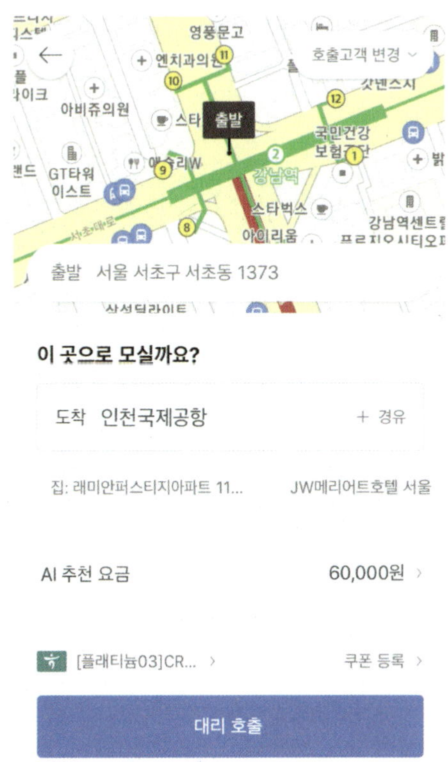

WHY DO KOREAN CARS HAVE BLUE SPONGES ON THEIR DOORS?

Driving around in Korea and you can see vehicles with little blue sponge blocks on their doors, and foreigners are curious about them because they aren't seen outside Korea. So, what are they? These little blue sponge blocks serve as a protection for the doors of the vehicle that's been newly released to the customer from the factory. Originally, the car manufacturer put them there to protect the vehicle from getting dents and dings in the lot from carelessly opening the door, but many owners decide to keep them because Korean parking lots are very narrow. It's a Korean way of being considerate of fellow drivers (and avoid having to pay for the repair for the damage caused).

WHY DO KOREANS TAKE A POOP SQUATTING?

Squat is the king of leg exercises, and Koreans have long been practicing this workout not at the gym but in the bathroom! While still found in some parts of Seoul and many parts in rural Korea, many young Koreans, and foreign tourists especially coming from the West, find it difficult to adjust to the different defecation apparatus, although it had been used in all parts of the world, including Southern Europe and Africa (it's called "French toilets" in some parts of the Middle East" and "Turkish toilets" in Western Europe). With the modernization effort, the Western-style "sit toilets" are replacing the "squatter toilets," and there's a rumor that the average leg strength of the Korean people has also been declining.

WHY DO KOREAN RESTROOMS ASK YOU TO TOSS TOILET PAPER IN A BASKET?

After doing your business (#2), you need to dispose of the used toilet paper. It's pretty much commonsense to just toss it into the toilet and flush them all down, but in some public bathrooms in Korea you might find a sign saying "Please toss the toilet paper in the trash can." This doesn't sound too appealing, right? Well, the reason for this practice is because many Korean public bathrooms, in order to conserve water, limit the water tank capacity under a certain level, and the amount of water used per flush is comparatively weaker than regular home toilets. To prevent toilet blockage, they recommend using the trash can instead. However, not only is it unsightly, it also poses a potential danger to public health. Nowadays, public bathrooms use more dissolvable toilet paper, and the flush-them-altogether method is becoming the norm.

WHY ARE CLEAVAGES A NO-NO! BUT MINISKIRTS ARE OK?

What's too "racy" or "revealing," according to your own standards? If you come from the West, the Korean notion is strikingly different from that of the West. In Korea, showing legs is okay, and recently, ***haeuishiljong* fashion 하의실종 패션** ("missing-pants fashion," or the "full-Donald") was all the rage among girls in Korea, and no one batted an eye. However, Korean girls are more conservative with their upper body, and clothes that reveal too much cleavage are considered too "racy," which is pretty much the opposite in the West. Some foreign fashion brands said they received a request to raise the V-neck line to cater to the needs of the Korean female consumers.

WHY ARE GUNS/KNIVES/TATTOOS BLURRED ON TV?

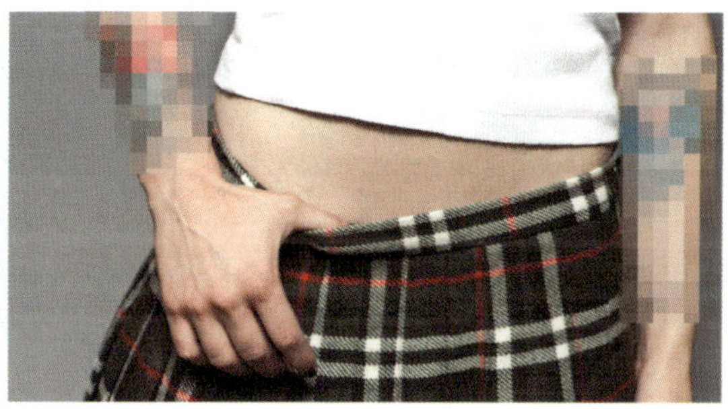

The rules set by **Korea Communications Standards Commission** prohibit but allow the following only if absolutely necessary for plot development.

Graphic depiction of : Beheading/decapitation and dismemberment / Scenes of brutal killing or direct physical damage using firearms, knives, and other murder tools / Mutilated body/body parts

Also blurred are **smoking scenes**, because the rules stipulate that: Broadcasting shall endeavor to create a sound civic spirit and lifestyle, and shall be careful when dealing with matters such as lewdness, decadence, drugs, drinking, smoking, superstition, gambling, profligacy, and etc.

As for **tattoos**, there are no rules that outright prohibit them from being displayed on TV, but TV stations voluntarily blur them out because it could still be under a related rule which stipulates: "Juvenile Viewing Protection Time Zone" should consider the emotional development of the audience.

Will it stay this way forever? Many doubt it. In the past, dyed hair of idol singers was prohibited to a degree where they had to hide their colorful hair with **bandanas** or **hats**, but the restrictions are long gone. On top of that, modern viewers complain that the current restrictions prevent them from fully appreciating the story.

THEN WHY ARE BRANDS/LOGOS BLURRED?

On the other hand, brands and logos are blurred and masked despite posing no potential threat/harm to the viewers. The reason they are hidden from viewing is due to business contracts with the program sponsors. The producers pay careful attention to prevent displaying the brands inadvertently other than those under contract. In some TV shows, you can see product-placement marketing (more widely referred to as "PPL" in Korea) in action, such as certain drink bottles placed on the table in front of the talk show panelists.

WHY DO KOREAN TV SHOWS HAVE SUBTITLES?

"Bam!" "Whack!" "LOL!" "You gotta be kidding!" Doesn't watching Korean variety TV shows, full of speech/thought bubbles and subtitles, feel like reading a comic book? First used in Japanese variety TV shows for added fun, a Korean producer introduced the system to the Korean viewers in the 1990s. At the beginning, it wasn't received well by the Korean viewers, but it's now an essential part of Korean variety shows. Not only does it provide relevant information like the names of the guests to the show, it also serves as a guide for the viewers to keep up with the plot development, in case it goes unnoticed. What makes it more interesting is that different shows have different flavors, depending on the styles of the show screenwriter. ***Muhandojeon* 무한도전 (*Infinity Challenge*, MBC, 2005)** is one of the shows that attracted a huge fan base thanks to the witty subtitles.

WHAT IS KAKAOTALK THAT EVERYBODY USES?

Katok hae*! 카톡해!** (Kakaotalk me!) has replaced “call me” in Korea, where everybody seems to be communicating through the iconic yellow smartphone app. Originally developed as a free instant messaging application, it now has numerous convenient services like voice talk, video chat, and group chat. Among all, a huge selection of emoticons that Koreans love to use to express their emotions is what sets them apart from other competitors. As of 2017, it’s used by 93% of Korean smartphone owners (de facto monopoly), and it keeps expanding into new markets with auxiliary services, including taxi-hailing, ***daerigisa (driver for hire) booking service, banking, and gifticons (electronic vouchers).

WHY DO KOREANS LOVE "KKK"?

If you have a Korean pen-pal, oops, we’re in 2020, so chat-pal, rather, then you might have received a message saying “**KKK**” from your Korean friend. Wait a minute… Is this a secret invitation to the notorious hate group? It possibly can’t be…! But you get more confused as you keep receiving the same message over and over… One day you take up the courage and decide to confront your friend, and learn that it’s totally different from what you thought - it’s actually the romanized spelling of **ㅋㅋㅋ**, the Korean equivalent of **LOL**. Why does your friend use it for someone who’s not Korean? Maybe your friend is too lazy to switch the keypad from Eng-Kor, or he/she thinks you are capable of understanding Korean. Now you know that your Korean chat-pal is completely innocent and is, well, just [laughing out loud in Korean]!

WHY DO KOREANS GET SO MUCH PLASTIC SURGERY?

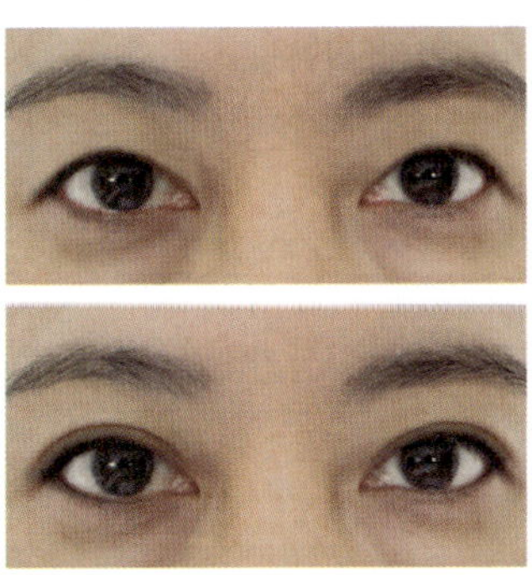

"Women are never guilty of their transformation." It's a popular copy line from a 1980s South Korean TV commercial. It wittily captures, not just women, but our basic desire for beauty, but also implies Korean people's tendency to put a lot of weight on the looks. As many foreigners believe, plastic surgery is very popular in Korea and is easily accessible to anyone, including foreigners who come to visit Korea just for that. But for many Koreans, it's not just the aesthetics they are after. The traditional belief of ***gwansang*** (physiognomy), which asserts that the harmony of the facial features determines a person's fate, play a role in the desire Naturally, a features determines a person's fate, play a role in the desire Naturally, a great number of people want to "improve" their appearance, as well as their odds, through simple plastic surgery before important events like a job interview. Only God knows how much of an impact that has on the interviewer, but if one can gain confidence from their "improved" look and live their life to the fullest every day, then their fate should be brighter than before. The double eyelid surgery and nose jobs, raising the tip of the nose and the nose bridge, are the most popular.

WHY DO KOREANS WEAR FACE MASKS?

Earth burned to the ground by nuclear war and those who survived live on wearing masks. These post-apocalypse scenes have long been a reality in Korea, where people embraced wearing masks as an essential part of their daily lives. The main culprit is the **fine dust** or **particulates matter**, partly coming from the factories located in China that use coal as energy, and partly from within Korea, as well as car exhaust fumes. Another major cause is the "**Yellow Dust**," where the dry soil particles from China and the Mongolian deserts get picked up to form dust storms. Ironically, the habit of mask-wearing played an important role in preventing the spread of pandemics such as the COVID-19 and MERS-CoV.

WHAT THE HECK DOES "GANGNAM STYLE" MEAN?

오빠 강남스타일! *"Oppa Gangnam Style!"* When the song "Gangnam Style" became a global hit back in 2012, everybody hummed and danced to the line "*Oppa Gangnam Style*," while doing the horse-riding dance. But 99% of the non-Koreans didn't know what *Gangnam Style* even meant, like how we danced to the tunes of the song "Macarena" when it was all the craze back in the days. Many non-Spanish speakers didn't have a clue what "Macarena" was. So, what the heck does *Gangnam Style* mean?

Gangnam 강남 means "**Region south of 한강 Hangang (the Han River)**," because *gang* 강 means "river," and *nam* 남 means "south" but often used to refer to the **most affluent area of Seoul**, also known as the "Gangnam 3(sam)-gu," which consists of **Gangnam-gu, 강남구, Seocho-gu 서초구**, and **Songpa-gu 송파구**. They are known for their house prices that are the highest in Korea, and the highest proportion of rich people in Korea, although a lot of "old money" *chaebol* families live in the north of the river, called Gangbuk 강북.

Gangnam (not to be confused with the singer with the same name) is the epitome of Korean affluence for its luxury boutiques, high-end department stores, entertainment establishments, and highly concentrated infrastructure, and often likened to Beverly Hills in the U.S. and Roppongi in Japan. It's a place where emerging CEOs, owners of small and medium-sized companies, and celebrities live. For many, having an apartment in Gangnam is equivalent to living a successful life. On the contrary, in Korean pop culture, people living in Gangnam are often depicted as snobs who only care about money.

Gangnam development was the first large-scale project of the development of a "planned city" in Korea and also the most successful example that has completely shifted the economic center of the nation. One of the main reasons as to why the south of the river was selected was due to the proximity factor from the Demilitarized Zone (DMZ), the borderline separating North and South Korea. To stay as far away as possible from the possible attack from the North, Gangnam was chosen as a strategically ideal place for development. So, back to the original question, "*Oppa Gangnam Style*!" can be translated as ***"Look at me, I'm ballin'!"***

HONG GIL DONG – THE JOHN DOE OF KOREA

Hong Gil-dong 홍길동 was the head of bandits in the Chungcheong-do area during the Joseon Dynasty, but he's more well known as the fictional character in the novel ***Honggildongjeon* '홍길동전'** (The Story of Hong Gil-dong) written by **Heo Gyun 허균**, which portrays him as a "righteous outlaw" who punishes corrupt officials and helps the poor, like **Robin Hood**. But the above story has little to do with the fact that his name is used as THE default generic name for official documents and forms. Then why Mr. Hong? There's no cut-and-dry rule as to designating it as the official placeholder name, but according to the person familiar with the subject, it might be because it meets the following criteria.

Such name must:

- Be well-known to everyone.
- Be the name of a fictional character so people mistake it for a real name (although he was a real person, most people think of the fictional character).
- Avoid historical characters to avoid possible claims from their descendants.
- Have a good public image and do not cause repulsion.

In addition, in the Korean alphabet system, which consists of consonants, vowels, and ***batchim* 받침** (final consonant that goes at the bottom of the syllable configuration), each syllable of his name Hong Gil-dong has all three components, thus suitable for an example. And who's the Korean Jane Doe? **Hong Gil-sun 홍길순**.

What Does A Korean Name Stand For? How Can I Decode it? P. 22

SYMBOL OF LOYALTY - JINDO DOG

Jindo 진도 dogs, a symbol of **Jindo Island** in **South Jeolla Province**, are known for their bravery, cleverness, and loyalty. Even when they meet wild animals in the mountains, they will never back down. And because they have the tendency of serving only one owner, it's very difficult for them to be adopted by another owner. There was a story that a Jindo dog returned to the original owner's house over a distance of more than 300 kilometers (186 miles) over seven months. The Jindo breed was designated as the **53rd 'Natural Treasure' of South Korea** in 1962.

EVERY KID'S DREAM - MAKE MONEY PLAYING VIDEO GAMES IN KOREA

It's every kid's dream – make money, not just some pocket money but a fortune, playing video games! Sounds too good to be true, right? Well, in Korea, video games (mostly PC games) are officially recognized by the government as "**eSports**," and professional gamer is a legitimate occupation that you can proudly put down on your resume. For example, **Lee Sang-hyeok**, a legendary '**League of Legends**' player better known by his in-game name "**Faker**," collected more than $1.2 million USD as his prize money from over 40 tournaments around the world in 2019 alone. Not only that, but team SKT, run by the namesake conglomerate, also got his back with a hefty salary. Add up the income he earns from endorsements and commercials, the number only gets bigger. Another iconic professional gamer known around the globe and is **Lim Yo-hwan**, better known as his in-game ID "**SlayerS_`BoxeR**" which he used for the real-time strategy game '**Starcraft**.' They were revered among the teenagers as heroes, and many kids put down "pro-gamer" as their dream job. Back in the heyday when eSports was at its prime, there were multiple cable TV channels dedicated to broadcasting video game tournaments. There were a lot of teams sponsored and managed by large firms, and the salary was similar to that of top sports players. In 2014, the final round of the world's most prestigious 'League of Legends' eSports competition was held at Seoul World Cup Stadium in Sangam, amid enthusiastic cheers from 40,000 spectators. Although "**YouTuber**" has replaced pro gamer as many kids' dream job, eSports is widely enjoyed by Koreans, regardless of age and gender.

PC BANG - THE TOTAL ENTERTAINMENT SOLUTION FOR THE DIGITAL GENERATION

If you're a fan of eSports, you might have wondered what the secret is behind the global dominance of the Korean players. Well, it's all about infrastructure! Anywhere you go, even in the most remote rural parts of Korea, they have a **PC bang 피씨방** (PC room). Once you enter, you will find a room full of computers, equipped with top-of-the-line hardware to cater to the needs of the gamers. With this, you might be hasty to come to the conclusion that these rooms, often large enough to hold hundreds of computers, are the secret training camp for the aspiring Korean gamers! You're partly right and partly wrong – because it's just an entertainment venue for those who want to kill some time playing games and also a decent dating spot. The best part? Most places have an awesome food selection, from self-service instant noodles to legitimate meals prepped by the PC bang staff. Sounds cool, right? For average couch potatoes like you and me, it's just awesome to have someone bring the meals while we're playing video games. Nowadays, some PC bangs even have shower and sleeping facilities, to cater to the needs of business people and hardcore gamers. For many, it's truly a home away from home.

"Everything about Korean PC Bang" by JAYKEEOUT x VWVB™

IT'S MIDNIGHT AND KIDS SHOULD BE AT HOME - "CINDERELLA LAW"

Do you know where your children are? **"The Cinderella Law/Act"** stipulates that **no access to PC games** should be allowed by the service providers to kids under the age of 16 during the late-night hours of between **12 a.m. to 6 a.m.**, and the in-game screens have to feature a warning sign about video game addiction.

MUKBANG - YOU CAN ALSO MAKE MONEY BROADCASTING YOUR EATING SESSION!

Becoming a pro-gamer seems like a long shot because you are all fingers and thumbs? Don't you give up just yet – there's another great opportunity to make money if you love food and have a healthy stomach! Known as ***mukbang* 먹방**, a compound word made up of ***meokneun* 먹는** ("eating") and ***bangsong* 방송** ("show/broadcast"), *mukbang* is a live online show/broadcast showing you eat! ! While the host of the show typically wows the viewers by eating typically wows the viewers by eating a large amount of food, which can be anything from instant noodles to super-sized pizza (**Tzuyang 쯔양** once ate 6 instant cup noodles in 10 minutes, and 170 McNuggets in one sitting), the main purpose of the show is to provide a vicarious gratification to the viewers and keep the solo diners company, and the fact that people watch other people eat on the screen accurately portrays the change in the lifestyle – it's a way of interacting with other people because you can join the chat screen on the side while being able to maintain personal space, perfect for young Koreans who are embracing the ***honsul/honbap* 혼술/혼밥** ("solo drinking/eating") culture. Famous *mukbang* stars make a lot of money, from YouTube advertisement revenue and donations from their fans. For instance, **MoonBoki 문복희** received over 1.8 million views on average on her YouTube channel alone. *Mukbang* has gained popularity around the globe, and many foreign YouTube personalities have been jumping on the bandwagon too.

TAEKWONDO

KOREAN MARTIAL ART AND NATIONAL SPORT

"The most difficult part of traditional Taekwondo is not learning the first kick or punch. It is not struggling to remember the motions of a poomsae or becoming acquainted with Korean culture. Rather, it is taking the first step across the threshold of the dojang door. This is where roads diverge, where choices are made that will resonate throughout a lifetime."

— Doug Cook, Taekwondo: A Path to Excellence

TAE	KWON	DO
"to stomp", "feet"	"to punch", "fist"	"discipline", "way"

"THE WAY OF THE HAND AND FOOT"

TAEKWONDO BY THE NUMBERS

MEMBER COUNTRIES	208
PEOPLE PRACTICING	OVER 80 MILLION
BLACK BELT HOLDERS	OVER 4 MILLION
TAE KWON DO STUDIOS IN KOREA	OVER 10,000

5 TENETS OF TAEKWONDO

COURTESY
예의 (*YE UI*)

INTEGRITY
염치 (*YEOM CHI*)

PERSEVERANCE
인내 (*IN NAE*)

SELF-CONTROL
극기 (*GUK GI*)

INDOMITABLE SPIRIT
백주불굴
(*BAEK JU BUL GUL*)

TAEKWONDO OATH

1. I shall **observe** the **tenets** of Tae Kwon Do
2. I shall **respect** my **instructor** and **seniors**
3. I shall **never misuse** Tae Kwon Do
4. I shall be a **champion** of **freedom** & **justice**
5. I shall **build** a more **peaceful world**.

1940's
1950's

FIRST SCHOOLS ESTABLISHED

Shortly after WWII, martial arts schools, named "*kwan* appear, but each *kwan* practices their own style of martial arts.

1952

EARLY FORMATION

South Korean President Syngman Rhee urges that the martial arts styles of the *kwans* be merged and standardized.

1959
1966

KTA AND ITF ESTABLISHED

Korea Taekwondo Association (KTA) is established to facilitate the unification of Korean martial arts.

In 1966, Choi Hong Hi establishes International Tae Kwon Do Federation (ITF), a separate entity incorporating his own style.

1973

WORLD TAEKWONDO FEDRATION

World Federation of Tae Kwon Do Is Established, with Kukkiwon 국기원 as headquarter.

2000

GLOBAL RECOGNITION

Tae Kwon Do becomes an official medal event at the 2000 games in Sydney

WHY ARE KOREAN WOMEN DOMINATING WOMEN'S GOLF?

Tune to any live golf tournament, I promise you that you will find a Korean name, if not names, on the leader board. As the four-time The **Ladies Professional Golf Association (LPGA)** champ, **Jessica Korda** said, "Korean women are dominating LPGA," and numbers back up her statement. From 1988 when **Ku Ok-hee 구옥희** became the first Korean to win the LPGA Tour, the trophy was lifted over 200 times by Korean female golfers, and the trend is likely to continue. So what's the secret behind the success of the Korean female golfers? It goes back to 1998, when **Pak Se-ri 박세리**, now a World Golf Hall of Famer, won the LPGA Tour with an incredible birdie shot. The victory meant so much to the Korean people who were suffering from the aftermath of the Asian Financial Crisis, or the "**IMF Era**." Many Koreans identified themselves with her and felt as if they won a difficult battle against the world. It was an inspiration and a consolation. Watching her rise to stardom, many Korean parents wanted their kids to become the next Pak Se-ri, and the generation of "**Pak Se-ri Kids**" became a reality. As of 2020, there are over 60 Korean golfers in the LPGA, a world of a difference from when Pak Se-ri was the only Korean player competing in the LPGA. Combined with the arduous training (we've already covered how zealous Korean parents are with education, so this should go without saying), and a large pool of aspiring players, the success is not that surprising.

WHY DO KOREANS DOMINATE ARCHERY?

The writing (painting) is on the wall! A Goguryeo mural painting ***muyongchong suryeopdo* 무용총 수렵도** depicts the Goguryeo people hunting animals with bow and arrow while writing on horseback.It looks so natural that many think the practice must have been a routine training activity for the bodies and the minds of Goguryeo people. In fact, ancient Chinese people used to call Korean people ***dong-i-jok*** 동이족 , which means "people who are good at shooting arrows." The DNA must have passed on to the descendants, which should explain why Korean archers dominate the world. And if the U.S. basketball team is the indomitable "Dream Team," the **Korean archery team** deserves the same status. The fact that the Korean archery team holds **12 of the 14 world records in the Olympic Games**, and sweeps the gold medals in world competitions, proves how formidable they are. The Korean archery team is a ruthless tyrant. Surprisingly, the Korean archery team wasn't all that good at the beginning. Until the 1970s, their performance was just so-so, compared to how Korea was doing in other sports. But with proper training methods, full support from the association, and the relentless efforts of the Korean archers, they were able to rise to the throne. Another important aspect is the creativity in their training methods – to cope with the loud noises coming from the audience, they practiced at a noisy baseball stadium full of audience, and even visited a cemetery at midnight, to have the nerves of iron. As a result, they developed the ability to maintain their cool, regardless of the situation. Awed by the Korean dominance, many foreign archery teams hired Korean coaches to transform their teams. At the 2016 Rio Olympics, 8 archery teams (Taiwan, Spain, Malaysia, USA, Japan, Mexico, Iran, Malawi) had Korean coaches.

WHO ARE THE "RED DEVILS"?

Seoul Plaza, 2002 FIFA World Cup

Founded in 1995, the original name was the '**Korea Supporters Club**,' and was renamed to ***bulgeun akma*** **붉은악마** the '**Red Devils**' in 1997. The name is said to have originated from the foreign media that used to call the **South Korean soccer team** who made it to the semifinals in a red uniform the "**Red Furious**" or the "**Red Devils**" at the 1983 U-20 World Cup (Fun fact, the nickname "Red Devils" was first used by the Belgian national soccer team). When the **2002 Korea-Japan World Cup** was held, the "Red Devils" earned the nickname the "12th player" thanks to their fervent cheering. Fueled by the Korean team's winning streak, the streets were flooded with people wearing red, and hundreds of thousands of people in red gathered at the **Seoul City Plaza** to cheer for the Korean team, creating a spectacular scene.

DID YOU KNOW THAT THUNDER STICKS WERE INVENTED BY KOREANS?

Have you ever wondered what it would be like to spend a day in the life of the hammer-wielding Norse God, Thor? With the mighty hammer *Mjolnir*, you can summon and control the powers of the storm. Among all, the coolest special effect must be the thunder and lightning combo which daunts all adversaries with its ear-splitting thunderclap. Well, if you envied his power, you can steal his thunder and experience the power yourself. In the early 1990s, a Korean firm invented and introduced the first generation of the so-called "Thunder Sticks" (a.k.a. Cheerstix, bangers, or bambams), made of polyethylene. It was a long tube to which air had to be blown into using a straw. It was then bent to form a V shape, and struck against each other, making noise that is 10 times louder than clapping. Despite its novelty, it also had a downside. The problem was that people just tossed away the straws they used to inflate the sticks. It made reusing the sticks cumbersome and created a huge pile of rubbish after an event. In 2001, another Korean firm introduced more eco-friendly sticks. Inspired by pool tubes, they used PVC for enhanced durability. The most significant improvement was that they could be inflated without a straw. To maximize user-friendliness, they installed air pumps at stadiums. After an event, they simply deflated the sticks and took them home to reuse during their next visit. They also gained popularity overseas. In 2002, the Anaheim Angels became the first to introduce these sticks to Major League Baseball. Fans loved them, and they became the hottest souvenir of the 2002 World Series. Today, you can see them used in many different occasions that attract large crowds such as political rallies or protests.Here is a fun fact about thunder sticks - In 1994, the LG Twins, the first team to introduce them, won the Korean Series (the Korean equivalent of the World Series). In 2002, the Anaheim Angels took home the World Series trophy, proving the mighty power of thunder!

WHY IS BASEBALL SO POPULAR IN KOREA?

Baseball is by far the most popular professional sport in Korea. The **Korean Baseball Organization (KBO)**, a professional baseball league in which 10 teams compete, attracts more than 10,000 spectators each game as of 2017. The history of Korean baseball goes back to when Philip Gillette, an American Christian missionary to Korea, introduced baseball to the members of the **Hwangseong Christian Youth Association** in 1905. As you may know, Koreans can learn things very quickly - The Korean baseball team won the **gold medal** at the **2008 Beijing Olympics**, third place in 2006, and was the runner-up in 2009 in the World Baseball Classic. At the **WSBC Premiere 12** held in 2015, they won the **championship** and finished runner-up in 2019. They also produced numerous star players who played in Major League Baseball and the stars who played in Major League Baseball also play in the KBO. In Korea, baseball is popular as a sport itself, but it's enjoyed more as a total entertainment experience. When you sing along to the cheering songs of your team, enjoy chicken and beer, and dance with the exciting cheerleaders' dance moves, it's the best way to laugh your stress away.

WHAT IS *SSIREUM*?

***Ssireum* 씨름** is a sport known to have been handed down from ancient times on the Korean Peninsula. On November 26th, 2018, South and North Korea jointly listed it as **UNESCO Intangible Cultural Heritage of Humanity**. It's a game in which two players, who stand on a sand arena with their waists wrapped with a ***satba* 샅바** (thigh band), grab the opponent's *satba* to knock or flip over the opponent with hand, leg or waist skills.It's a very simple game because it ends as soon as any part of the opponent's body except the sole of the foot touches the ground. It's also a sport of psychological warfare because one simple mistakc and miscalculation will lead to losing posture and balance. As a traditional sport, village-wide competitions were held during the holidays, and national competitions were broadcast on TV. The champion, called ***cheonha jangsa* 천하장사** ("The Strongest Man On Earth"), earned fame, honor and wealth. The popular entertainer and MC **Kang Ho-dong 강호동** is also a former *cheonha jangsa*. Recently, however, *ssireum* lost their fan base as the number of professional teams has declined as it failed to keep up with the latest trends. The younger audience tends to think of the sport as "outdated" and turned their eyes to Mixed Martial Arts.

JEJUDO

Jejudo 제주도, or **Jeju Island** is Korea's largest island off the southwest coast of the Korean Peninsula and is the most popular tourist destination for newlyweds, couples, and families. Palm trees, basalt, and beautiful beaches make exotic sights that are hard to see anywhere else in Korea.

Mt. Halla 한라산 stands tall at 1,947 meters high (6,387 feet) in the center of the island and is the highest mountain in South Korea. It was formed from a lava eruption at the end of the 3rd Cenozoic Era. On top of the mountain is a beautiful lake called **Baekrokdam 백록담**. While the mountain looks peaceful on the outside, it's actually dormant - the most recent volcanic activity was 1,000 years ago during the **Goryeo Dynasty**, according to history.

DOLHARUBANG

Hey, guys! My name is ***dolhareubang* 돌하르방!** (*dol* = "stone," ***hareubang*** = Jeju dialect for "grandfather/senior"). As the name suggests, we are statues carved from porous basalt (volcanic rock) and we can be as tall as three meters (10 ft)! Our face has bulging eyes, a long broad nose, and a hint of a smile. Like our friends ***jangseung* 장승**, you can find us outside of town gates, working 24/7, protecting the townspeople from the awful demons! We're very popular among women because we're a symbol of fertility - There's a myth that if pregnant women touch our nose, they will have a son. The way we place our hands has a meaning too. We rest them on the bellies, in sets of two, one higher than the other. If our left hand is higher, it symbolizes a writer/scholar, and a military figure if the right hand is placed higher. According to the ***Tamraji* 탐라지**, a historical town chronicle of Jeju Island, we made a debut in 1754, and some of our friends stood outside the Eastern, Western, and Southern gates of the Jeju City fortress as guardian deities. Today, we're made into awesome souvenirs, including chocolates, miniatures, and key chains!

What Are The Huge Korean Totem Poles In Korean Folk Villages? P. 211

HAENYEO : KOREAN MERMAIDS

There is a mermaid in Jeju Island! The women in the iconic black diving suit are called ***haenyeo* 해녀** ("Sea **Woman**"). Amazingly, they dive and collect seafood without oxygen tanks (there's a law set to prevent over-fishing and preserve the ecosystem, and as a result, their ability to hold their breath is outstanding). Thanks to the Jeju mermaids, we can enjoy local delicacies like abalone and sea cucumber!

GIFT IDEAS : WHAT DO TOURISTS BUY?

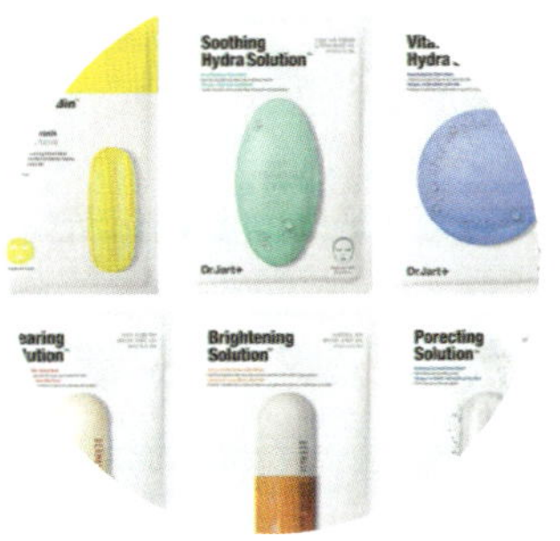

COSMETICS / BEAUTY MASKS

CHARACTER SOCKS

KOREAN LIQUOR

KOREAN SNACKS

K-POP CD/POSTERS

KOREAN RED GINSENG

KOREAN SEASONED SEAWEED

HANJI CRAFTS

HANBOK

KOREAN DOLLS

HONEY YUJA (CITRON) TEA

KEY RINGS/JEWELRY

SEOUL METRO FACTS

- World's longest multi-operator metro system by route length.
- Rated as one of the world's best subway systems by CNN and Jalopnik.
- Nearly all stations have platform screen doors, adding an extra layer of security.
- All lines are equipped with the T-money smart payment system which incorporates RFID and NFC technology for convenient and speedy automatic payment.
- It is the world's only subway system with full-color LCD screens that display real-time arrival time of trains.
- All stops are announced in Korean and English, and some major stops in Japanese, and Mandarin Chinese.

seoulmetro.co.kr

KOREAN BUSES - WHAT DO THE DIFFERENT COLORS MEAN?

BLUE	GREEN	RED	YELLOW
- TRUNK BUS	**- BRANCH BUS**	**- RAPID / EXPRESS BUS**	- CIRCULATION BUS
- LONGER DISTANCE	- SHORTER DISTANCE	- CONNECTS METROPOLITAN AREA TO DOWNTOWN SEOUL	- CIRCLES PARTS OF SEOUL AND STOP AT STATIONS NEAR ESSENTIAL AREAS LIKE BUSINESS, TOURIST, SHOPPING SPOTS
- CONNECTS SUBURBAN AREAS TO DOWNTOWN SEOUL	- CONNECTS MAJOR SUBWAY STATIONS / BUS TERMINALS OUTSIDE DOWNTOWN		

WHAT'S THE FASTEST GROUND TRANSPORTATION IN KOREA?

Korea Train eXpress (KTX)
330 km/h (205 mph)

letskorail.com

THE TALLEST BUILDING IN KOREA?

LOTTE WORLD TOWER
A 556-METER (1824 FT)
123-STORY SKYSCRAPER

Oppa

HALLYU
KOREAN WAVE

WHAT IS *HALLYU* 한류 (KOREAN WAVE)?

EARLY 1990s

SEO TAIJI AND BOYS - CHANGING THE HISTORY OF KOREAN MUSIC INDUSTRY

WATCH
Seo Taiji and Boys' Debut Performance

When discussing the history of K-Pop, the attempt is meaningless if it doesn't include **Seo Taiji and Boys**, because they were the pioneers who first transplanted American Pop to Korea. Fast beat music, rap, and powerful dance were something that no one had ever tried to put together on stage before. Were they way ahead of their time? When they first debuted in 1992, they received discouraging comments from critics. But it didn't take much time to prove them wrong. A huge fandom sprung up, and groups that imitate them begun to emerge in droves. And just like that, they became the touchstone of K-Pop, and the Korean music industry was forever changed. (For your information, **Yang Hyun-suk**, one of the members, is the president of **YG Entertainment.**)

THE 1990s

THE BIRTH AND BEGINNING OF *HALLYU* / KOREAN WAVE

The term ***Hallyu* / Korean Wave** began to emerge in the late 1990s when H.O.T., one of K-Pop's legendary idol groups, became popular in China. In February 2000, after H.O.T. successfully finished their performance in Beijing, "*Hallyu* Hits China" hit the headlines of Chinese newspapers. Ever since then, the word *Hallyu* / Korean Wave officially became known as the term for Korean Pop culture. Meanwhile in Taiwan, **Clon**, a powerful dance duo made a splash. In China, **NRG**, a pretty-faced-boys idol dance group, also rose to fame while Korean TV dramas captivated the Chinese viewers. Back at home in Korea, the three-member female idol group **S.E.S.** made a meteoric rise, and shortly after, a four-member female idol group, **Fin.K.L**, debuted to form a rivalry. **G.O.D**. and **Shinhwa**, all-male groups with powerful choreography and trendy tunes, also raised the bar.

WATCH
H.O.T Perform "Candy"

EARLY TO MID-2000s

FULL-FLEDGED LANDING OF KOREAN CULTURAL CONTENT IN JAPAN, THE *YONSAMA* CRAZE, AND *DAEJANGGEUM*.

Now, the next stop of the Korean Wave is Japan! Will the Korean Wave be popular in Japan, the powerhouse of trendy pop culture, which has been influencing all over Asia with J-Pop and bubbly romantic dramas? It was the movie ***Swiri* 쉬리** (1999) that showed the possibility. The suspense thriller, which depicts the romance between a South Korean national security agent and a North Korean spy, was a huge hit in Japan, showing the potential of Korean cultural content in Japan. After that, the melodrama ***Gyeoul Yeonga* 겨울연가 *(Winter Sonata,* 2002)** became a mega-hit, generating a sensational response from the middle-aged female viewers in Japan. Through this drama, **Bae Yong-joon** got a nickname, "***Yonsama* ('Emperor Yon),**" and was adored as the "first love" of the Japanese women, treated as a state guest at the airport, surrounded by thousands of

Swiri 쉬리 (1999)

Gyeoul Yeonga 겨울연가
(*Winter Sonata* KBS, 2002)

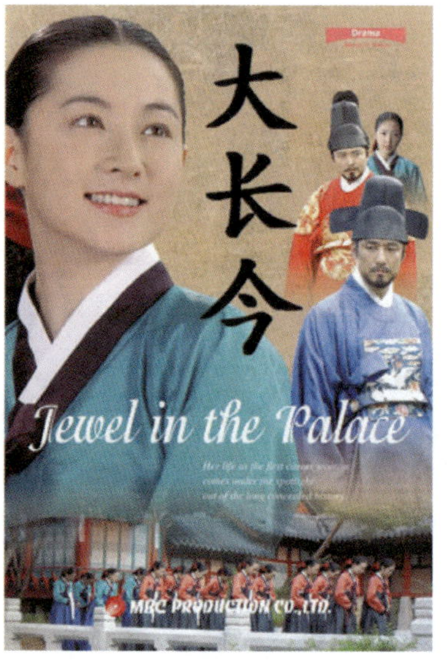

Daejanggeum 대장금 (MBC, 2003)

fanatic fans. From then on, the word "*Hallyu*" appeared in Japan, and "*Hallyu* Syndrome" swept Japan. In the music industry, **BoA**, a teenage female singer from **SM Entertainment** who had been active in the Japanese music scene since her early age, became a huge success, dominating the Japanese Oricon charts, setting the cornerstone for K-Pop's soft landing in Japan. However, the Korean Wave content that was truly popular around the globe, reaching the audience outside Asia was, unarguably, ***Daejanggeum* 대장금 (*Jewel in the Palace*, MBC, 2003)**. This historical drama about the success of the first female royal physician of the Joseon Dynasty was popular among foreigners because it charmingly presents the outstanding scenery of Korea, the beauty of *hanbok*, and Korean cuisine. Besides taking the viewers by storm in China, it was also popular in Africa as well as the Middle East (especially Iran). It was even remade in many countries including Japan and Turkey.

LATE 2000s - 2010s

CONTINUED OVERSEAS EXPORT OF KOREAN CULTURAL CONTENT AND THE GROWING INFLUENCE OF K-POP

TVXQ's Asia Tour Concert Poster

It was **Dongbangshinki 동방신기 (TVXQ)** that succeeded the K-Pop craze in Japan in the late 2000s, whose sold-out concerts at the mega dome stadiums were nothing to be surprised about. Idol bands with innocent boyish charms like Super Junior and **SHINee** gained huge popularity, and trendy Hip-Hop/dance-based groups such as **Epik High, Big Bang**, and **Brown Eyed Girls** continued to expand their fandom overseas. But most of all, the advent of **Girls' Generation** changed the K-Pop scene that boy bands were dominating. **Wonder Girls**, **KARA**, **After School**, **f(x)**, and **T-ara** were among the top contenders vying for the crown. And while **U-Kiss** gained popularity with their youthful charms, **2AM**, **2PM**, and **B2ST**, the boy bands with masculine charms, expanded the spectrum of the K-Pop boy band. "Girl Crush" bands like **4Minute** and **2NE1** appeared and were well received by fans around the globe. At the same time, variety show programs such as ***Running Man*** and ***Infinite Challenge*** were exported overseas and received positive responses.

WATCH

2NE1 Performing in New York MTV IGGY's Best New Band in the World

WATCH

Gangnam Style Music Video

In the early 2010s, idol groups such as **ZE:A**, **CN BLUE, SISTAR**, **Miss A**, **Girl's Day**, and **APink** continued to appear, and dominated the K-Pop scene. It wasn't a big step, but it was a time when the Korean Wave continued to secure fandom around the world with small but steady steps. At that very moment, something that no one ever expected happened - and people all over the world were suddenly captivated by K-Pop madness! That's right, it was **Psy**'s "**Gangnam Style!**" The addictive melody and horse-riding dance helped the song go viral through social media, pushing it to the second place on the Billboard chart, an unprecedented achievement in the history of K-Pop. Including a **New Years' Eve performance at Times Square** and collaboration stage with **MC Hammer** at **American Music Awards (AMA)**, **Psy** was the busiest person in the world in 2012, and his presence helped shattered the stereotype that K-Pop is only about idol groups.

2012 ~ PRESENT

HALLYU'S CONTINUING POPULARITY AND SPREAD INTO THE GLOBAL MARKET

***Taeyangeui Huye* 태양의후예**
(*The Descendants of the Sun* KBS, 2016)

***Gisaengchung* 기생충**
(*Parasite*, 2019)

So far, the Korean Wave has been a huge success in Asian markets, but in North America and Europe, it has only formed a small fandom. However, from this time on, the Korean Wave finally moved beyond its geographical limits, and people around the world began to enjoy K-Pop. The globalization of the Korean Wave continued with the emergence of talented groups such as **EXID, EXO, AOA, BTS, GOT7, AKMU, RED VELVET, LOVELYZ, iKon, Mamamoo, ASTRO,** and **BlackPink**. The reason for success was that K-Pop, which began in the beginning by imitating American Pop music and J-Pop's *idol* system, has now created its own flavor through active convergence and transformation. Now, K-Pop is not a child of American Pop and J-Pop, but a unique brand with a "cool and hip" feeling that only K-Pop has to offer. In addition, dramas and movies were also very popular. ***The Descendants of the Sun* (KBS, 2016**) became a sensation in Asia and has sold copyrights to many countries in Europe and in 2020, director **Bong Joon-ho**'s ***Parasite* (2019)** surprised the world by winning four **Academy Awards**, setting a milestone in Korean film history!

WHAT DOES THE FUTURE OF *HALLYU* / KOREAN WAVE LOOK LIKE?

While some critics hold negative views about the sustainability of the Korean Wave for it being too heavily skewed towards K-Pop and K-Dramas, no one can deny that they played the most important role in sparking an interest in Korea. And the efforts are coming to fruition - the Korean Wave is gradually expanding its presence in various areas such as fashion, cosmetics, food, tourism, martial arts, movies, literature, and education, making the spectrum of the Korean Wave wider and diverse. Experts say that K-Beauty and K-***Webtoon*** are emerging as the golden boy of the next generation of New *Hallyu*, and it would be interesting to see what the New *Hallyu* Wave will evolve into.

WHAT MAKES K-POP POPULAR?

1) Addicting Melodies
2) Amazing Choreography That Is Perfectly Executed In Sync
3) Trendy Fashion And Make-Up
4) Stellar/Appealing/Eye-Catching Music Videos With In-depth Storylines
5) Multi-talented Idols Who Can Appeal To Diverse Audiences

WHAT DOES IT TAKE TO BECOME A K-POP IDOL?

"***Trainee***" literally means an aspiring K-Pop singer who enters into a contract with an entertainment agency and goes through a rigorous professional training course (vocal, dance, language, and so many others) with a dream to become a K-Pop idol star one day. Most of them start in their teenage years and the training period can last as many as 7~8 years, but it's not a guarantee as the entertainment companies have the right to release them if they believe their trainees don't have what it takes to become a K-Pop star. However, being a K-Pop idol is not a job for everyone, and it's ultimately a professional agency's job to determine whether the gemstone is a diamond in the rough or not, and it's also their role to process it into a sparkling diamond. But if they can make it, they have a great shot at wealth and fame. For this reason, many teenagers pick K-Pop idol as their dream job. But what happens when everyone wants the same job? Becoming a professional idol singer, let alone becoming a trainee, is as difficult as getting into an Ivy League school.

TOP K-POP ENTERTAINMENT COMPANIES

SM ENTERTAINMENT

EXO
SUPER JUNIOR
RED VELVET

YG ENTERTAINMENT

BLACKPINK
TREASURE
BIG BANG

JYP ENTERTAINMENT
LEADER IN ENTERTAINMENT

TWICE
MISS A
ITZY

Big Hit Entertainment

BTS
GLAM
8EIGHT

SWING ENTERTAINMENT

WANNA ONE
KIM JAE HWAN
X1

rbw
Rainbowbridge World

MAMAMOO
ONEUS
VROMANCE

CUBE ENTERTAINMENT

APINK
BTOB
(G)I-DLE

PLEDIS ENTERTAINMENT

SEVENTEEN
AFTER SCHOOL
ORANGE CARAMEL

woollim Entertainment

LOVELYZ
INFINITE
ROCKET PUNCH

WHY IS BTS SO POPULAR?

"UNLIKE MANY OTHER KOREAN ARTISTS, BTS HEAVILY RELIED ON USING YOUTUBE AND TWITTER TO PROMOTE THEMSELVES ONLINE, FROM THEIR HUMBLE BEGINNINGS TO TODAY'S SUCCESS. THIS METHOD CONTRADICTED THE NORMS OF THE INDUSTRY SINCE K-POP IDOLS TYPICALLY USE KOREAN NEWS CHANNELS AND TV SHOWS TO MAKE A NAME FOR THEMSELVES."

("BTS IS A SOCIAL MEDIA SUCCESS STORY" JADE HOOKAHM, UC SAN DIEGO VIA STUDYBREAKS)

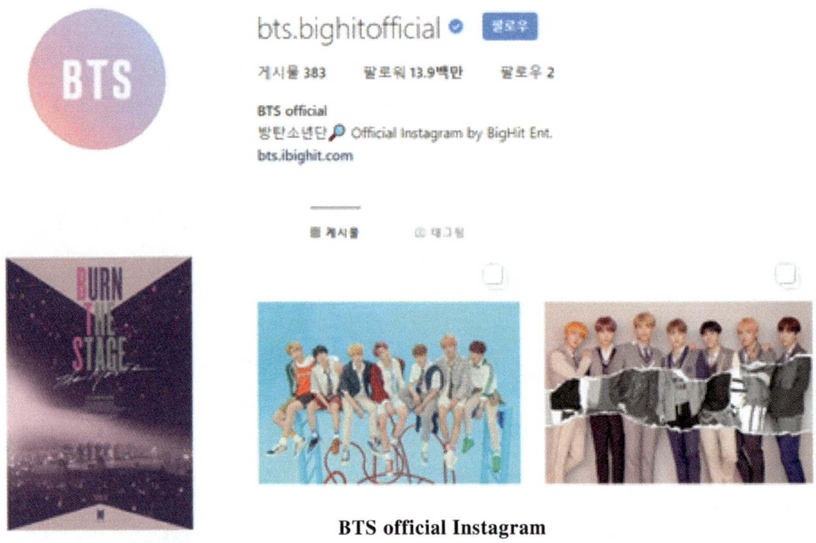

BTS official Instagram

A prime example of this revolutionary change is **BTS (Bulletproof Boy Scouts/Beyond the Scene)**, which has a gigantic global fandom called **A.R.M.Y (Adorable Representative MC for Youth)** and has become the epitome of K-Pop. But many people wonder what makes BTS so different from other K-Pop groups and how they became a global phenomenon. Handsome face? A perfectly synchronized choreography? This is actually true for other K-Pop groups. Then what? Based on the fact that BTS has also been officially selected as the most-mentioned artist on Twitter and scores an overwhelmingly higher active engagement index than other celebrities, we should be able to sense a change in the production and consumption of pop culture. Previously, it was an unilateral process where pop culture was created by the entertainment agencies, and fans (consumers) passively "consumed" it. But now fans (consumers) can interact with the agency and the artists through new media channels, providing inputs and feedback during the production phase. Therefore, the role of fans (consumers) has evolved from "passive consumption" to "pro-active participation." Through platforms such as Twitter, Instagram, and V-Live, fans can share every move of BTS and stay in touch with them, and fans fully embrace BTS as part of their life and identify themselves with them. Not only that, but the inspiring values BTS also preaches, love, effort, and beauty of youth, have created absolute empathy in teenagers' minds. In other words, BTS has become a life mentor and a BFF and that's something no one has ever tried before.

KOREAN MOVIES AND THEIR HOLLYWOOD REMAKES

Old Boy (2003) / *Old Boy* (2013)

Yeopgijeokin Geunyeo 엽기적인그녀 *(2001) / My Sassy Girl (2013)*

Janghwa Hongryeon 장화홍련 (2003) / *The Uninvited* (2009)

Shiwolae 시월애 (2000) / *The Lake House* (2006)

Geoulsokuro 거울속으로 (2003) / *Mirrors* (2018)

VIDEO GAME INSPIRED BY KOREAN CULTURE

KARMA KNIGHT by UltramrineSoft
available on Steam Network

REFERENCES

WHY IS THERE A PEPSI LOGO ON THE KOREAN FLAG?
대한민국의 국기 ko.wikipedia.org/wiki/대한민국의_국기
태극기의 변천 theme.archives.go.kr/next/symbolKorea
Flag of South Korea en.wikipedia.org/wiki/Flag_of_South_Korea
조선민주주의인민공화국의 국기 ko.wikipedia.org/wiki/조선민주주의인민공화국의_국기
Flag of North Korea en.wikipedia.org/wiki/Flag_of_North_Korea
Package Design Trivia: Why is the Pepsi logo red, white, and blue? core77.com/posts/12821

KOREAN NAMES
우리나라의 성씨는 몇 개나 될까? (통계청)
http://kostat.go.kr/file_total/nkids/kids_pp/story_pdf130603.pdf
Sato most common surname in Japan (Japan Today) japantoday.com/category/national/sato-most-common-surname-in-japan
List of the 1000 Most Common Surnames in the U.S. namecensus.com

DO KOREANS SPEAK CHINESE OR JAPANESE?
Hangul en.wikipedia.org/wiki/Hangul [위기의한글①] '반대를 위한 반대' 한글 탄생 가로막다 (뉴스1) news1.kr/articles/?3730958
"국한문 혼용으로 돌아가자…한국어 품격 높아진다" (동아일보)
donga.com/news/Culture/article/all/20141010/67068211/2

HISTORY OF KIMCHI
Kimchi en.wikipedia.org/wiki/Kimchi
뮤지엄김치간 kimchikan.com
김치에 대한 진실 혹은 거짓 (서울식품안전뉴스)
fsi.seoul.go.kr/webzine/seoulFood201801/2017_02_002.html

YUGYO
Korean Confucianism en.wikipedia.org/wiki/Korean_Confucianism
한국유교 – 성균관 skk.or.kr
삼강오륜 bupdori.com
조선아동교육 남녀칠세부동석 (한국콘텐츠진흥원) culturecontent.com

WHAT DOES A KOREAN FAMILY LOOK LIKE?
삼종지도, 칠거지악 encykorea.aks.ac.kr

KOREAN ETIQUETTE BASICS
경례(敬禮)와 악수(握手) (한국전례연구원) wooriyejeol.or.kr
절하는 방법 (네이버 백과사전) terms.naver.com

HANSKIK
여름철, 보양식, 유래는 아시고 드시나요? (열린창업신문) rgnews.co.kr
Dog Meat en.wikipedia.org/wiki/Dog_meat
7 Proven Health Benefits of Ginseng healthline.com
Ginseng en.wikipedia.org/wiki/Ginseng
우황청심원 namu.wiki/w/우황청심원
[우리의 맛 장(醬)] 장의 종류 (식품음료신문) thinkfood.co.kr
떡의 유래와 의미 (여러가지 떡) (전통문화콘텐츠연구소) noriyon.co.kr
비 오는 날, 막걸리에 부침개가 당긴다…왜 그럴까?
yna.co.kr/view/AKR20160705179300064
코로나19에 "숟가락 섞지 말아야"…겸상 문화가 한국 거라고?
hankookilbo.com/News/Read/202005020399057581
한국인만 유독 쇠젓가락을 사용하는 '똑똑한' 이유 heftykr.com/chopstick_culture

WHY DO KOREANS LOVE SOJU SO MUCH?
한국의 소주 ko.wikipedia.org/wiki/한국의_소주
선비들이 술을 마시는 의례 - 향음주례(鄕飮酒禮) dongheon.or.kr

WHY DO KOREANS WORK SO DARN HARD?
Miracle on the Han River en.wikipedia.org/wiki/Miracle_on_the_Han_River

FUN & QUIRKY KOREAN SUPERSTITIONS & BELIEFS
삼신할머니 (한국콘텐츠진흥원) culturecontent.com
Mongolian spot en.wikipedia.org/wiki/Mongolian_spot
사주팔자 namu.wiki/w/사주팔자
[관상의 과학] 부자 관상·왕이 관상 타고니지만, 살면서 바뀔 수 있다? (아시아경제)
asiae.co.kr/article/2018061511532486737
풍수지리 namu.wiki/w/풍수지리
무당 (한국민속신앙사전) folkency.nfm.go.kr
선풍기 사망사고의 진실은? (연합뉴스) yna.co.kr/view/AKR20080715194900003
[취재파일] '손 없는 날' 믿어야 하나? (SBS 뉴스) news.sbs.co.kr/news/endPage.do?news_id=N1001636632
혈액형 성격설 namu.wiki/w/혈액형%20성격설
내 얼굴, 큰 것일까 커 보이는 것일까? (한국경제) hankyung.com/news/article/201206055778

DEATH & AFTERLIFE
전통장례절차 (예다함) yedaham.co.kr
장례식 namu.wiki/w/장례식
한국의 제사 ko.wikipedia.org/wiki/한국의_제사
제사상 차리는 방법 (서울시설공단) sisul.or.kr

WEDDINGS IN KOREA
혼례(婚禮) (한국민족문화대백과사전) encykorea.aks.ac.kr

WHY ARE THERE TWO NEW YEAR'S DAYS?
신정과 구정의 차이를 아십니까…음력 설의 수난사 (시사저널)
sisajournal.com/article/173856
Korean New en.wikipedia.org/wiki/Korean_New_Year
보신각 종, 33번 치는 까닭은? (한문화타임즈) hmhtimes.com/news/articleView.html?idxno=1626
제야의 종 namu.wiki/w/제야의_종

HANBOK THE TRADITIONAL KOREAN CLOTHES
삼국 시대의 복식 blog.daum.net/yonghwan6158/1421
한국 복식: 삼국시대 (고구려, 백제,신라) blog.naver.com/mongjja_/221099996686
한복디자이너[삼국시대의 복식] blog.naver.com/PostView.nhn?blogId=abcde3965&logNo=50145936239
[한복] 시대별 한복의 변화 instiz.net/pt/5317188
한복 ko.wikipedia.org/wiki/한복
Hanbok en.wikipedia.org/wiki/Hanbok
한국민족문화대백과 (네이버 백과사전) terms.naver.com
Voyage en Corée 2. (Voyage in Corea Section 2) anthony.sogang.ac.kr

TAE KWON DO
Taekwondo en.wikipedia.org/wiki/Taekwondo

JEJUDO
마을의 수호신 돌하르방
jeju.go.kr/culture/folklore/religious/religious05/religiousHarubang.htm

DEATH & AFTERLIFE
전통장례절차 (예다함) yedaham.co.kr
장례식 namu.wiki/w/장례식
한국의 제사 ko.wikipedia.org/wiki/한국의_제사
제사상 차리는 방법 (서울시설공단) sisul.or.kr

WEDDINGS IN KOREA
혼례(婚禮) (한국민족문화대백과사전) encykorea.aks.ac.kr

WHY ARE THERE TWO NEW YEAR'S DAYS?
신정과 구정의 차이를 아십니까…음력 설의 수난사 (시사저널)
sisajournal.com/article/173856
Korean New en.wikipedia.org/wiki/Korean_New_Year
보신각 종, 33번 치는 까닭은? (한문화타임즈) hmhtimes.com/news/articleView.html?idxno=1626
제야의 종 namu.wiki/w/제야의_종

HANBOK THE TRADITIONAL KOREAN CLOTHES
삼국 시대의 복식 blog.daum.net/yonghwan6158/1421
한국 복식: 삼국시대 (고구려, 백제,신라) blog.naver.com/mongjja_/221099996686
한복디자이너[삼국시대의 복식] blog.naver.com/PostView.nhn?blogId=abcde3965&logNo=50145936239
[한복] 시대별 한복의 변화 instiz.net/pt/5317188
한복 ko.wikipedia.org/wiki/한복
Hanbok en.wikipedia.org/wiki/Hanbok
한국민족문화대백과 (네이버 백과사전) terms.naver.com
Voyage en Corée 2. (Voyage in Corea Section 2) anthony.sogang.ac.kr

TAE KWON DO
Taekwondo en.wikipedia.org/wiki/Taekwondo

JEJUDO
마을의 수호신 돌하르방
jeju.go.kr/culture/folklore/religious/religious05/religiousHarubang.htm

ACKNOWLEDGEMENT

Parts of the text have been adopted in full or with modification for optimal reading experience from the following sources under the CC-BY-SA license.

WHAT IS THE THREE KINGDOMS PERIOD?
wikipedia.org/wiki/Three_Kingdoms_of_Korea

GOGURYEO, THE LARGEST DYNASTY IN KOREAN HISTORY
wikipedia.org/wiki/Goguryeo

BAEKJE, THE CULTURAL POWERHOUSE
wikipedia.org/wiki/Baekje

SILLA, THE GOLDEN KINGDOM
wikipedia.org/wiki/Silla

GORYEO, THE GOLDEN AGE OF KOREAN BUDDHISM -
wikipedia.org/wiki/Goryeo

JOSEON - THE LAND OF THE MORNING CALM
wikipedia.org/wiki/Joseon

GYEONGBOKGUNG - "Palace Greatly Blessed by Heaven" -
wikipedia.org/wiki/Gyeongbokgung

CHANGDEOKGUNG - "Palace of Prospering Virtue" -
ikipedia.org/wiki/Changdeokgung

CHANGGYEONGGUNG - "Palace of Magnificent Joy" -
wikipedia.org/wiki/Changgyeonggung

DEOKSUGUNG- "Palace of Virtuous Longevity" -
wikipedia.org/wiki/Deoksugung

GYEONGHUIGUNG - "Palace of Joy and Harmony" -
wikipedia.org/wiki/Gyeonghuigung

DREAMING OF A MODERN STATE, THE KOREAN EMPIRE -
wikipedia.org/wiki/Korean_Empire

SAD HISTORY - JAPANESE OCCUPATION -
wikipedia.org/wiki/Korea_under_Japanese_rule

WHY IS KOREA DIVIDED? - wikipedia.org/wiki/Korean_War

Printed in Great Britain
by Amazon

8a9274da-042d-4c88-aecd-8bd8da57c61dR01